Beyond Dependency

edited by
Guy F. Erb and
Valeriana Kallab

Prepared with the
support of the
Charles F. Kettering Foundation
and published
in cooperation with the
Overseas Development Council

The Praeger Special Studies program—
utilizing the most modern and efficient book
production techniques and a selective
worldwide distribution network—makes
available to the academic, government, and
business communities significant, timely
research in U.S. and international economic, social, and political development.

Beyond Dependency
The Developing World
Speaks Out

Praeger Publishers   New York   Washington   London

PRAEGER PUBLISHERS
111 Fourth Avenue, New York, N.Y. 10003, U.S.A.

Published in the United States of America in 1975
by Praeger Publishers, Inc.

© 1975 by the Overseas Development Council
Library of Congress Catalog Card Number: 75-23960
Printed in the United States of America
ISBN: 0-275-55580-1

Table of Contents

Beyond Dependency

Acknowledgments

The Overseas Development Council wishes to express its appreciation to Phillips Ruopp of the Charles F. Kettering Foundation, whose vision and dedication to improved international communication were the foundation of the North-South Dialogue project that has culminated in this book. Special thanks are likewise due to the authors who contributed essays to the volume, as well as to Abdoul Barry, Pathé Diagne, El-Sayed Dohaia, Maria Teresa Moraes, Neville Kanakaratne, and Raimi Ola Ojikutu, all of whom made valuable contributions to the Dialogue project.

The Editors wish to thank their colleagues at the Council—particularly Denis Goulet, James P. Grant, Roger Hansen, Robert Johnson, John W. Sewell, Stephen Taran, and Mildred Weiss—as well as Robert E. Hunter and Robert Seidel, for valuable criticisms offered in various draft stages. Special thanks for editorial assistance go to Nancy Krekeler, Rosemarie Philips, Carol Hoban, and Judith Johnson, and to Marta Arruda for translation and administrative assistance. Both the book and the project benefited from the administrative assistance of Michael O'Hare, ODC Comptroller; and the final manuscript could not have been prepared without the assistance of Ferne Horner, Diana Capers, Susan Epstein, Deborah Everett, Phyllis Jansen, Patricia Neace, and Kandi Triner.

Introduction

When the Overseas Development Council three years ago issued the first of its annual assessments of U.S. policies toward the developing world—the ODC *Agenda for Action* series—we recognized that while our own recommendations are prepared mostly by U.S. analysts, development is of course a two-way street, and we announced at that time our intention to ensure that the views of those in developing countries are heard more widely in the United States. With this objective in mind, and with the support of the Charles F. Kettering Foundation, we are issuing this collection of essays by authors from developing countries as a "companion volume" to our *Agenda for Action* series.

This direct encounter with developing-country opinions comes none too soon. During the past two years, the views held in industrialized and developing countries on development and international relations have become increasingly polarized. A variety of developing-country actions—ranging from those of the oil exporting nations and of a few other producer groups to the greater collective assertiveness of developing countries in international organizations—have had a significant impact on those in the United States and in other developed countries who had long regarded themselves as sympathetic to developing-country objectives. Many persons in the industrialized world have found their attitudes and preconceptions challenged by the new objectives of increased sharing of trade and production and of a greater voice in international decisions that the developing countries have added to their traditional goals of internal economic and social development. The increasing solidarity and common actions of the developing countries on such noneconomic issues as the Arab-Israeli dispute and Southern Africa have intensified the atmosphere of confrontation and the growing rift between the developing countries generally and the "old rich."

The recent large developing-country majorities within the United Nations have given rise to U.S. complaints about a "tyranny of the majority." However, these developing-country majorities are a reflection of the failure of consensus politics. In the late 1960s and early 1970s, the developing countries—aware of the futility of approving principles and resolutions that were unacceptable to the developed countries—made vigorous efforts to reach a consensus with developed countries on international economic decisions. Since then it has become apparent, however, that even those decisions reached by consensus have not been any more readily implemented than earlier resolutions, and that they often have become meaningless as a result of negotiated compromises. Another factor underlying the procedures followed by developing countries—as well as their lengthy and sometimes excessive lists of demands—is the result of their need to maintain cohesiveness vis-a-vis the industrialized world. Indeed, developing-country solidarity often is maintained by endorsement of the specific goals of individual, or groups of, developing countries. Consequently, intra-"Group of 77" political considerations and the "one nation, one vote" procedure encourage developing-country unanimity and declarations that accentuate the divisions between North and South.

Some commentators have stated that the recent actions and rhetoric of the developing nations herald a new "cold war" that threatens to diminish the living standards and political influence of the industrialized world. These observers see the present situation in confrontation terms. Another view—expressed in recent months by Secretary of State Kissinger—is that the developing countries "in their quest for their own progress . . . present a challenge to the rest of the world—to demonstrate that the international structure can give them a role, a fair share, dignity, and responsibility."[1]

All nations now face issues whose resolution will fundamentally alter the world economy during the rest of this century. In my view, efforts to address the problems before us should be made cooperatively by developed and developing countries with such ingenuity that all parties may ultimately gain. To achieve that goal, much greater mutual understanding is required. Our intent in issuing this collection of essays by individuals from developing countries is to contribute to increased understanding and a greater appreciation in the United States and other industrialized nations of the problems, aspirations, and objectives of the developing countries.

What are the main issues that rich and poor nations must address together? *First*, there is considerable uncertainty as to when or even whether the high growth rates experienced during the 1960s and early 1970s can be recaptured. Important obstacles to continued growth have emerged in the past few years, and major changes are required in world economic systems involving the cooperation of both rich and poor countries if potential scarcities and economic tensions among nations are to be managed successfully.

Second, in a world where the disadvantaged peoples of both poor and rich nations demand more equitable shares from the gains of economic growth, greater attention will have to be paid to issues of distribution within and among nations, particularly if slower growth rates accentuate social conflicts in all countries. On grounds of equity alone, the developed countries need to foster a greater sharing in decision making and the benefits of growth; it is equally important, however, that the developing coun-

---

[1]Address to the Institute of World Affairs of the University of Wisconsin, Milwaukee, July 14, 1975.

tries strengthen their claim by providing greater assurance that rising resource transfers will benefit primarily their poor majority rather than just the privileged few.

Third, increasing economic interrelationships and the importance of economic factors in a situation of nuclear stalemate have forced a widening of the concept of security in the United States beyond traditional political-military concepts to include areas in which the cooperation of at least some, if not all, developing countries is vital. The successful management of international economic systems for trade, finance, investment, food production and distribution, and the environment is now part of a wider definition of national security that has heightened the importance of another major transformation: the shift of some economic and political power toward resource-rich countries, many of which are members of the Third World. Control by developing countries over key resources, their economic and technical advancement, and their political sophistication now give them greater capacity to achieve some of the changes that they have been demanding of rich countries since the early 1960s.

The perceptions which underlie the changes taking place in the developing world are the subject of compelling personal essays contributed to this volume by experts from the Third World. The book is divided into four sections. The first, "Self-Reliance and Interdependence," sets out the major internal and external changes necessary to bring about a more genuinely effective and equitable interdependence between rich and poor nations. The second, "Critical Problem Areas," reviews several of the major issues now confronting both the rich nations of the "North" and the developing nations of the "South." All of the five chapters in this section treat urgent short-run problems as well as the need to seek solutions that will contribute to the longer-run changes required for a more equitable relationship between North and South. Part three of the book, "Toward a North-South Bargain," opens with a chapter by Guy F. Erb that draws together the major issues in the present debate between developing and developed nations and provides the historical perspective that is essential in assessing the present "challenge" from the South. Mr. Erb—ODC Senior Fellow and Director of the North-South dialogue project that stimulated most of these essays—is the only developed-country contributor to this volume. His chapter analyzes the current positions of the developing countries in the light of their past relationships with Western societies. Mr. Erb's review of the policy options open to both sides of the North-South debate is followed by the closing chapter—an essay by Mahbub ul Haq that sets out some of the elements of a possible bargain between rich and poor countries.

The volume's final section of annexes presents some of the major statements and declarations that document the North-South debate of the mid-1970s. 1974 and 1975 saw many efforts, both private and official, to set out objectives and attempt a reconciliation of the positions of developed and developing countries. Annex A presents several public statements—the Belmont Statement (March 1974), the Cocoyoc Declaration (October 1974), and the Communique of the Third World Forum Conference in Karachi (January 1975)—prepared by groups of private experts, mainly from the developing world, seeking to contribute to the inter-governmental negotiations that must implement the aspirations of their peoples. Annex B contains four of the most important official statements on North-South issues made during 1974-75. The first document included is the Declaration and Action Programme on the Establishment of a New International Economic Order adopted at the Sixth Special Session of the U.N. General Assembly in April/May 1974—at the General Assembly's session on raw materials that began the debate about to be resumed at the time of writing at the Assembly's Seventh Special Session on Development and International Economic Cooperation. The highly controversial 1974 Declaration and Action Programme and the Charter of Economic Rights and Duties of States adopted in December 1974 were the result of negotiations between representatives of developed and developing countries. They were not, however, adopted unanimously, as a number of developed countries—including the United States—could not accept some of the points held by the developing nations. The two other statements included in the annexes— the Dakar Declaration of the Conference of Developing Countries on Raw Materials and the Algiers Declaration by OPEC Heads of State—both resulted from negotiations toward a common position among developing countries. It is a striking thing that these last two documents—although characterized by what many in the West dismiss as "rhetoric"—present views that receive serious, considered support both in the essays contributed to this volume by men and women from the developing world and in the Belmont Statement included in Annex A.

The present challenge from the developing world should not be interpreted as merely a passing phase in international relations. If the industrialized countries are to meet this challenge constructively—so that *all* nations may gain from changes in the world economy—they must attempt a fuller understanding of the nature of the aspirations of the developing countries. Some of the latter's views will appear unreasonable or extreme to readers in the United States and other rich nations—just as the demands of the American Populists at the turn of the century and the early demands of the American labor movement appeared extreme to the then existing power structure in this country. In the United States, many of those early calls for greater opportunity have been incorporated in legislation and in management-labor relationships. Can a similar global evolution be hoped for from the present confrontation between rich and poor countries?

James P. Grant, *President*

August 1975   *Overseas Development Council*

Beyond Dependency

Part I

Self-Reliance and Interdependence

Chapter 1

Self-Reliant Development in an "Interdependent" World

Samuel L. Parmar

While "global interdependence" is receiving increasing attention in developed countries, "self-reliant development" is becoming a major concern in the developing nations. What specific objectives does each of these broad principles encompass? And are these objectives complementary or antagonistic? These questions are important, for if the goals of "interdependence" and "self-reliant development" should prove to be opposed to each other, the prospects of increased international cooperation would indeed be bleak.

The Quest for Self-Reliant Development

The experience of the developing countries with the development process over the last two decades or so has made them wary of two things: concepts, policies, and patterns of development borrowed from developed nations; and patterns of international economic cooperation that continue to make trade, aid, investment, and the transfer of technology instruments of domination by the developed nations. For these reasons, developing countries are now far more inclined to fashion their economic policies in terms of their own needs, problems, and experience. This trend does not imply a lessening of their interest in international cooperation but rather a striving to make North-South relations reflect *genuine* interdependence and international economic justice.

From the standpoint of developing economies, it is natural that strategies and programs relating to domestic social and economic problems should govern the nature and extent of their participation in the world economy. International trade, for example, is not an end in itself but a means for the development of an economy. However, since international trade involves the interests of more than one economy, it should confer benefits among all concerned. Only thus can it reflect a mutually advantageous interdependence. In theory this is precisely what international specialization and trade are supposed to do. But in practice the history of trade has been one of domination by the strong and deprivation of the weak. It has been both an "engine of growth" for developed nations and an instrument of exploitation of the developing. To the nations of the world's South, this appears to be true not only of past economic history but also of the contemporary situation.

Interestingly enough, the newly manifested concern of the developed nations about interdependence and a global approach to problems appears to stem from their own domestic needs. Problems such as scarcity of raw materials and energy resources, international monetary crises, pollution and ecological imbalance, and unregulated use of ocean resources have generated an awareness that cooperation between North and South is an essential prerequisite of constructive solutions. Progressive economic thinking on international cooperation in the developed countries underlines the importance of egalitarian patterns of trade, aid, and investment in order to promote the long-term interests of both rich and poor nations. Perhaps most instrumental in forcing a change in the outlook of developed nations is the realization that they really need the help of developing countries for even their short-term economic well-being. The current oil crisis provides a case in point, clearly showing that in developed as in developing nations, international trade is subordinated to the needs of the domestic economy.

Thus it would be a mistake to view the developing countries' pursuit of self-reliant development as necessarily leading to their withdrawal from world economic systems and to the subordination of international trade to programs dealing with domestic social and economic policies. From the mercantilist era to the present, international trade has always been subordinated to domestic policies. This should not be a matter of debate, for it expresses the logical relationship between the internal and the international economies. Instead, the critical test of a policy should be whether it leads to trade restriction or liberalization.

In general, the two analyses of North-South relations referred to throughout this chapter—the Brookings Institution's *Reassessing North-South Economic Relations*, prepared by thirteen experts from developed nations, and the Overseas Development Council's annual policy assessment, *The U.S. and the Developing World: Agenda for Action*—favor the liberalization of trade and other forms of international cooperation.[1] This

[1]*Reassessing North-South Economic Relations, A Tripartite Report by Thirteen Experts from the European Community, Japan, and North America* (Washington, D.C.: The Brookings Institution, 1972); and *The United States and the Developing World: Agenda for Action, 1973* (Washington, D.C.: Overseas Development Council, 1973).

view would find support in developing countries, provided that the patterns of international economic relations between North and South were radically altered to divest them of their exploitative features. It is true that developed nations need to recognize that "the poor countries want accelerated economic development, an acceptable level of autonomy, and fair participation in the growth of the international economy," and that international policy "must take into account the interests of developing countries on . . . issues such as coordinating trade and monetary measures and exchange rate policy, adopting measures to deal with international capital movements, solving the problems posed by large foreign holdings of dollars and sterling."[2] It is likewise true that "trade policy may well be the primary test of North-South relations"—that developed nations are in fact challenged to consider whether they can achieve a more productive and dynamic worldwide division of labor. The important test is thus "not a question of rich countries giving assistance to poor countries, but of assuring greater mutual gains."[3]

It would, however, be an optimistic oversimplification to conclude that a facile complementarity can be brought about between the interests of developing and developed nations by making a few changes in the patterns of international economic relationships. As has already been suggested, these links have to be judged from the standpoint of domestic social and economic policies. If the interests that prompt developed nations to liberalize trade and extend other forms of international cooperation are at variance with the developing nations' basic objective of self-reliant development, then the latter cannot be expected to be enthusiastic about international economic relations. But if developed nations actually translate their affirmation of interdependence into support for more egalitarian structures in the international economy, there should be no fundamental conflict between self-reliant development and increased international economic cooperation.

Clearly any search for mutually beneficial North-South cooperation— indeed, for any real North-South dialogue—must be based on a deeper understanding by both sides of a) the meaning of self-reliant development and its implications for international cooperation, and b) the intent and likely impact of the developed nations' present emphasis of "interdependence" on already controversial aspects of the international economic order.

The Meaning of Self-Reliance

The terms "self-reliance" and "self-reliant development" are used interchangeably in this paper. This is valid only if one does not adhere to the

---

[2] *Agenda for Action*, op. cit., pp. 41 and 32.
[3] *Reassessing North-South Economic Relations*, op. cit., p. 10.

narrow sense of "self-reliance," which merely refers to policies that will, over time, ensure a balance in the foreign exchange budget commensurate with a satisfactory rate of growth. In this view, if export earnings become equal to import expenses plus debt repayments, so that no foreign aid is required, the economy may be said to have achieved self-reliance. To a large extent this corresponds to the idea of "self-sustaining growth." While the attainment of such a balance in external accounts is very important, it is only one component of self-reliant development. It is therefore a limited, resource-oriented approach whose central concern is that the country earn enough foreign exchange resources to be free of foreign assistance.

In contrast, a more comprehensive understanding of self-reliance assigns central importance to the process of structural change—which involves much more than the mere balancing of accounts in the foreign trade sector of the economy. A developing country could succeed in maintaining growth without foreign assistance, but that would not by itself ensure structural changes. Thus where growth fails to promote social justice, to utilize the economy's most abundant resources, to engender public participation in the development process, to reduce the concentration of economic power, or to assist in the establishment of more egalitarian patterns of international economic relationships, there may be self-reliance in the narrow sense but not in the deeper, structural sense.

This difference may be illustrated by the experience of India, where efforts to reduce reliance on foreign assistance through policies of export promotion and import substitution have met with some success, but have not helped realize other important goals of planning, such as social justice. Import substitution has led to the establishment of certain consumer-goods industries that cater to the high-income group in the country. As a result, inequalities have increased; there has been a widening of the consumption gap between the small affluent class and the large lower-income group. Other negative features also are becoming evident. Increased expenditures on less essential consumer goods weaken the savings ratio. A "demonstration effect" has been generated in the economy that is strengthening the desire for less essential goods and services even in those segments of society which lack adequate purchasing power for necessities. These trends have resulted in a diversion of resources from the production of socially necessary commodities to that of less important goods, causing distortion in investment and production patterns. At the same time, an increase in the influence and power of private foreign investment and of the multinational corporations—as well as of the domestic groups with which they are closely linked—has concentrated economic power in the hands of a few. This is diametrically opposed to one of India's important social objectives of development. Finally, because new industries tend to favor capital-intensive technology, their potential for absorbing the surplus labor force is very limited, which runs counter to another important objective of Indian planning.

India's efforts to promote exports manifest a number of contradictions. Thus the export of certain essential commodities which are in short supply domestically (for example, sugar, cement, oilseeds, leather goods, and steel) pushes up their domestic prices and puts them beyond the reach of low-income consumers. The consumption gap between the rich and the poor therefore widens, with a consequent receding of the goal of a reduction in economic inequalities. Export promotion of this kind also often implies depriving the needy in a poor country in order to add to the range of goods available in a rich country—a case of the weak subsidizing the strong. The result is a strengthening of the nonegalitarian character of the world economy. Even though this is a consequence of the poor country's decisions and initiatives, it represents exploitation through the mechanism of trade. The problem is compounded by the tendency of export promotion programs to adopt a *quantitative* approach to increasing aggregate foreign exchange earnings and frequently to fail to differentiate between goods on a *qualitative* basis. Certain resources (especially minerals) that are nonrenewable are exported recklessly, to the jeopardy of future development. The quantitative benefits of enhanced foreign exchange earnings are more than offset by the qualitative depletion of national resources and the consequent weakening of productive capacity over time.

Moreover, a number of new industries with a high foreign exchange component have been set up in India with the intention of creating a more diversified export base. But because of their high prices and the flourishing sellers' market in that country, these tend to become import substitutes that cater only to a privileged domestic minority. At the same time, the initial foreign exchange investment and recurring expense of imported inputs (which generally are financed through loans), become a heavy burden on the economy, as they do not set into motion a process to earn foreign exchange to repay debts. Finally, most of these new export industries have relied on capital-intensive technology. Their role in the alleviation of unemployment and underemployment therefore is marginal. Even more serious is the fact that they weaken the quest for technology that is relevant to the needs of the domestic economy.

The intention of these arguments is not to decry India's or any other country's export promotion and import substitution objectives as such or to minimize the importance of these policies to the process of self-reliant development. But trade policy must be formulated in such a way that it does not ignore the other vital social and economic objectives of a developing country. Increased foreign exchange earnings represent additional resources for development. More important than the quantum of resources, however, are the uses to which these are put and the objectives they help to attain. The basic objective of a poor country is to overcome poverty. This is possible only through a radical social transformation, which new power and property relations and new institutions can ensure. A narrow understanding of self-reliance either ignores this vital concern or operates on the unacceptable premise that adequacy of foreign exchange resources somehow helps to bring about basic structural changes. Certainly the experience of developing countries does not provide evidence to support this presupposition.

Important Components of Self-Reliance

Perhaps the most important element of self-reliance in developing nations is the formulation of concepts and policies of development based on their own socio-economic realities rather than on ideas inherited from the North. Developing nations have much to learn from the experience of the developed—the most important lesson being that the latter have formulated theories and policies with reference to their own special conditions. But imitation will prove disastrous, as is already becoming evident, because it means misshaping one's own framework to make it conform to the realities and interests of others.

A disturbing feature of almost two decades of organized developmental efforts in many countries of the South is the emergence of serious contradictions in these economies. These contradictions are undermining the growth process. The Indian economy can again be used to illustrate this situation:[4]

> (a) National and per capita incomes have increased (although at a slower rate than envisaged in the Five-Year Plans), but there has been an increase in the extent and intensity of poverty. More than 40 per cent of the population is still living below the "poverty line," which is generally identified as being an annual per capita income of Rs. 240 (about $33) at 1960–61 prices in the urban sector, and Rs. 180 (approximately $24) in the rural sector. Official statements confirm the fact that economic inequalities have increased, with the rich growing richer and the poor feeling more deprived in a relative sense—even though they may be slightly better off than before.
>
> (b) Although India has been commended for the success of its "green revolution," there nevertheless is a shortage of foodgrains (despite a doubling of foodgrain production between 1951 and 1971), and prices of agricultural produce are rising sharply. At the same time, increasing inequality in rural areas is generating social discontent and unrest. In 1972, one bad monsoon seemed to neutralize the benefits of the green

---

[4]This section is taken from Samuel L. Parmar, "The Environment and Growth Debate in Asian Perspective," *Anticipation* (World Council of Churches, Geneva) August 1973, p. 5.

revolution and created near-famine conditions in large drought-affected regions.

(c) India's industrial progress is impressive, but it is accompanied by increases in industrial unrest, unemployment and underemployment, rising prices of manufactures, unused capacity, power shortages, and monopolistic tendencies. The traditional sector of small-scale and cottage industries, which not only utilizes available resources and skills but also is more employment-generating per unit of invested capital, is in a state of crisis despite government subsidies and encouragement.

(d) The value of annual exports is now over two and a half times the 1961 level, with an impressive diversification in both composition and direction. But balance-of-payments deficits continue, and debt-servicing will soon consume one third of export earnings.

(e) Although literacy has more than doubled—which is an impressive achievement—70 per cent of the population remains illiterate, and more persons are in that category today than were twenty years ago.

(f) As regards the country's "self-reliance" (in the narrow balance-of-payments sense of the term), it appears that "the donor [countries] rather than the Planning Commission determine the degree of our self-reliance."[5]

The Brookings Institution's study, *Reassessing North-South Economic Relations*, gives an excellent picture of such existing contradictions in the economies of developing nations. After referring to achievements such as GNP growth rates of 5 per cent and more in "developing countries taken together" in the 1960s, to the fact that "exports of manufactures seem to have crossed a threshold," and to the progress of the green revolution, which signifies a "promising start . . . in the development of technologies specifically related to the economic and social conditions of the South," the study rightly points out that "averages obscure some stubborn facts." These "stubborn facts" highlight the contradictions and give a glimpse of the realities of developing nations. Among those cited are: the lack of resources, the lack of experience in the arts of production or administration, overpopulation, the inefficiency inherent in small markets, the large number of the "desperately poor,"[6] unemployment and underemployment, and undernourishment and disease.

The Overseas Development Council's *Agenda for Action* also refers to this dialectic of poverty. It stresses the fact that "many developing countries . . . are hard pressed even to retain the achievements they have already made in providing lives of decency and hope for their people. And many are failing." Commenting favorably on the high average rate of

[5]V. M. Dandekar, "Democratic Socialist Path to Economic Development," *Mainstream*, January 19, 1974, pp. 10–11.
[6]*Reassessing North-South Economic Relations*, op. cit., pp. 2–3.

growth achieved by the developing world during the 1960s—"a rate of growth unequalled by the rich countries at a comparable stage of their development"—this analysis also then points to some of the grim realities: "many developing countries' unemployment levels are still increasing . . . the income gap between the poorest half of the population and those well-off is actually widening." Finally, "if the debt burden that has built up in a number of major developing countries continues to accumulate, it will become insupportable."[7]

Yet after recognizing such contradictions, both reports surprisingly seem to fall back upon the standard cure prescribed by developed nations in terms of their own concepts and interests: more growth, more aid, more trade, and so on. The Brookings study expresses a strong conviction that "economic progress in the developing countries is an objective that is both attainable and right."[8] No one in the South would question such sentiments. But the question to be asked is: Why have the standard cures failed? And why have they not only failed but also generated the contradictions that aggravate the disease?

We in the South have to reexamine the presuppositions and norms on which our understanding of development and developmental policies have been based. The frame of reference must be our own socio-economic realities. There is today a legitimate debate about "liberation" versus "development." It is suggested that the first step in the process of "liberation" is to formulate social and economic goals and strategies that are relevant to domestic realities and needs. This is one of the basic elements of self-reliance. With this objective of authenticity in mind, it is possible to identify some of the specific components of self-reliant development.

1. *Rejecting Imitative Approaches.* The ambition to become a high production/high consumption society—another Japan, West Germany, or United States—is not in keeping with developing-country needs and possibilities. Increases in production and consumption have to be given high priority in the poor countries, where a large proportion of the population lives at a submarginal level. But only a high rate of growth with just distribution of total national product can ensure basic necessities to these people. There is a fundamental difference between such socially useful production and consumption and the "pursuit of affluence" that characterizes most countries of the North.

One of the most significant statements in the Overseas Development Council's *Agenda for Action* is: "We Americans should take a hard look at our ceaseless pursuit of affluence, and seek new ways to ensure that the goal of economic growth, both domestic and international, incorporates greater social justice." It is becoming increasingly evident that the world

---

[7]*Agenda for Action*, op. cit., pp. 7 and 58.
[8]*Reassessing North-South Economic Relations*, op. cit., p. 3.

does not have enough resources to allow all nations the consumption and production patterns prevalent in the developed countries. As the *Agenda* points out, "currently, the United States, with only 6 per cent of the world's population, consumes about 40 per cent of the world's raw materials and energy outputs."[9] As another study reveals, in the decade 1959-1968, the American people used more of the resources of the world than all the people of the earth consumed in all previous history.[10] And yet we find that the United States is directing its economic efforts to further increases in its standard of living. It will continue to appropriate a steadily larger share of the world's resources, some of which are nonrenewable and may be reaching the point of exhaustion. Can the world afford more U.S.A.s? Since other developed nations are pursuing similar goals, there is not much chance for the South to acquire enough resources to join in this race.

Most developing countries lack the purchasing power to bid for essential resources in a situation in which prices are rising sharply, as in the case of oil. Nor do they have sufficient political influence and economic bargaining power to get a fair share (in terms of their numbers and needs) of the world's resources. There are no indications, moreover, that the developed nations will give up their hold on these resources. Therefore, one of the harsh realities confronting most nations of the South is the paucity of available resources.

Whether or not the North itself accepts "the apocalyptic arguments which call for an end to economic expansion because of the alleged impending exhaustion of the earth's physical endowments,"[11] there already are serious "limits to growth" for the South. Should not the developing nations therefore recognize this reality and fashion their development objectives and efforts accordingly? Should they not do so even if the world community has not yet accepted a new understanding of what constitutes economic progress and well-being?

The current oil crisis underscores some of these problems. As a result of the phenomenal rise in oil prices, the bulk of foreign exchange earnings of many countries of the South will go for oil imports. India, for example, may have to use almost 80 per cent of its export earnings for that purpose. That this will put the projections of the Five-Year Plan into complete disarray is obvious. At the same time, however, despite affirmations of coordinated action, many developed nations—notably Japan, the countries of Western Europe, and the United States—are pursuing unilateral policies, guided only by their limited, individual interests, to ensure adequate oil supplies. Arrangements between France and Saudi Arabia, or between

---

[9]*Agenda for Action*, op. cit., p. 3.
[10]Charles Birch, "Three Facts, Eight Fallacies and Three Axioms about Population and Environment," *Anticipation*, September 1972, p. 9.
[11]*Reassessing North-South Economic Relations*, op. cit., p. 5.

the United Kingdom and some oil producing countries, illustrate the "each for himself" approach. In such a ruthless political-economic scramble, what chance do the developing countries have to secure even the bare minimum necessary for their survival?

In addition to the force of realism itself, which suggests that developing countries would be ill-advised to operate on the notion that development means becoming like the developed countries, this issue also has an ideological side. Some thinkers in the developed nations are pointing to the "poverty of affluence" and raising fundamental questions about the correlation between material prosperity and human well-being. Does ceaseless growth ensure human happiness? Economists generally have shied away from such "philosophical" questions, but today these are being forced upon us by socio-economic realities. It may also be said that such questions should be raised only after a society has attained some degree of material affluence and not when the majority is still living in misery and deprivation; this line of thinking is not uncommon in the developing nations. But human experience seems to indicate that a yearning for affluence only leads to insistence on still greater affluence. Therefore, the time for developing nations to consider these basic questions is *now*, before they are caught up in the "affluence syndrome." Why should we become enamored of a new kind of poverty when we have still to overcome the old?[12]

Closely related to the idea that development means imitating the developed countries is the "catching-up" fallacy. Considerable stress has been laid on the importance of reducing the gap between the North and the South, yet the gap keeps on widening. "Of the nearly $1.4 trillion of global production in 1950, about $1.1 trillion was in the rich countries and about $260 billion in the poor. By 1970, the rich countries had added $1.8 trillion to their production, while the poor countries had added only $480 billion."[13] During the last twenty years, the increase in per capita income of developing countries as a whole has been less than $1 per year. However, the difference between the average per capita incomes of developed and developing countries was around $2,220 in 1970, and it is likely to increase to $3,220 by 1980.[14] According to another projection, by the year 2000, the present 1:40 ratio between India's per capita income and that of the United States is likely to become 1:80 while the India-West Germany and India-Japan ratios become 1:40 and 1:165 respectively.[15] It also has been calculated that the increase in U.S. per

[12]On this question see also Parmar, "Environment and Growth Debate," op. cit.
[13]*Agenda for Action*, op. cit., p. 102.
[14]Mahbub ul Haq, "The Crisis in Development Strategies," *Anticipation*, December 1972, pp. 3 and 4.
[15]Donella H. and Dennis L. Meadows et al., *The Limits to Growth: A Report for the Club of Rome's Project on the Predicament of Mankind* (New York: Universe Books for Potomac Associates, 1972), based on Table 3, p. 43.

capita GNP in one year is equal to the increase that India may be able to manage in 100 years.[16] These rather dramatic figures—even if one assumes them to be somewhat exaggerated—point to the illusory nature of the "catching-up" motivation of development.

Why should developing countries accept a yardstick of development that makes them appear poorer the more they progress? By subscribing to such a viewpoint, the South would deliberately mortgage its future well-being. Self-reliance requires that developing countries relinquish such dubious concepts and evolve their own measuring rod of progress, using their own economies as the frame of reference. As long as a country's effort is an improvement on its previous best, as long as quantitative increases in output correct maldistribution, and as long as policies of development generate people's participation, it is immaterial whether there is a widening or a narrowing of international gaps. For developing countries to allow the economic conditions of the industrial nations to determine and measure their performance is a kind of self-imposed neo-colonialism.

Yet there is one sense in which the "catching-up" viewpoint can have significance. The concern for reducing the gap between rich and poor nations has relevance in a framework of international economic justice. Emphasis on justice within and between nations is an important element of self-reliance. But there is a difference between "catching-up" just to keep up with the Joneses of the North and "catching-up" as a corrective of an international maldistribution of resources and economic power.

2. *Ensuring that Social Justice Accompanies Growth.*[17] The experience of a majority of developing nations shows that increases in GNP have aggravated rather than decreased economic inequalities. Inflationary tendencies, rising unemployment, and the slow pace of welfare-oriented programs generally impose heavy burdens on the weaker sections of society and reduce their share in the social product while a small privileged group appropriates the major share.

But development should first improve the lot of the poor people in a country, not strengthen the hold of a privileged minority, as growth seems to have done. The broad classification under which a country is labeled "poor" obscures the existence in the same country of a small affluent group that controls the means of production and the levers of economic and political power. Through a built-in process of maldistribution, this small segment of the population is able to usurp an inordinately large part of the increases in GNP. That is why it is said that under the current pattern of development the rich tend to become richer and the poor,

---

[16]Haq, "Crisis in Development Strategies," op. cit., p. 4.
[17]See also Parmar, "Environment and Growth Debate," op. cit., pp. 6–7.

poorer. Such an unfair distribution in effect precludes people's participation in developmental efforts. This not only impairs the productive capacity of the economy but also generates serious social and political discontent, which in turn subverts efforts to maintain a desired rate of growth.

Yet there still are many proponents of the view that policies of social justice generally divert resources from investment to welfare and thus slow down the rate of growth. This position reflects a misunderstanding of social justice. Rightly understood, social justice is not a dole for the poor but an investment to increase the productive capacity of people—who, after all, are the most important factors of production and are, at the same time, the ones for whose benefit development is undertaken. Unless they are drawn fully into the process of production and acquire a stake in development, all efforts to maintain high growth rates will prove fruitless. There is evidence in some developing countries that impressive growth rates have been possible without social justice, if only for a short period. Such an unbalanced process tends to generate numerous contradictions (such as the examples from the Indian economy cited earlier), which ultimately have an adverse effect on production and cause a sharp slump in the growth rate. What is more serious, these contradictions create widespread instability and disorder and jeopardize future growth.

Thus the recent experience of developing countries indicates that balanced growth can be achieved only through social justice. Instead of thinking of development as a process in which growth will automatically bring about social justice, it should be affirmed that social justice should be considered a necessary precondition of growth.

The GNP-oriented view of development is aggregative and has two basic shortcomings. The first is that when it equates a higher average income with development, it bypasses the important question of *distribution*. By itself, an increase in production is a purely quantitative phenomenon. Just distribution, in contrast, relates to a society's values and institutions, and the developing countries lack institutions through which increased GNP can be transferred to lower-income groups. It is wrong to assume that increased output will "trickle down" to the poor. Developing countries consider planned action necessary for promoting production, but they have shown a strange reluctance to plan the process of distribution. Yet planning the production process and not the distribution process is a contradiction in terms. The market mechanism, on which reliance is often placed to bring about better distribution, favors groups with adequate purchasing power, i.e., higher-income groups. The demand of these groups determines what will be produced. Low-income groups by definition lack sufficient purchasing power. Hence their needs are not transformed into effective demand that can influence patterns of production. Even if the forces that increase GNP somewhat enhance the income of the poor, they still are not able to influence production to any significant degree. Under such conditions it is unsound to accept the automaticity implied in the "trickle down" idea.

From the standpoint of the developing nations, only those increases in GNP which result from a massive increase in production for those below the poverty line can be indicative of development. In other words, production priorities in developing nations must be determined in terms of social needs calculated on the basis of desirable minima. Since the resources available for development are limited, it is necessary to impose a national maximum per capita consumption level in order to release resources for the production of essentials.

The second weakness of the GNP approach stems from overlooking certain *qualitative* aspects of the use of resources. All increases in production, whether of luxury goods or basic necessities, add to the GNP. But in terms of the needs of our societies, priority should be given to the production of essentials. Slum clearance is more important than high-cost housing; increases in the production of essential commodities are more important than expansion of the luxury goods sector; increases in health and educational facilities are more important than night clubs; and small viable projects are more important than prestige projects. These vital distinctions in the application of resources do not receive sufficient weight in the aggregative GNP concept of development. Consequently, increased production becomes the cause of increased waste and misdirection of resources. From the societal standpoint, a pattern of production and consumption that fails to assign priority to essential goods and services is nonegalitarian and development-restricting, and makes growth counterproductive.

3. *Giving Priority to Social and Institutional Change.* Theories and policies of development generally have been concerned with quantities of resources and have tended to ignore the social framework (consisting of economic, political, and social institutions). If values and institutions that constitute this framework are change-resisting, then resource use is linked to the status quo. In many developing countries, existing institutions are still based on feudo-colonial values. One should not, therefore, be surprised if increases in resource inputs have strengthened nonegalitarian tendencies, creating conditions in which poverty continues to increase despite a growing output. None of the basic objectives of development—social justice, self-reliance, or growth—are possible without a radical transformation of the social framework.

Unfortunately for developing countries, most of them became enamored of quantitative and resource-dominated views of development. Take for instance the concept of the "capital-output ratio." It long was assumed that once this magic ratio had been calculated, all a country would need to do would be to procure the capital required to sustain a desired rate of growth. Thereafter, the development process itself would acquire the necessary momentum to lead the economy to the point of "take-off." Since in this view domestic savings cannot be expected to provide capital in the required amounts, developing economies were advised to seek foreign assistance and foreign investment. After almost two decades of nursing such illusions, it is now realized that unless there is a change in the structure of society—more specifically, in the institutions through which resources are used—development will not take place. A change of this nature calls for a change in values and attitudes. Realities in the South seem to indicate that some kind of cultural revolution (a radical change in values) must proceed simultaneously with the social and economic revolution.

Recently the quantitative and resource-dominated approaches to development have been subjected to considerable critical analysis. One line of thought emphasizes the importance of institutional change to ensure increasing social justice and growth: if resources are wisely allocated and brought within reach of the lower-income group, increases in production and improvements in distribution take place side by side. Although this approach itself represents a significant advance in development theory, it does not go far enough. Institutional change has to be planned and pushed through, and this necessarily involves political decisions. Economists by habit tend to shy away from political questions—which is rather strange, considering that economics is essentially *political economy*.

Resources have their own hidden values. The mighty multinational corporations which increasingly dominate the foreign investment field operate on a profit basis, owe allegiance to shareholders rather than to the developing country they enter, and establish links with owners of the means of production in the host country who are themselves motivated by possibilities of profit and increased economic power. The nature of these firms is nonegalitarian, hence their impact cannot be otherwise. We should not assume that financial resources are neutral. The values and institutions that these resources promote depend on who owns and operates them and with what objectives, as well as on the social framework in which they originate.

The widespread disillusionment with foreign aid in both donor and recipient nations provides a good example of the ineffectiveness of financial resources per se. The failures of aid generally can be attributed to two main causes. *First*, aid originates in patterns of international economic relations that reflect international inequality and flows into a traditional, feudo-colonial framework resistant to change. Therefore it has often injected the wrong impulses into the recipient economy and into international economic relations. *Second*, while aid's quantitative aspect has been stressed, very little attention has been paid to the need for supportive changes in the structures of donor nations, recipient nations, and the international economy. Thus if aid increases the productive capacity and export potential of a developing country in manufactures, this represents an important element of structural change. But this alone is not enough if it is unaccompanied by donor-nation acceptance of a new international division of labor related to the emerging pattern of production in the recipient nations. This calls for adjustments in the internal economic structure of the donor nations as well as in the international economy. All these steps have important consequences for the trade policy of developed nations. But this kind of continuing interaction between resource transfers and structural changes generally has been lacking, thereby impeding the efforts of aid recipients to achieve self-reliant development.

Conflicting Understandings of "Interdependence"

As mentioned earlier, developing countries have good reasons to support the liberalization of trade and other changes in the economic relationships between North and South, provided that these links promote international economic justice and thereby contribute to a process of self-reliant development. Unfortunately, much of what goes on in the name of international cooperation and interdependence is heavily loaded in favor of the North. If the world community desires to promote genuine interdependence, there will have to be a deliberate "tilt" toward developing nations. Such a tilting would require: a) removal of those aspects of international economic relations which act as restraints on the development of the South and b) willingness on the part of the North to make the "interdependence" concept not a mere "cover" for projecting its own interests, but rather a means to bring about a genuine complementarity of Northern and Southern interests.

But trends in international economic relations over the last two decades and the current pulls and pressures give little hope that such complementarity will be achieved. International economic relations have been and continue to be governed by the economic and political power of individual nations and groups of nations. Developing countries in general—leaving aside the newly powerful oil producing countries— have inconsequential power and are therefore at the losing end. This is evident from some of the burdens that various forms of interdependence have imposed on them.

The Present Burdens of "Interdependence" for the South. One impediment to the South's development today is the *debt burden.* "Out-payments on foreign debt threaten to increase at an average of 15 per cent or more during the 1970s and to be an extremely heavy burden for some countries."[18] Since 1966, the external debt of poor countries has doubled. "In India, for example, eight bilateral aid programs plus the IBRD with-

---

[18]*Reassessing North-South Relations*, op. cit., p. 23.

drew more from India in repayments on past aid than they gave India in new aid last year [1972]."[19] Even debt renegotiation, which is supposed to help developing nations, "is likely to be costly . . . since in many cases they will find that their credit worthiness and ability to borrow will have been damaged."[20]

In order to achieve balance in their external accounts and to reduce their reliance on foreign aid, many developing countries have embarked on policies of import restriction and export promotion. Both of these impose heavy sacrifices on their economies. Restriction of imports prevents trade from augmenting meager domestic supplies of commodities and thus contributes to scarcity, high prices, and reduced consumption, all of which generally add to the burdens on the poor. Export promotion, on the other hand, requires that exportable surpluses be squeezed out of an economy of scarcity, thereby aggravating shortages. Moreover, since some of these surpluses do not command competitive prices in the world market, their export requires subsidization. This further aggravates already heavy fiscal burdens. Developing countries are reconciled to these burdens as a necessary price of development. But existing patterns of trade and foreign assistance and the restrictive trade policies of developed nations contribute substantially to the high costs of export development.

The *trade policies of developed nations*, generally most oppressive for the developing countries, represent another burden of interdependence. Industrial countries impose "quantitative restrictions on a wide range of manufactured products, sometimes with meager justification." There are a "large number of import quotas in contravention of the GATT." The United States has been using "the technique of voluntary export restraint agreements." Japan maintained many import quotas "even in the face of a balance-of-payments surplus that assumed embarrassing proportions."[21] In the past, "negotiations on trade have been largely a rich-nation affair—as in the Kennedy Round of tariff negotiations, which provided benefits for the industrialized states but in some cases actually penalized developing countries." "Until now, the growing export trade of developing countries has been matched by a growing tendency in rich countries to seek protection of markets from 'low wage' imports." What is even more serious, "the many international economic systems that do exist actually tend to transfer resources from *poor* nations to rich—not the other way around . . . Private investment and private money flows typically follow this pattern."[22]

---

[19]*Agenda for Action*, op. cit., p. 52.
[20]*Reassessing North-South Economic Relations*, op. cit., p. 24.
[21]Ibid., p. 12.
[22]*Agenda for Action*, op. cit., pp. 10, 34, and 48.

Technology received from developed countries as part of the inter-dependence effort likewise imposes burdens by creating new problems for recipient nations.[23] Such technology often fails to relieve the burdens of unemployment and underemployment, as it is usually capital-using and labor-saving. It distorts the use of factor endowments by creating a greater demand for capital and weakening the demand for labor, which is relatively abundant. Technology imported from the developed nations also frequently aggravates the existing maldistribution of income by in-creasing the share and power of capital relative to labor. Moreover, technological dependence on the developed nations weakens efforts to achieve self-reliance. Once the leading sectors of an economy became committed to imported technology, it is far more difficult to evolve a technology more relevant to the country's social as well as economic goals.

Imported technology also generally brings with it elements of the system in which it originates, such as high consumption patterns and an inclination toward built-in obsolescence. In terms of the realities of developing countries, these represent a misdirection and waste of resources.

The Indifference of the North to the South's Problems. There is a fairly widespread feeling in the developing countries that developed nations advocate faith in interdependence when their own immediate interests are involved but tend to be indifferent when international economic relations adversely affect the interests of the South. Such feelings may appear to be parochial or chauvinistic, but they are based on considerable empirical evidence. Let us consider some examples.

In the North, there is currently great concern about the stability of the international monetary system. The Brookings Institution study certainly is not the only one to mention that "in our highly interdependent world, a well-functioning international monetary system is important for all countries, not just the principal financial powers."[24] But why has this realization dawned on the North only after the recent crises? Since the early 1950s, many developing nations have had their own variety of "dollar crisis" caused by insufficiency of dollars, gold, or other hard currencies. Why have the developed nations for so long not considered this urgent problem faced by the developing countries? Indeed, if the prob-lem of Eurodollars and Japanese surplus dollars had been tackled within a framework of North-South needs and possibilities, the international monetary system might not have been so seriously dislocated. Dollar surpluses which Western Europe and Japan found embarrassing could

---

[23]Parmar, "Environment and Growth Debate," op. cit., p. 11.
[24]*Reassessing North-South Economic Relations*, op. cit., p. 6.

have provided precious foreign exchange to developing countries to bridge their payments gap. In the process, the U.S. economy also would have been helped, as developing countries would have spent most of these dollars in the U.S. market. Yet instead of giving a chance to interdependence of the right kind, surplus dollars were used to spark off speculative activities and to disequilibriate the rates of exchange.

Consider also the inequitable distribution of the International Monetary Fund's special drawing rights (SDRs). "Nearly 75 per cent of the SDRs have been given to the 25 industrialized countries that are members of the IMF. The remaining 25 per cent went to the 88 participating poor countries."[25] So far, however, this has not received widespread recognition as an important problem—perhaps, again, because it relates to the interests of the South.

The current oil crisis that has engulfed the world economy is in fact an even greater problem for developing nations than for the developed. The former have to curtail essential production and consumption; the latter can manage by cutting down on less essential items. Countries of the South lack purchasing power to secure even their minimum requirements; countries of the North do not. As oil prices rise, the rich nations are likely to corner world supplies, leaving less for the poor—unless, of course, the oil producing nations show special consideration for their "poor cousins" in the Third World! Furthermore, the general increase in the prices of essential inputs imported from rich nations is bound to have an adverse effect on the development efforts of poor nations. Despite declarations supporting a global policy to resolve the energy crisis, some of the important developed nations are resorting to unilateral measures to protect their particular interests. It seems that the interests of the South will receive nothing more than lip service.

One final instance of the North's indifference to the problems of the South is the fact that while the oil price rises have been condemned as sudden and shattering, the steep price rises of essential commodities supplied by *developed* nations have created no similar stir. Could that be because such increases had an adverse effect mainly on developing countries and not on the North? The price of wheat went up by over 300 per cent between 1972 and 1974, placing a heavy load on food-importing developing countries, yet this awesome trend did not evoke concern and protest in developed nations on the scale of their response to the oil price increases—until the crisis reached famine proportions in many countries and spurred belated emergency measures.

In the face of such experiences, it is difficult for developing countries to believe that interdependence as envisioned by the North will not remain a cover for the self-interest of developed nations. Very little has been done in recent years to resolve the existing crisis of confidence.

---

[25]*Agenda for Action*, op. cit., p. 49.

A Projection of the North's Self-Interest? Even Northern analyses that are as sympathetic to the needs and aspirations of the South as *Reassessing North-South Economic Relations* and *Agenda for Action* offer some reasons in support of interdependence that are disquieting to the skeptical mind of the South. Considerable emphasis is placed on "collaboration on a global scale"[26] to deal with ecological threats. Other problems identified as requiring "a greater degree of common effort if they are to be successfully met" are energy supply, environmental difficulties, narcotics control, security of travel, and raw-material supply.[27]

While there can be no dispute about the importance of these problems and the need for common action by the world community, most are fallouts of the socio-economic systems of developed countries—some resulting directly from the continuing pursuit of super-affluence. To people in the South, surrounded by unrelieved poverty, these problems appear remote. For them, "poverty is the primary pollution to be eliminated,"[28] because "environment cannot be improved in conditions of poverty."[29]

It is true that an environmental disaster will not distinguish between rich and poor nations, but developing nations have become accustomed to bearing transferred burdens. Therefore, they cannot easily see why international cooperation to deal with problems originating in developed nations should have first claim on their own efforts. There also is some apprehension that the North's concern about environmental problems may push aside its concern about poverty in the South. It sometimes even seems that problems of the North are being presented as global problems so that the mechanisms of international cooperation may be used to serve the interests of rich nations. Thus, for example, interdependence has been advocated "to better provide for our own prosperity" on the doubtful assumption that "steady growth and high employment in the industrial countries are essential conditions for . . . economic progress in the nonindustrial nations."[30] Neither the evidence of the last two decades nor the spirit of self-reliant development supports this assumption. Similarly, it is advanced that while one of the principal concerns of the United States in trade negotiations is to improve its export opportunities in *developed* markets, "the United States also stands to gain a great deal from measures that would further increase its exports to the developing nations." In recent years, the U.S. trade surplus with these countries has averaged about $2 billion per year.[31] It should be remembered, however, that these countries are struggling to have an export *surplus* with the United States and other creditor

---

[26]*Reassessing North-South Economic Relations,* op. cit., p. 5.
[27]*Agenda for Action,* op. cit., p. 6.
[28]*Reassessing North-South Economic Relations,* op. cit., p. 5.
[29]Prime Minister Indira Gandhi, in an address to the United Nations Conference on the Human Environment, Stockholm, June 1973.
[30]*Reassessing North-South Economic Relations,* op. cit., pp. 5 and 6.
[31]*Agenda for Action,* op. cit., pp. 29 and 30.

nations. In this context, efforts by the United States to enlarge its exports may make the payments position of debtor nations even more difficult. In any case, there is no guarantee that an increase in U.S. exports to these countries will lead to a corresponding rise in the exports of the developing countries, particularly in view of recent trends in U.S. import policy. Expansion of trade would then serve the interests of the stronger partner.

These fears cannot be allayed by the references to positive measures for mutually advantageous trade given in the two policy analyses issued by the Brookings Institution and the Overseas Development Council. Good advice about genuine interdependence has not been lacking. But in general, developed nations have heard but not heeded it. What grounds are there for assuming that there will be a better response in the second half of the 1970s?

There is still a tendency to look upon poor countries as important "sources of raw materials, as hosts to foreign private investors, and as debtors of developed countries and international institutions." It is suggested that "with increasing U.S. demand for minerals and petroleum from abroad, it will be highly desirable to ensure adequate supplies through private investment in extractive industries. In addition, the returns on that investment would add significantly to the U.S. balance of payments, somewhat offsetting the costs of greater imports."[32] Shades of colonial trade and investment!

It is even being suggested that "the poor countries, with their far less developed economies, may well have a comparative advantage in capacity to absorb waste products for some time to come," and that "this comparative advantage may become important." Thus Japanese industrialists, for example, "are considering the location of pollution-intensive industries in poor countries."[33] From the point of view of developing countries, it is difficult to think of a more distorted application of comparative advantage. The trade policies of developed nations have raised all kinds of obstacles to deny the comparative advantage which poor countries actually enjoy in various lines of production. But when a comparative advantage allows a pollution outlet, developed nations seem to accept it with alacrity. Professions of interdependence notwithstanding, it appears that developed countries are still using existing patterns of international economic relations to serve their own narrow interests.

Toward a Long-Term Realism

International economic relations between North and South are still very much in the traditional mold and do not promote complementarity be-

---

32Ibid., pp. 32 and 44.
33Ibid., p. 102.

tween the respective priority concerns of developing and developed nations. It is difficult to suggest a way out of the impasse. The best one can do is to point to certain issues and problems that should claim the attention of the world community.

1. *If trade liberalization and other adjustments in international economic relations are to the long-run advantage of developed nations, why have they not been pursued?* Since the recent international monetary crisis, there has been a definite shift toward more restrictive trade policies, reduced foreign assistance, and a weakening of the impulse for participating in the development efforts of poor countries. The *Agenda for Action* and *Reassessing North-South Economic Relations* both present persuasive rationales for genuine interdependence. Some of their suggestions are in line with suggestions made by international organizations, progressive social scientists, and statesmen over the last two and a half decades. It has been stressed that the "enlightened self-interest" of the North requires that trade, aid, and investment relations be adapted to also promote the interests of the South. But developed nations still show a strange reluctance to move in this direction.

"Lack of political will" has sometimes been mentioned as one of the main reasons for rigidities in international economic relations. This observation is puzzling in view of the fact that nations daily exercise political will to safeguard and further their own interests. Why should there be a lack of political will if the long-term interests of developed nations demand a different pattern of economic relations than has prevailed? The answer may be that the rigidities express not a lack of political will, but the nature of the political-economic systems that operate in developed nations. Under such systems, *short-term* interests are given precedence. Therefore, instead of decrying a lack of political will, might it not be better to think of reshaping the economic system so that it could generate political will in terms of *long-run* interests based upon just economic relations between countries? The *Agenda for Action* emphasizes that the United States "will have to recognize the *political* need for a new set of attitudes and actions."[34] Since that is not possible without basic changes in the *economic* system and its goals and processes, it follows that an essential precondition for genuine interdependence between North and South is change itself. Before asking why developed nations have been reluctant to pursue more progressive policies, it may be more relevant to ask whether these nations are willing to accept economic patterns that will promote mutuality and justice between rich and poor nations.

At present, each crisis appears to bring a resurgence of narrow self-interest. This was evident after the international monetary crisis of

---

[34]Ibid., p. 19.

1970-71 and is even more evident in the current oil crisis. Chances are that a world economy built upon national rather than global interests will continue to experience more crises. Developed countries, because of their greater economic and political power, have a more significant role in determining how the world community deals with these crises. It should be recognized that concern for safeguarding existing interests and structures amounts to protecting many nonegalitarian elements in international economic relationships. This will naturally run counter to the interests of the poor nations.

2. A still more fundamental question needs to be raised. Even if it is assumed that favorable conditions exist for promoting international co-operation, it does not follow that there is complementarity between the concerns of the developing countries and those of the developed. *What is the objective of developed nations in furthering interdependence?* Is it to maintain their economic progress along present lines, i.e., as part of the "ceaseless pursuit of affluence"? If that is indeed the intent, relations between North and South will continue to be characterized by a domination of the strong over the weak, a drain of important resources from poor nations to rich, and appropriation of an increasing share of the world's resources by those who are already prosperous. This is a travesty of cooperation and interdependence. Elements of inequality and exploitation in the international economy would increase—contrary to the hopes expressed in both the *Agenda for Action* and *Reassessing North-South Economic Relations.*

A basic shortcoming in the approach of these reports, however, is that they favor more egalitarian patterns of international economic relations but fail to show how closely such changes depend on the adaptation of the economic systems and patterns of production and consumption in developed nations. While it is stressed that "the success of development also depends upon a willingness of rich countries to see a greater share of the world's resources flow to the developing countries," there is insufficient appreciation of the fact that this is not possible unless the developed nations themselves accept a new style of life—in effect, a new economic system. The lesson of economic history is that "those nations which are most powerful, and whose interests are best served by the *status quo*, have valued stability far more than change."[35] Today, stability of developed nations means a continuance of their material prosperity. This, however, is the most important cause of instability in the world economy. Unless this fundamental question is dealt with, terms like "international cooperation" and "interdependence" will merely continue to camouflage economic and political aggrandizement by the powerful groups in the world.

[35]Ibid., pp. 17 and 23.

24

3. In this setting, *how able are the developing countries to influence international decisions?* Some of them, like the oil producing countries, have found new leverage. This very leverage, however, has caused as many, if not more, problems for the South as for the North. In its efforts to arrive at a settlement with the small group of oil producing nations, the North is likely to ignore the interests of other developing countries. Increased prosperity could even lead oil producing countries into the orbit of the North as their trade and investment relations with the developed countries increase. Can the South "manage confrontation" in a way that will protect and promote its legitimate interests?

Since the basic interest of poor nations in international economic relations is to secure international economic justice, one constructive course remains available to them. They must work to establish or strengthen *domestic* structures in order to increase economic justice. Unjust international patterns influence developing countries through unjust internal patterns. Therefore, the struggle against the former must begin by reshaping internal patterns in keeping with the spirit of self-reliance. If the international climate is unfavorable to more egalitarian patterns in the international economy, the South may have to reduce its participation. Foreign assistance, foreign investment, and imported technology have not helped in the solution of its basic problems. It may be wiser to get out of the habit of depending on such relief in order to face the problems more realistically. Moreover, such links with the North have helped to perpetuate change-resisting forces in developing economies. The intention of these suggestions is not to advocate isolation. But if, after nearly twenty years of lip service to "partnership" and "sharing," the world's economy still remains unjust and nonegalitarian, what option is left the weaker segment?

4. The mood of these observations is pessimistic. It may even appear defeatist. I suggest, however, that the right adjective to describe them is "realistic." In recent years there has been a weakening of support of international organizations and an increase in unilateral action by important nations and blocs. One cannot be sanguine about the present lack of policies based upon a dynamic *international* outlook. Those who stand for such policies should concentrate on programs for arousing supportive public opinion to push governments into action. Public opinion in developed countries, especially among the working classes, is not in favor of any curbs on rising rates of growth in their own economies. Hence there will be strong resistance to a fairer use of the world's resources—since this may slow down the production process in the North and require a simpler pattern of consumption. *Without the underpinning of favorable public opinion, governments will continue in their old ways.* The thrust of this argument is to suggest that measures to create the right climate of public opinion in developed nations are as important as measures for

genuine international cooperation. They are a precondition for necessary structural changes. At this point developing countries cannot do much in this regard, nor should they try to. However, if a restructuring of domestic economies goes on in both developing and developed countries, this will complement efforts to restructure the world economy.

5. One of the important omissions of both the *Agenda for Action* and *Reassessing North-South Economic Relations* is their *failure to assign more than marginal importance to both the direct and indirect implications for development of world defense expenditures and the arms trade.* Colossal sums are spent annually by the North on armaments. Exports of armaments have become a normal part of world trade. Perhaps it is not realized that this draws developing nations into mini-armaments races against each other, causing a gross misuse of resources in their situation of poverty. A further danger is that the sophisticated technology that comes into defense industries in developing countries generates impulses that incline the economy toward such technology. Attempts to evolve a relevant technology, which is an essential part of the technological revolution that these countries badly need, are thereby seriously jeopardized.

While détente between big powers is most welcome, it may—as has already happened—encourage confrontation by proxy in the South. This is a deleterious form of international interdependence that can obliterate positive efforts to achieve better economic relations between the North and South. Discussions on development must give to questions of world peace and disarmament an importance equal to that given them in the early 1960s when the dangers of the cold war and East-West confrontation were more serious and the "one world" ideology was only emerging. Despite setbacks, the "one world" ideology is still valid and needs to be affirmed.

6. Finally, there is the matter of moral imperative. *The basic rationale for continuing to support and strive for international cooperation* (in the best sense of the term), despite an inhospitable world climate, *is neither economic nor political but moral.* "Gross inequalities in the international distribution of wealth are morally unacceptable and incompatible with world peace and prosperity." "Conscience is, of course, a large part of the problem, for there are massive and portentous inequities in the distribution of the world's wealth and income."[36] The *Agenda for Action* refers to "a great reservoir of moral concern in America," which "argues for helping developing countries to meet their critical human problems— simply because it is right." That is why the hope has been expressed that the American people will "respond to these challenges and opportunities . . . in a spirit of compassion."[37] This is the appropriate plank on

---

[36]*Reassessing North-South Economic Relations*, op. cit., pp. 4 and iii, respectively.
[37]*Agenda for Action*, op. cit., pp. 1, 7, and 3.

which efforts to make the concerns of the North and the South complementary should be built.

In fact, the most hopeful feature of the present world situation is the recently widening acceptance of justice as an objective in economic relations. But moral concern should move from sentiment to strategy. For this reason it is important to work for policies of social justice within and among nations, despite all the setbacks that have been experienced. It has wisely been suggested that "the idealist alone is the long-term realist." Our world needs to progress from the realism of the immediate to "long-term realism." This is in essence the challenge facing international economic cooperation today. The struggle for self-reliant development and genuine interdependence must be continued, not because it is readily feasible, but because it is desirable; not because it is expedient, but because it is right.

Chapter 2

Reflections on Nonalignment in the 1970s

Soedjatmoko

Like many institutions, movements, and policies that took shape during the cold war, nonalignment has been, and is still, in the process of redefining itself in the face of the changing conditions resulting from the shift toward multipolarity taking place in international politics. The concerns expressed at the 1970 Lusaka and the 1972 Georgetown Conferences of Heads of State or Government of Non-Aligned Countries reflect the awareness that of the many leverages on major powers developed by Third World countries, exploiting cold war rivalries had fallen away as a result of détente. Henceforth, in principle at least, mutual big power accommodation without any regard to Third World interests, and even at the expense of the Third World, had become possible. In general, the response of the Third World countries has been to press their demands for the changes in the international economic system expressed in the Final Act of the third United Nations Conference on Trade and Development (UNCTAD), to emphasize the need for much closer political and economic cooperation among the nonaligned nations themselves, and to emphasize the need for increasing self-reliance. On the whole, despite its many complications for the nonaligned world, détente was seen as a vindication of the basic premises of nonalignment.

It is the purpose of this chapter to explore some of the broader implications of multipolarity for nonalignment and to discuss some problems that the nonaligned countries will have to face in order to maintain their thrust

NOTE: This chapter is an elaboration of a paper originally presented to the Seminar on Non-Alignment, organized by the Indonesian Institute of International Affairs in Jakarta in May 1973 and issued in *The Indonesian Quarterly* in July 1973. Reprinted with permission of the author.

and coherence in the new fluidity that characterizes international politics in this post-cold-war thaw.

This new fluidity in international politics is the result of many factors. There is the erosion of the credibility of superpower deterrence and the substantial loss of cohesiveness of the security-oriented coalitions and structures of the cold war; the emergence of Japan, Europe, and China as more-or-less autonomous centers of power, still uncertain of their role but too strong to be ignored; a continuing shift in the balance of power and of competitive capability among the major industrial countries and regions, as well as shifts in the political balance and prevailing value orientations within some of the major powers. All that can be said with certainty about this new fluidity in international politics is that no valid prediction can be made about either the real significance or the ultimate direction of the changes that are now in progress.

It is conceivable, for instance, to think of the future in terms of a relatively stable multipolar balance. In this light, the breakdown of the international monetary system might be viewed as a short-term crisis and the trend toward the further liberalization of world trade might be seen as only temporarily interrupted by sectoral claims for protectionism in a number of industrial countries. Present manifestations of a new economic nationalism among some of the industrial countries could in this context be overcome by the codification of new "rules of the game" for international trade, reconciling "free trade" with some irreducible requirements of national economic integrity. Such a development would also reduce the danger of the world system falling apart into spheres of economic and political influence in which the Third World countries would inevitably be split up and arranged in neocolonial structures along various North-South axes. This scenario also would make possible the gradual reduction of those built-in features of the present system of international trade that discriminate against the developing countries, and might also—though not necessarily—lead to improvements in the kinds of aid and the terms of aid, as well as in the effective transfer of technology and science.

This rather hopeful scenario is not, however, the only one that should be considered. Other scenarios are possible, and the nonaligned nations can ignore them only at their own peril. For a variety of international and domestic reasons, it is not entirely beyond the realm of possibility that no new viable international monetary system will be agreed upon, and that makeshift remedies will continue to break down. The resulting uncertainties, speculations, and protectionist pressures could lead to a long period of neglect of the problems of international poverty. This in turn might lead to a strong political radicalization in the Third World and to political upheavals in a number of developing countries that would threaten the security of raw-material supplies to a number of industrial countries. If we assume continued internal confusion in the United States and the collapse of its political will to assert its power internationally, it could be argued, as some American analysts do, that this would leave the Soviet Union, as the superpower least dependent on external resources, in the strongest position to shape a new international system—insofar as it is possible to speak of an international system at all under such conditions. This scenario of course assumes that the Soviet Union can overcome its dependency on grains from the capitalist world and remain invulnerable to domestic pressures arising out of its nationalities problem and the desire for political liberalization.

A third and rather grim scenario was presented in a very provocative article by Lord Gladwyn in the April 1973 issue of the *Ecologist*. Commenting on the general conclusions of *The Limits to Growth*,[1] published under the auspices of the Club of Rome, Lord Gladwyn suggested that continued growth might not end in worldwide collapse, but in "regional totalitarianism, with Japan allied economically and philosophically with China, a new social and political system in the socialist countries, the industrial economy of the United States in collapse, Western Europe living within its resources, and the populations of the Third World victims of a series of natural disasters."[2]

It is of course possible and necessary to shoot holes in such scenarios as well as to think up others. The main significance of such scenarios lies not in their degree of probability, but in their implicit suggestion that we are quite possibly only at the beginning of very profound changes in the international structure and dynamics of the world, and that it would be a mistake to look at the changes that are taking place now only in terms of their difference from older patterns, or in terms of their immediate implications. Such scenarios bring out very clearly that there is no automaticity in the emergence of a new international system to replace the one that has shaped international politics in the years since World War II. They also suggest how great is the stake of the nonaligned countries of the Third World in a viable international system that gives sufficient scope to meeting the soaring expectations of the Third World. They demonstrate the essential need for the nonaligned countries to help shape such a new international system.

In order to do so, it will be important for the nonaligned countries to develop the analytical tools needed for an understanding of how such a new system might work and what its requirements for viability might be. And subsequently, it will also be important to forge the operational instruments that will make it possible for the nonaligned countries to play such a creative role. Analysts like Alastair Buchan have written about the con-

---

[1]Donella H. and Dennis L. Meadows et al., *The Limits to Growth: A Report for the Club of Rome's Project on the Predicament of Mankind* (New York: Universe Books for Potomac Associates, 1972).

[2]Lord Gladwyn, "The Logic of Growth," *Ecologist*, Vol. 3, No. 4 (April 1973), p. 130.

cepts of "multiple coexistence" and "mutual interpenetration" as important tools for understanding and shaping multipolar balance under conditions of interdependence. The concept of multiple coexistence denotes the working out of arrangements for coexistence not only among the major powers, but also for cooperation among smaller countries with different social and political systems and for cooperation between smaller countries and neighboring large ones. The concept of mutual interpenetration points to the requirement that no area in the world is to be considered the exclusive sphere of influence of any major power. All regions should be accessible to all major powers, though possibly with different mixtures of such external influences. The emergence in the wake of détente of nonsecurity problems such as monetary and economic problems, problems of cultural and scientific exchange, and those arising out of the new concern for environment—all within the general setting of interdependence—will undoubtedly give rise to new country groupings that partially overlap and crosscut in a variety of ways. The possibility that is now open of membership in functional as well as regional groupings of various kinds serving a multiplicity of specific objectives and cutting across traditional ideological boundaries is bound to enhance the overall stability of such a new international system, given at least an adequate measure of stability in the strategic relationship between the major powers. All this does not necessarily mean that such mutual interpenetration actually will take place. The tendency not to take risks for the sake of an uncertain future—or, more concretely, for a new but not entirely predictable international system—is still a real one, and the world may fall back on older patterns of coercive diplomacy simply for lack of imagination or as a result of the inadequacy of political will on the part of some key nations.

It is very obvious that the nonaligned nations have a primary interest in stopping the tendency toward new types of bipolarization and inward looking regional groupings. They will have to strengthen all impulses toward a new global system. The requirements for multipolar dynamic equilibrium in a global setting of multiple coexistence give a new relevance to the concept of regional arrangements. The term regional arrangements is not used here in its traditional cold war sense of alliances directed against a particular country or alliances such as NATO, CENTO, or the Warsaw Pact, but in the sense of Article 52 of the United Nations Charter—that is, in the sense of a regional system for the peaceful resolution of conflict. It might, for instance, at some point be found useful for all countries in the Asia Pacific region and all the major powers to have a common forum in which to air their differences, to express their misgivings and fears, to account for their actions and policies as they impinge on the interests of other countries, and to try to conciliate incipient conflicts. Such regional arrangements might be able to deal more effectively than previous ones with regional problems, without the distorting impact of outside voting blocs. Problems of the Asia Pacific region could then be handled without reference to African voting patterns. An Indian Ocean Basin regional structure could profitably ignore Latin American voting patterns. Similarly, given a successful outcome of the European Security Conference, an Atlantic-European regional arrangement could operate on the basis of and within the United Nations Charter. The existence of such regional arrangements would give new vitality to the United Nations in problems of security and the peaceful resolution of conflicts.

Within such arrangements, the impact of a region's nonaligned countries would very much depend on their ability and willingness gradually to harmonize their policies on foreign policy problems and to vote together. This may not always be easy to arrange, despite the fact that these countries have in common the problems of poverty; there is in various places also a heritage of traditional rivalries, dynastic conflict, and residual border disputes often exploited in the past by the colonial ruler. Moreover, most of the nonaligned countries are still searching for or developing the social, political, and economic systems that will enable them to surge forward and sustain a rapid pace of development. Most of them also have to contend with the disaffection and political discontent of various ideological orientations and degrees of radicalization. Some processes of change and even some forces pressing for change cut across national boundaries, creating a number of intraregional problems and constituting a threat to the integrity of the nations concerned. The need to develop regional cohesiveness and the need to vote together in the United Nations and in the regional arrangements discussed here may well necessitate the promulgation of a new "code of conduct" and may call for the establishment of mechanisms for conflict resolution within the various regions.

Such regional cooperation would also require very close cooperation in developing the intellectual concepts and common language that are needed to come to grips with the security problems of the region in the new conditions of multipolarity. It is possible to put the relationship between such regional arrangements and the struggle of the nonaligned nations in more precise terms. Such regional arrangements could only be of benefit to the nonaligned nations to the extent that these nations do develop their capacity to vote together on most issues of common interest. It would therefore be in the interest of the nonaligned nations to press for such regional arrangements only as fast as their capacity to work and vote together evolves. If such cooperation and identity of views can be achieved, the existence of such a broader formal regional forum might not even be essential for the purposes of the nonaligned world. It might, under certain conditions, be conceivable that a meeting of the nonaligned nations in a particular region on a particular set of problems of interest to them all might have considerable impact. In fact, Yugoslavia's idea of a meeting of nonaligned nations on the problems of the Mediterranean basin falls within this category.

In speaking about regional arrangements, however, one cannot escape the question of how such regional groupings could be prevented from deteriorating into the kind of autarkic regional organizations that would condemn the weak and small nations to a position of neocolonialist subservience. It is of the greatest importance that such regional arrangements should have no exclusive claim on the loyalty of their members—which used to be the case in the hierarchical structure of the cold war coalitions. If a new international system is to come into being at all, it will have to be based on a combination of such regional as well as functional, transregional relationships or coalitions involving major powers, nonaligned countries, and other weak and small nations. It is also of the greatest importance that the nonaligned members of a regional forum participate in other organizations or coalitions serving specific purposes in the fields of trade, industry, aid, scientific and technological cooperation, environment, etc. The best guarantee against the development of closed systems—and for the openness of a new international system—would be the establishment of a dense network of partially overlapping organizations and coalitions, with cross-cutting memberships.[3] This leads us to consider the question of the forging of new global organizations.

The so-called "energy crisis" in the United States and the concern of Western Europe and Japan about oil supplies on the one hand, and the efforts of the oil producing countries to bring about overdue adjustments in price and production relations on the other, point up the growing need for a more rational system of raw-material and energy-supply management before politically dangerous competitive drives set in. The Conference on the Law of the Sea provides another example of the need for the creation of global structures for the management and equitable distribution of the benefits of global resources. Another example of the need for worldwide regulation is the role and social and political responsibilities of the multinational corporations. These giant concentrations of managerial skill, technology, and capacity to mobilize capital are already important factors in the growth of the world economy. In the world of the future, as manifestations of a new type of sovereignty, they may well be equally or almost as important in shaping and giving direction to the international system as are nation states. The attempts in the United Nations to establish a legal code governing the behavior of the multinational corporations, and the new U.N. Charter of Economic Rights and Duties of States are both efforts to deal with this problem.[4] The need for global systems has also become obvious in other fields, such as monitoring and regulating the use of the globe's atmospheric, water, and terrestrial resources, and in global communications.

---

[3]See Seyom Brown, "The Changing Essence of Power," *Foreign Affairs*, Vol. 51, No. 2 (January 1973), pp. 286–99.
[4]See Annex B-2, p. 203.

It is obvious that the nonaligned nations must ensure adequate representation for themselves in the international regimes that will have to be created, to enable them to protect their own interests and the interests of the weak in general, as well as to see to it that these international authorities become effective vehicles for the creation of a more equitable international order. This struggle is bound to be a political one and one that will require a concentration of the limited expertise and scarce intellectual resources of the nonaligned nations.

If this struggle bogs down in irreconcilable demands, the prospect is one of a long period of heightened conflict between the industrial countries and the poor nations of the Third World. In that case, there would seem to be no other recourse but to start thinking in terms of the establishment of producer cartels for those products of the Third World that are in relatively short supply—such as copper, tin, and perhaps manganese, coffee, and cocoa—possibly financed out of the large reserves built up by some nonaligned countries from their oil revenues in order to ensure a stronger bargaining position for the nonaligned world, with a view to press more effectively for such global systems. In any case, the nonaligned nations have a large stake in the development of such global systems, and their preoccupation with the very real and continuing problems of colonialism and imperialism should not blind them to the urgency and magnitude of this other struggle—one which may make a crucial difference to the future of the Third World.

The Lusaka Conference of nonaligned nations adopted the thesis that, in order to achieve greater autonomy and to have a greater impact on the international system, the nonaligned nations themselves would need to attain greater self-reliance, and that the road to greater self-reliance was through greater economic cooperation *within* the nonaligned world. However, as yet, not much has come of such economic cooperation; nor has there been any significant implementation of the call of President Kaunda of Zambia for the establishment of the machinery for maintaining contact with one another. There is no doubt about the urgency and importance of creating such machinery, both at the governmental and especially at the nongovernmental level. It is simply not enough for government leaders to meet regularly and listen to each other's speeches. What is needed is a continuing flow of information among the nonaligned countries, as well as an infrastructure that makes this possible. There is no sense in closing our eyes to the appalling ignorance that exists among our countries about each other and about each other's regions. It is not an exaggeration to state, for instance, that the countries of Southeast Asia need to know a great deal more about each other before regional cooperation can take on substantial meaning. The problem is much worse, moreover, when it comes to knowledge available in Southeast Asia about the nonaligned countries of Africa or Latin America. All this points to the need for formal and informal structures that can make possible regular and frequent meetings between parliamentarians, editors, scholars, businessmen, and trade unionists from the nonaligned countries.[5]

Intergovernmental structures generally do not come to life unless a constituency is created—often deliberately—in the countries concerned. In each country, for instance, at least one university or research institution should specialize in studies related to the nonaligned world. This would be one way of providing relevant data on a continuing basis. Apart from concentrating on some of the problems discussed here, and on the whole range of problems that have become the concern of UNCTAD, special emphasis should be given by such institutes to the identification of divergences and possible conflicts of interests, and ways in which these differences could be resolved. Conflict resolution and the conciliation of policy differences are concerns that will eventually help widen the options open to nonaligned statesmen in their efforts to weld the closer inter-nonaligned cooperation that is desired. All this will require special funding, and centers such as those proposed here could also usefully undertake to study and suggest some alternative ways of financing work in this area.

Implicit in the resolutions on self-reliance adopted at the Lusaka Conference of nonaligned nations and since has been the recognition that the reasons for the slowness of development are related not only to the difficulties of resource flows from the rich industrial countries to the poor, to the problems of transfer of science and technology, or to the discriminatory character of the international trade system, but also to social-political structures within the nonaligned countries themselves. Three problems have become particularly clear in this connection.

The first is that in former colonies, concentration on economic growth—prior to changing the structure of the economy from a colonial one geared to serving the needs of the colonizer into a national, modern growth economy—only strengthens the foreign sector at the expense of the domestic sector. In the process of transformation, the role and rapid development of the indigenous entrepreneur, whether private or public, is one of the most important instruments. Such entrepreneurial capability has come to be recognized as the crucial factor determining the growth capability of the domestic sector of the national economy.

Second, for the more populous poor countries, the adoption of the consumer patterns and consumption levels of the rich industrial countries before the development of an adequate domestic industrial base, and the broad proliferation in the countryside of modern technology not adapted to the needs and resources of the rural area are bound to perpetuate and even increase dependency on the rich industrial countries and to widen the

---

[5]*Editors' note:* The creation of the Third World Forum is one recent response to this need. See Annex A-3, p. 178.

gap between the modern elite and the society at large, with serious political consequences.

Third, it has become obvious that development is not so much economic growth as it is the cultivation of the *capacity* to grow—the capacity to respond creatively to new challenges. This is not possible without modernizing and democratizing the traditional social-political structures and without overcoming the vestiges of feudal or colonial relations within the nonaligned societies themselves. Self-reliance needs social-political structures capable of releasing the creative energies of people and conducive to responsible, autonomous activity and decision making.

There is thus an internal dimension to nonalignment which is increasingly making a claim on our attention and efforts. It is not going too far to conclude that, while nonalignment is a reflection of the deep alienation from the world as presently structured, it has even deeper roots in the yearning not only for independence and economic betterment in a more equitable world order, but also for freedom, justice, and progress within their own societies. Nonalignment is merely the external projection of that yearning.

In conclusion, it may be said that the period of the 1970s is one of great promise, opened up by great-power détente. At the same time, it is also a period of great danger for the nonaligned world. None of the major powers is in a position of providing the intellectual and moral leadership now so needed to give shape to a new international system, and to prevent a drift toward regressive structures and methods of coercive diplomacy, which can only operate to the detriment of the Third World. It is therefore of the greatest importance that the nonaligned world not simply continue to give expression to the broad consensus on external problems already achieved—such as the struggle against colonialism, imperialism, and facism, and the struggles for the right to national self-determination and territorial integrity, for disarmament, and for a more equitable system of international trade. In order to increase its capacity for effective action, the Third World also will have to pay more attention to its own weaknesses and to develop ways to reduce them. Many of these weaknesses are the result of legitimate differences in ideological orientation, differences in concept and stage of development, as well as of differences in regional preoccupations, leading to different emphases and priorities in the various regions of the Third World. As recent events have shown, the nonaligned nations will have to take much more seriously the likelihood of conflict and even wars between nations of the Third World. They will also have to look for ways to improve their capacity for joint political action, not only in connection with the problems discussed here, but also in relation to questions of how to help prevent further nuclear proliferation and of how to prevent the arms trade from industrial countries to the Third World from destabilizing and weakening it further. At the same time, some reconsideration of the relationships and modes and intensity of cooperation between the nonaligned nations and the other medium-sized and small nations that so far have stayed outside the nonaligned world seems to be in order as the consequence of multipolarity. The nonaligned world also will have to take into account the likelihood—especially in case of a failure to establish early on a new international monetary system—of more and sharper conflicts between the rich industrial nations and the Third World. Nevertheless, opportunities do exist for the nonaligned nations to give shape to a more satisfactory international system, providing that they can broaden their vision and develop the additional capabilities needed to wage that noble struggle for a just and viable world community.

Chapter 3

The New Interdependence

Ali A. Mazrui

The first three quarters of this century have come to a close. Nineteen seventy-five is a year of reflection about whether the remaining quarter of a century will witness that level of international economic justice which the rest of the century had thought about and talked about—but never found the will or even the inclination to pursue.

At the heart of this question is the old issue of equality, which in history has always been linked to the tensions of interdependence. The degree to which men have needed each other has been at the core of their interrelationships. Theories about the consequences of the division of labor, and about the origins of caste, class, and hierarchy, essentially have been concerned with issues of equality and issues of interdependence. It is quite clear from both the history of social institutions and the history of social ideas that interdependence could either create or destroy equality. The critical factor concerns the precise nature of that interdependence.

Ever since the energy crisis hit the headlines of the world press, a new agonizing reappraisal of interdependence among nations has been under way among both scholars and policy makers. Discussions have gone on between the European Community and the Arab oil producers concerning the possibility of exchanging European technology for Arab oil in a bid for mutually induced economic development. The U.S. government has explored ways of strengthening relations between Western Europe and the United States in search of a new economic basis for the Atlantic partnership. The United Nations has discussed the problems of raw materials in relation to

NOTE: This chapter is reprinted, with permission, from James W. Howe and the staff of the Overseas Development Council, *The U.S. and World Development: Agenda for Action, 1975* (New York: Praeger Publishers, Inc., 1975).

international trade, and one eminent speaker after another has called for a new definition of international interdependence.

But what was central to all these discussions and debates was an ancient moral problem: the problem of equality—at once simple and taxing, at once topical and perennial.

In this paper, three stages of interdependence are distinguished: primitive, feudo-imperial, and mature. The *first* of these stages, primitive interdependence, exists in conditions of rudimentary technology and limited social horizons. In most parts of the world, primitive interdependence within individual societies is a matter of the past, with only a few residual elements surviving to the present day. But there are small societies in the developing world that are still characterized by very limited and narrow social horizons, and by very rudimentary and primordial technology. To the extent that their members are mutually dependent for the fulfillment of their needs, such societies do exhibit precisely what we here mean by primitive interdependence.

The *second* stage is feudo-imperial interdependence, which seeks to combine some of the characteristics of feudalism and some of the attributes of imperialism. A central characteristic of this kind of interdependence is *hierarchy*, and hierarchy is of course founded on the premise of inequality.

The *third* stage of interdependence is one which combines sophistication with symmetry. The sophistication comes from enhanced technological capabilities and expanded social and intellectual awareness; the symmetry emerges out of a new egalitarian morality combined with a more balanced capacity for mutual harm. The different parties in this stage of interdependence must not only need each other—their different needs also must be on a scale that enables serious mutual dislocations in case of conflict. The combination of an egalitarian ethic and reciprocal vulnerability within a framework of wider technological and intellectual frontiers provides the essence of mature interdependence.

Technological Change and Social Imbalance

Relations among nations in the first three quarters of the twentieth century have been primarily feudo-imperial or hierarchical—without either the kinship solidarity of primitive interdependence or the sophisticated symmetry of mature interdependence. One of the most important questions confronting the last quarter of the twentieth century is whether the human race is at last about to evolve a genuine pattern of mature interdependence before this momentous century comes to a close.

The most basic factor behind the West's rise to imperial preeminence was the technological revolution in Europe. The rise of new techniques of production and the utilization of new forms of energy and mechanical implements set the stage for the West's expansion and territorial colonization. A basic paradox soon revealed itself. While the industrial revolution in Europe prepared the way for domestic equality within each country, it at the same time established the basis of major international disparities between the industrialized world on the one hand, and much of the rest of the world on the other. From the eighteenth century onward, technology helped to lay the foundations of a more egalitarian England and an even more egalitarian America; yet that same technology, by increasing the inventive and productive capabilities of these societies way beyond those attained by others, initiated a process of massive disparities of income and power among the nations of the world.

At the global level, the United States grew to become the richest and most industrially developed country. The distance between the United States and a country like Niger, Mali, or Tanzania in terms of affluence and technological sophistication illustrated the powerful tendency of modern technology to widen disparities far more than was conceivable a few generations ago. These levels of affluence had their repercussions on the global plane. The Northern hemisphere as a whole consumed a staggeringly disproportionate share of the scarce resources of the world, conducted the bulk of international trade, controlled much of the world's finance, and enjoyed the highest standards of living as yet attained by man. Asia, Africa, and Latin America were overshadowed in both living standards and outright power.

To some extent, this world order did involve a form of interdependence. Primary producers contributed raw materials and oil and other sources of energy to the manufacturing and industrial plants of the Northern hemisphere, and they received processed goods and products of highly sophisticated technology in return. It was claimed that this was indeed a sound basis for partnership between the poorer societies of the world in Asia, Africa, and Latin America, and their more affluent neighbors to the North. Copper from Zambia and Chile, coffee from Brazil and Uganda, oil from the Middle East and Venezuela, tea and jute from Pakistan, rubber from Malaya, uranium from Niger, cloves from Zanzibar, and cocoa from Ghana all provided a pattern of contributions from the Southern hemisphere to the life style and methods of production of the people of the North. Back from the North came radios and bicycles, typewriters and train engines, knives and forks, padlocks and tractors. A partnership was presumed to have grown out of the natural processes of economic and industrial change. It was indeed a system of interdependence, but the interdependence was once again feudo-imperial. The richer countries seemed to be getting richer still; the poorer seemed to remain in indigence. "Nothing prospers like prosperity"—so the international system of the world seemed to affirm. An old adage thus discovered a new and ominous vindication. Under the impetus of technological success, the North was widening more than ever the gap existing between itself and the less fortunate sectors of the human race.

And then one day the term "energy crisis" entered the vocabulary of international affairs. A developing-country poet might have written, as William Wordsworth did of the French Revolution:

> Bliss was it in that dawn to be alive
> But to be young was very heaven!

Economic Power and New Strategies

The October 1973 war in the Middle East helped the process of reawakening in the developing world. The war was fought at two levels—the military and the diplomatic. From the point of view of the Middle East, both levels were perhaps equally important. The relatively modest military successes of the Arabs were politically important beyond their military significance. They certainly helped to restore Egyptian and Syrian morale, and contributed toward destroying the belief in some circles of the world that Israel was invincible.

But while these military factors were quite fundamental to the Middle East itself, it was the *economic* war waged by the Arabs that fired the imagination of the developing countries. From the point of view of the rest of Asia, Africa, and the Middle East, it was neither the tank battle in the Sinai nor the air battle over the Golan Heights that was basic to their own destiny. Rather, it was the utilization of oil as a political weapon, with all its implications for relations between the affluent industrial world and the primary producers of the Southern hemisphere.

From this economic point of view, the term "October War" is somewhat inaccurate. The Arab *economic* war for the restoration of Arab lands lasted for several months longer than the Arab *military* challenge to Israel. In a sense the use of Arab economic power in order to recover those lands still continues.

What the Arab economic war revealed were two potentially critical strategies for creating a new economic order in the world: the strategy of *counter-penetration* by the Southern countries into the dominant countries of the North, and the strategy of *inter-penetration* between the different sections of the South itself. Before examining these two approaches in greater detail, another school of thought should be mentioned that has many adherents in the developing world: the strategy of disengagement.

Disengagement: An Elusive Dream

Those who promote a strategy of disengagement seek to explore the maximum possibilities of "emancipation" from the international capitalist system. But here one must distinguish between domestic and international capitalism. There are developing-world theoreticians who assume that by eliminating capitalism at home, they would necessarily "disengage" from the international capitalist system. What they overlook is that a country can abolish private enterprise and even private property at home and still be wholly dependent on the vagaries of trade with the capitalist countries and the fluctuations of the capitalist monetary system.

The Soviet Union, domestically socialist in at least economic organization, has been groping for ways to strengthen its links with the capitalist system. It has negotiated the involvement of Japanese firms in the exploitation of mineral resources in Siberia and has sought Japanese expertise in related economic endeavors. It likewise has been keen on expanding trade with the United States. The attainment of most-favored-nation status, which signifies eligibility for concessions gained by all participants in international trade negotiations, has been one of the Soviet Union's economic ambitions in the process of consolidating detente with the United States. Even the 1971-72 grain deal between the Soviet Union and the United States was envisaged by both sides as a step toward strengthening Soviet links with U.S. private enterprise. In that grain deal, Soviet commercial skills in the art of "maximizing returns" were impressively revealed. What all this meant was that a superpower like the Soviet Union, while committed to domestic socialism, might nonetheless find it moral and prudent to strengthen its links with international capitalism.

A similar trend is discernible in the economic attitude of the People's Republic of China. It is true that China pursued a policy of isolation for over twenty years, yet its isolation did not take place entirely by choice. The United States took the leadership for that period in ostracizing the People's Republic. When, under former President Richard M. Nixon, the United States at last decided to end its policy of ostracism, and to court Chairman Mao's China instead, the latter did not resist the overtures. Since then China has begun to respond to economic explorations from Japanese and Western European as well as from American business firms. China has not yet moved as enthusiastically as the Soviet Union to strengthen links with international capitalism, but the trend is in that direction.

If "disengagement" from the international capitalist system is difficult even for such socialist giants as the Soviet Union and China, it is bound to be an elusive dream for most developing countries.[1]

The Strategy of Southern Counter-Penetration

As already mentioned, one of the two major strategies for changing the existing international economic order is that of Southern counter-

---

[1]The strategy of disengagement should not, however, be confused with yet another important school of thought in some developing countries which counsels developing countries not to imitate the values, methods, and institutions of the North but to design or discover and adapt indigenous ones. This school does not seek to isolate or disengage the South from economic transactions with the international capitalist system.

penetration. In 1975 the oil producers will have many billions of dollars available for investment abroad. Should they use it for investment in the developing world or in the Northern hemisphere? The answer would seem to be that they should do *both*—since their increasing investment in the European Community and in the United States clearly will advance their objective of counter-penetration.

Japanese counter-penetration of the United States is an illustration of how a former appendage of American capitalism became a serious economic rival to the United States. Japanese businessmen have recently been manipulating aspects of the American economy almost as effectively as American businessmen once manipulated Japan. The strategy of counter-penetration in Japan's relations with the West so far has been dramatically and convincingly vindicated.

Compared with Japan's capabilities for counter-penetration, those of the developing countries still seem very modest; yet the oil producers may help to create a kind of leverage that could one day transform the world economic order. Disengagement from the capitalist system would only weaken countries such as Libya, Iran, Nigeria, and Saudi Arabia. Moreover, it is their potential influence within the system that much of the rest of the South really needs. Parts of the Northern hemisphere are beginning to feel the countervailing power of parts of the South.

Even as the Arab world celebrated the first anniversary of the October 1973 war, two trends were already discernible among the industrialized nations. One was a campaign to get the petrodollars recycled—a campaign led by the United Kingdom, which was eager to persuade the oil producers to invest their surplus capital in countries such as itself. This approach had already met with some success. Both Iran and the Arab world were evolving an aggressive commercial enthusiasm and had begun widespread soundings for new investment opportunities. Chancellor Helmut Schmidt of the German Federal Republic announced in November 1974 that a Middle Eastern government had bought a substantial share of the Daimler-Benz Corporation, the manufacturer not only of Mercedes cars but also of some military vehicles. It later transpired that the government concerned was Kuwait, which had acquired a 14 per cent interest in the firm. A few months earlier, Iran had acquired a 25 per cent interest in the steel division of the massive Krupp Enterprises. Other industrial and commercial enterprises in the Western world which had entered, or were reported to have entered, into discussion with oil producers included Lockheed Aircraft Corporation in the United States, Pan American World Airlines, and Grumman Aerospace Corporation.

But precisely because the oil producers were beginning to take seriously the Western invitation to recycle and reinvest their dollars, a second trend was also discernible in the West—a groping for ways to "contain the threat of excessive foreign investment." At a news conference early in December 1974,

Secretary of State Henry Kissinger indicated that the U.S. government wished to study "the implications of substantial investments" by the oil-producing countries in the United States, "how we can keep track of them," and the identification of the "dangers against which we must guard."[2]

More specifically, the American government was becoming concerned that some oil-producing countries might attempt to take over financial control of critical defense industries. The anxieties were partly an outgrowth of Iran's summer 1974 offer of a loan to help financially troubled Grumman Aerospace Corporation. Iran's offer originally envisaged the acquisition of a potential equity position in the company. A controversy flared up, influenced by the fear that some oil-producing countries might attempt to take over control of industries that are critical to American defense needs. The Defense Department resolved the Grumman case by insisting that Iran should not be given equity control of this traditional producer of fighter planes for the U.S. Navy. A full-scale study was ordered a few months later by the Ford Administration about the wider implications of this new wave of foreign investments into the United States. A distinction was beginning to be made behind the scenes between investment from military allies such as Western Europe and Japan, and investment from non-aligned developing countries with different political and economic imperatives. In the words of a December 1974 report in the *The New York Times*:

> In contemplating a possible invasion of Arab oil money, the Defense Department finds itself trying to walk a line between an over-all Administration policy of welcoming foreign investments and a desire to protect the defense sector against foreign control. In the past year, there have been some rumblings of discontent in the Congress over foreign investment in American industry—faint echoes thus far compared to the cries in Canada and Europe over alleged domination by American investments. . . . At a news conference last Friday, James R. Schlesinger, Secretary of Defense, said his department would examine any attempt by a foreign government to acquire a major or controlling interest in an American contractor doing classified work "with great caution and on a case-by-case basis."[3]

If the strategy of counter-penetration achieves nothing else, it should at least increase American understanding of the fears of those who have previously expressed anxieties about the U.S. economic presence in other lands. Such a fundamental reexamination by the United States of the role of

---

[2]See *The New York Times,* December 8, 1974, and December 10, 1974.

[3]*The New York Times,* December 10, 1974. Consult also Paul Lewis, "Getting Even: A Redistribution of the World's Wealth," *The New York Times Magazine,* December 15, 1974, pp. 13, 76-93.

foreign investment in world affairs could itself have far-reaching implications. Yet that would only be the beginning. The long-term potential of counter-penetration lies in creating conditions which would help to force the creation of a new international economic order.

What should be borne in mind is that counter-penetration consists of more than just the recycling of petrodollars into the developed world. An even more fundamental aspect of the strategy is the conversion of developing-country resources from their oil role as sources of dependency to a new role as sources of power. Part of this conversion is merely a change in the level of political consciousness and economic astuteness. For as long as the Arabs did not realize that their oil was a potential source of immense power, their oil became a pretext for their own exploitation by others. But as the oil producers attained new levels of economic awareness and political consciousness, they first began demanding bigger percentages of profits from the expatriate oil companies. As they obtained larger and larger percentages of the profit, and as the consumption of oil in the developed world increased, an awesome realization dawned upon the consciousness of the oil producers. If they were united, they could transform their dependency into power. The Organization of Petroleum Exporting Countries (OPEC)—originally conceived primarily as an instrument for pressuring the foreign oil companies—was soon to enter the mainstream of world economic diplomacy. Without their realizing it, the age of counter-penetration by the South had begun.

In addition to these two aspects of counter-penetration (recycling petrodollars and converting primary resources from a symptom of dependency to a tool of power), the strategy of counter-penetration also requires a sensitivity to the implications of the international monetary system. The immense foreign reserves in the hands of the oil producers should be used to force changes in the international monetary system in the direction of easing the burdens of the developing countries. The potentialities of this monetary power in the hands of oil-producing countries was illustrated in December 1974. A major oil company almost casually revealed that Saudi Arabia no longer wanted to be paid in sterling for its oil. Until then, Saudi Arabia had received about a quarter of its oil revenue in the form of the British pound. The new decision created consternation in London. The pound descended to an all-time low in Western markets, and the stock exchange in London reverberated with gloom. The Bank of England had to supply millions in support of the pound. The only silver lining of that cloud was the possibility that Saudi Arabia would continue to invest in Great Britain, even when it no longer accepted pounds for its oil. The future of sterling as a world currency was briefly under cloud simply because one Arab country was unilaterally reconsidering its financial options. The world thus caught a glimpse of the potential power of the oil producers to force major changes in the international monetary system.

Finally, the counter-penetration strategy also has a demographic element related to population distribution. The "brain drain" from the developing into the developed world could one day become a source of Southern influence within the North—comparable in principle to the role played by Jewish intellectuals and businessmen in Europe and North America in defense of Israeli interests. Given that Israel has been so dependent on the United States, especially for economic and military support, and therefore has been deeply penetrated by America, the Jewish presence within the United States is a case of demographic counter-penetration. There are other examples of such demographic counter-penetration in the United States, including the political influence of Irish Americans made evident in varying degrees since the last quarter of the nineteenth century. The more recent influence of Greek Americans on U.S. policy in the Mediterranean is another case in point.

As for the more humble migratory patterns from poorer countries to richer countries, these too might one day serve comparable purposes. The world of the future will include interlocking population centers—Blacks in the Americas and Europe, Whites in Africa, Jews in North America and the Middle East, Arabs in Africa, East Indians in the Caribbean, and perhaps one day even Chinese in Australia. Some population exchanges will be symmetrical, for example, Blacks in the White world "in exchange" for Whites in the Black world. Other demographic migratory patterns might be less symmetrical—for example, the Chinese in Malaysia. Where there is lack of symmetry, or where the immigrants are more privileged than the indigenous peoples, tensions are inevitable. But despite some examples to the contrary, such as General Idi Amin's expulsion of Asian ethnics from Uganda, the central long-term world trend is toward the emergence of an interlocking population system between now and the end of the twenty-first century. Demographic counter-penetration from the Southern into the Northern hemisphere would be only one aspect of such a system.

Inter-Penetration Within the Developing World

Clearly relations between the Southern and the Northern hemispheres are only part of the quest for a new economic and political order. In matters of migratory patterns, as well as in other areas of international life, relations among different parts of the South itself are equally important.

The birth of developing-country solidarity came as a result of a marriage between two movements—Afro-Asianism and non-alignment. Solidarity between Africans and Asians started as a racial assertion, but by the late 1960s it was based less and less on the sentiment of being colored peoples and more on the recognition of shared economic and diplomatic weaknesses.

The non-aligned movement was also changing its emphasis—away from preoccupations about keeping out of the "cold war" and refusing alliances with the major powers, and toward a struggle to try to create a new economic order in the world. Issues of race continued to be central as long as southern

Africa continued to be dominated along racial lines. A conference of non-aligned countries was held in Lusaka, Zambia, partly to dramatize the commitment of the movement in support of the remaining wars of national liberation. But both the Lusaka conference in 1970 and the Algiers conference in 1973 clearly revealed that the non-aligned movement had become more committed to the cause of economic justice in the world than in the old days of Tito, Nehru, Nasser, and Nkrumah, and less preoccupied with issues of avoiding military alliances—since the superpowers themselves were now pursuing a policy of detente.

As Afro-Asianism became "deracialized" and non-alignment demilitarized in emphasis, a new synthesis emerged based on the concept of the Third World, or the "Group of 77" developing countries. This synthesis provided a transition from "pan-pigmentationalism," an affinity based on color, to "pan-proletarianism," an inchoate solidarity based on shared indigence and underdevelopment. While Afro-Asianism had by definition limited itself to two continents, the Group of 77 also encompasses Latin America. It is thus a tricontinental phenomenon, forging a limited interdependence among underdeveloped countries in Asia, Africa, and Latin America. Although this interdependence is relatively rudimentary for the time being, it is once again transnational and still provisionally influenced by an egalitarian ethic among the constituent countries, and increasingly conscious of the possibilities of cooperation in the future.

Developing-world transnationalism has found expression in a variety of sub-movements, ranging from the radical left-wing tricontinental movement to the United Nations Conference on Trade and Development (UNCTAD). Also increasingly significant have been the alliances of primary producers, ranging from the Organization of Petroleum Exporting Countries to the new informal arrangements among producers of copper. Most of these primary producers are competitors and thus vulnerable to tactics of divide and rule. Yet in their relationship to the consumers of their primary products, there has been growing a sense of solidarity, however fragile and inchoate it is for the time being.

The doctrine of equality among developing countries is also fragile and uncertain. Technological imbalances are important not only in relationships between the North and the South, but also in relationships among the Southern countries themselves. Countries such as Brazil and India are technologically in a different category from countries such as Libya and Uganda. The weight and leverage exerted by the technologically and demographically more powerful developing countries carries the risk of feudo-imperial influences among them.

Brazil has long had a vision of a leadership role—first in Latin America and then in the developing world as a whole. It has seen the establishment of a constituency of influence within the South as a step toward the attainment of superpower status. For some time, Brazil even appeared to entertain the possibility of sharing a feudo-imperial role with Portugal in Africa. The Portuguese colony of Angola briefly seemed to be developing into a condominium under the joint hegemony of Portugal and Brazil.

There were occasions when some developed countries sought to influence Portugal's policies in Africa through the intervention of Brazil. Brazil's former Ambassador to Washington, Roberto de Oliveira Campos, claimed soon after the coup in Portugal in the spring of 1974, that in 1963 the Kennedy Administration—apprehensive about the possibility of a repetition in "Portuguese Africa" of the chaos that had befallen the former Belgian Congo on attainment of independence—had offered financing for Brazilian welfare and economic projects in Angola, Mozambique, and Guinea-Bissau. According to Campos, the United States was reluctant to approach Portugal directly, fearing a negative reaction from Lisbon that might shake the Atlantic alliance. The Kennedy initiative, if Campos's report is correct, failed partly because Brazil was unsure about the wisdom of the American initiative, and partly because Portugal was predictably unenthusiastic once the danger of a Congo-type collapse had receded.

By 1963, Brazil was already sensing the broad difficulties of feudo-imperialism in the modern period but still continued to play a role basically supportive of Portugal. By the end of the 1960s, however, its shift from serving as a co-imperial power in an informal sense to serving as a developing-world partner in Africa began to be discernible. While it was still reluctant to be associated with African liberation movements as such, it nevertheless sought to establish new economic relations not only with the countries still under Portuguese control, but also with countries in the independent sector of the continent. On the one hand, Brazil's economic and technological development was widening the gulf between itself and many of the other developing countries. On the other hand, the new policies pursued by Brazil in the developing world emphasized a spirit of egalitarian solidarity and seemed to lay the foundations for a new developing world transnationalism.

The Arab world was also exploring possibilities of enhanced solidarity with African states and the Moslem world. Some of these movements could conceivably split the Group of 77 along continental, religious, or ideological lines. But they could also be seen as additional manifestations of the new mood of transnationalism among the poorer and weaker countries of the globe.

The new interdependence of Arabs and other developing countries continues to be fitful and inconclusive. The Arab oil producers have been reluctant to concede special concessions in oil prices to fellow developing countries. In the case of the African states, the only commitment undertaken by the Arab oil producers was to provide development aid and subsidies from a new Arab fund for Africa, but even this aid fell far short of meeting the extra costs of increased oil prices.

There was a possibility of special concessions to Moslem countries from

Arab oil producers, but the Islamic Summit Conference of Lahore in 1974 failed to realize such a spirit of economic generosity and solidarity between the haves and the have-nots. What all this means is that the struggle for an effective and operational developing-world transnationalism has only just started. There are enormous obstacles in the way of its fulfillment. These obstacles range from a residual dependency complex among those developing countries dominated by their former metropolitan masters to excessive greed among those developing countries which have become staggeringly rich without evolving a commensurate scale of developing-world solidarity.

The bulk of economic interaction in the world so far has been between the Northern industrial nations themselves (upper horizontal relations). Next in importance has been interaction between the industrial North and the less developed Southern hemisphere (vertical relations). The least significant has been interaction within the Southern hemisphere itself (lower horizontal relations). Because of this latter deficiency, the bonds among developing countries have been weak. Until recently, there was only a very limited sense of interdependence and little awareness of each others' problems. A strategy of increased mutual economic penetration between developing countries, ranging from trade to technical assistance, could raise their level of interdependence and enhance the possibilities of an organic solidarity among them.

In the economic domain, a form of partnership based on interlocking economic systems may be defined as "organic solidarity." An alliance for purposes of collective bargaining with a third party may be defined as "strategic solidarity." The developing countries have already discovered the virtues of strategic economic solidarity against the industrial North. Most developing-country economic dealings are with the industrial North rather than with other developing countries. By "ganging up" against the industrial powers in forums such as the U.N. General Assembly's Special Session on raw materials, or the U.N. Conference on Trade and Development (UNCTAD), the Group of 77 has begun to develop some skills of strategic solidarity. But only effective inter-penetration among developing-world economies could create a solid organic form of interdependence.

In the new era of counter-penetration, there is need to use petrodollars for investment in such efforts as irrigation in the Sahel or in Sudan, not only in Daimler-Benz and International Business Machines (IBM). The oil-exporting developing countries must be the vanguard of the Third Development Decade, as well as the remainder of the Second. They are in a position to demonstrate that what could not be accomplished under Northern economic leadership in the 1960s can be accomplished with the imaginative initiatives of the Organization of Petroleum Exporting Countries in the 1970s and the 1980s. The South's underprivileged status in relation to the industrial North may at last be transcended as the developing world itself creates a genuine organic and symmetrical solidarity among its own members in the South.

But what is likely to be the balance between vertical counter-penetration (from the South into the North) and horizontal inter-penetration (among Southern countries themselves)? For a while, the oil-rich developing countries will be tempted to invest much more in the industralized countries than in less developed nations. This is partly because of the tempting short-term returns of investing in Western Europe and North America, and partly because the industrialized countries can in any case *absorb* more capital than can the less developed economies.

But investment by developing countries elsewhere in the developing world will nevertheless grow and expand. So will foreign aid from resource-rich developing countries into resource-poor less developed economies. There are already strong indications of such a trend, in spite of all the skepticism one finds in the North. In the words of the Washington correspondent of *The Financial Times* of London:

For the very poor [countries], there is no alternative to charity. The O.P.E.C. countries are starting to face up to their responsibilities here, although their reaction has been slow and they often show a preference for the Islamic poor over the rest. All the same, their development aid is already up to the target level set by the United Nations—something which cannot be said for the rest of the industrial world and particularly for the United States, which is not only the world's richest nation but its meanest. As yet O.P.E.C. aid may be insignificant in terms of the size of the difficulty the oil-price rise has created for the very poorest countries such as India and the Central African nations, which have neither oil nor many other marketable commodities. But the fact that they are making some kind of an effort helps them maintain the political support of the rest of the Third World, and there is some fragmentary evidence that they may already be doing rather more than appears in any of the figures.[4]

Among the oil-rich developing countries, some differences in orientation are inevitable. Investment by the conservative oil-rich regimes is more likely to fit the pattern of vertical counter-penetration than that of horizontal inter-penetration. Kuwait, Saudi Arabia, and Iran will either favor Western Europe and North America or give priority to fellow Moslems. Algeria and Libya, on the other hand, may prefer developing-world solidarity to profits gained in Europe or America. They may still show a preference for helping fellow Moslems, but are also likely to show sensitivity to the needs of other developing societies in Africa and Asia. Therefore, while conservative regimes such as Kuwait and Saudi Arabia enhance the process of vertical counter-

---

4Paul Lewis, "Getting Even," op. cit., p. 84.

penetration, radical or militant regimes such as Algeria and Libya should in time accelerate the process of horizontal inter-penetration among the Southern countries themselves. What should be borne in mind is that these are predictions about probable future behavior rather than interpretations of the aid record so far.

But neither kind of regime is likely to limit itself to only one direction of investment and general economic activity. Destiny has placed on the shoulders of the oil-rich developing countries an historic role in the transformation of the world's economic order.

Policy Options for the United States

It is in the enlightened self-interest of the United States, as well as of other powers, that the age of feudo-imperial or hierarchical interdependence should come to an end. *How can the hierarchy come to an end without also destroying the interdependence?*

For a while the West will experience an immense temptation to maintain the hierarchy. The energy crisis could provide the pretext for either gunboat diplomacy or outright resurgence of full imperial annexation. President Ford's hard-line speech at a Detroit conference and the speeches of Secretary of State Kissinger at the United Nations and the University of Chicago in the fall of 1974 were widely interpreted as implying the threat of military intervention in the Middle East should the energy situation reach economic "strangulation." Both speakers have denied that they ever intended such a threat, but official denials in matters of this kind are not adequate proof of lack of calculation in that direction.

One scenario involves an initiative by Israel with tacit Western encouragement or in outright collusion with the West. The precedent of 1956 when Israel was encouraged by France and Britain to launch an attack against Egypt in the hope of overthrowing President Nasser is still widely remembered. Israel's warning in November 1974 to countries such as Kuwait, Libya, Iraq, and Saudi Arabia that sending token contingents to Syria and Egypt in the next war would be taken by Israel as a declaration of war upon itself was interpreted in some developing-world circles as a diplomatic preparation for the invasion of oil-rich Arab countries in the next war. Israel might not be able to maintain control over such newly occupied distant oilfields for very long, but the new situation which this would create could enable the major powers to define new conditions for the price and availability of oil in return for the restoration of the oilfields to their Arab owners.

Such a scenario assumes that the Soviet Union would limit itself to making noises of protest without directly intervening on the side of the Arabs. If by any chance such military options are being considered by some of the back-room scenarists in the State Department and the Pentagon, they should be abandoned speedily. First, such options raise the risk of a nuclear war—

should either the Soviet Union or the United States miscalculate about the intentions of the other. Second, they risk the widespread sabotage of oil installations in the Arab world, causing for at least a short while a more devastating energy crisis than anything experienced so far. Third, they risk ruining the chances of a Middle East settlement for the rest of this century. And fourth, they risk hardening the lines of confrontation between the developing world as a whole and the West for at least another generation.

One realistic initial response by the United States would be to pursue further the implications of the Shah of Iran's suggestion that oil prices should be related to world prices of manufactured products, food, and other commodities. The Shah has argued that oil prices account for only 2 per cent of the total inflation of 20 per cent in the world—much of the rest of the inflation (18 per cent) having been caused by domestic factors in the industrial world. He has further argued that there is little likelihood of reduced oil prices for as long as the other causes of inflation in the industrial world are left unchecked. The projected collective discussions and negotiations between oil producers and oil consumers in 1975 should provide a useful forum for airing and beginning to resolve this issue.

A second potentially profitable response by the United States would be to encourage more emphatically the whole strategy of recycling petrodollars. The United States is no longer as negatively oriented toward the strategy as it was at the beginning of 1974, but the Ford Administration still shows considerable skepticism and caution.

If counter-penetration is partly designed to make the North as vulnerable to economic pressure from the South as the latter is to the North, why should the United States not remain cautious, skeptical, and even hostile to such a trend? One answer lies in the principle of *reciprocal vulnerability*. Two trends in December 1974 were potentially mutually negating. One trend was captured in the Charter of Economic Rights and Duties of States adopted by the General Assembly of the United Nations in that month—a new international doctrine virtually legitimizing future nationalization without compensation of any foreign industry in the developing world. The other trend was the increasing readiness of oil-rich developing countries to invest heavily in Northern industry. The General Assembly's Charter seemed to threaten Northern investment in Africa and Asia—while Arab and Iranian investments in the North were at the same time providing alternative safeguards for the future.

In the past, Northern investments abroad had to rely primarily on overall Northern domination of the world for security. In the future, however, Northern investment will increasingly need to rely on reciprocal investment by others in the industrialized world. If Saudi Arabia today acquired a large stake in Northern industry, and if tomorrow a socialist revolution took place in Saudi Arabia, the new government would be circumspect about nationalizing foreign firms in Saudi Arabia without compensation. The principle of reciprocal economic vulnerability would help to consolidate genuine symmetrical interdependence. The price of such interdependence is the ability to harm each other as genuine equals. The fear of such reciprocal harm should help to deter irresponsible and one-sided ventures. The industrialized world should therefore not only continue to encourage the oil-rich developing countries to bank their billions in the North, but it should also promote a genuine interlocking world economy by permitting massive Southern investment in their own industries. Just as the Northern hemisphere has a direct stake in many of the economies of the developing countries, so some of the latter should establish a direct stake in the economies of the industrial giants.

A third factor in promoting an interlocking world economy is to link food, energy, and technology policies. The European Community has already started exploratory discussions with the Arab League about a system of exchanging European technology for Arab oil. The discussions were interrupted as a result of the Arab desire to include the Palestinian Liberation Organization as a participant in the negotiations, but this interruption is likely to be of relatively short duration. A technological "quid" for an oil "quo" seems destined to be the basis of future economic relations between Europe and the Arab world.

A particularly critical area of convergence for the three elements of technology, energy, and food production would lie in such ambitious projects as the containment of the Sahara desert. How can areas like the Sahel be saved from the Sahara's expansion? How can countries bordering or encompassing the desert be made more productive? An alliance linking Arab petrodollars, Western technology, and African endeavor could help in finding positive answers to such ominous questions. Petrodollars *earned* in the deserts of Arabia could help *transform* the deserts of Africa. In the difficult enterprise of making the Sahara bloom, the developing world might find one project worthy of inter-penetration—made the more effective with the technological expertise of a more responsive Northern hemisphere.

But until the Sahara does bloom, there are lives to be saved from starvation. At the World Food Conference in Rome in the autumn of 1974, the American delegation was split over tactics and over immediate action to be taken for the alleviation of drought and famine. The official position of the Ford Administration was far behind countries such as Canada, Norway, and Australia in readiness to meet the food aid challenge. Canada committed over 15 per cent of its food production for the next three years to food aid. If the United States would like to see the oil producers become more sensitive to the problems of others, the United States itself, as the world's largest food producer, should display a similar sense of global responsibility. Those who consume resources on a per capita scale greater than anybody else should learn to make commensurate contributions to the alleviation of human misery. The United States has yet to rise to that challenge.

Perhaps the conference of oil producers and oil consumers in 1975 can be used as an occasion for American commitment on food supplies, as well as OPEC commitment on energy prices. A formula does need to be found not only to enable oil prices to float with the prices of other commodities, but also to link the energy crisis to the broader crisis of basic human survival.

What is at stake is indeed the belated but still sorely needed transition from an interdependence based on hierarchy and Western charity to an interdependence based on symmetry and mutual accountability. The last quarter of the twentieth century stands a chance—modest, but still a chance—of traversing the remaining distance toward such a world order.

Part II

Critical Problem Areas

Chapter 4

Multinational Enterprises and North-South Relations

Félix Peña

The oil crisis shows clearly that changes in the international system are not limited solely to East-West relations and the interaction of the major powers but also affect North-South relations. The international bargaining power of at least some of the countries of the Southern hemisphere has increased as a result of a reassessment of their contribution to the economic systems of the great powers. This reassessment is based largely on a recognition of their market potential and their importance as raw-material suppliers.

This study examines the changes in North-South relations and the increased bargaining power of the South in order to clarify the significance of the activities of multinational enterprises from the point of view of developing countries.

The activities of the large international corporations in developing countries represent what Stanley Hoffmann has conceptualized (in a different context) as a "principal line of tension" in relations between two segments of the international system. To illustrate, at the height of the nuclear confrontation, the outcome of East-West relations was contingent upon the manner in which nations resolved their competition for nuclear superiority. Similarly, during the present North-South industrial and technological confrontation, the future status of developing countries within the forum of nations will depend to a large extent on the way they resolve the challenge—both positive and negative—of the increasing participation of international corporations in their own economic and political activities.[1]

[1]Some of the ideas presented in this paper are elaborated further in Celso Lafer and Félix Peña, *Argentina y Brasil en el sistema de relaciones internacionales* (Buenos Aires: Nueva Visión, 1973). See especially "Aportes a una perspectiva latinoamericana del sistema internacional."

The North-South Power Dichotomy

Apart from their geographical connotations, the terms "North" and "South" generally differentiate between the rich and the poor countries, the fully industrialized and those in process of industrialization, the developed and the developing, or the major and the marginal countries. Granting the existence of intermediate categories between these extremes, the North-South division relates to the existence, on the one hand, of countries that have achieved a high level of economic development that allows them to offer their inhabitants general and widespread welfare, and, on the other hand, of countries whose economies lack the potential required to achieve this level—at least on such a wide scale. The dichotomy is generally stated in terms of welfare and measured by, among other indices, per capita income.

Although it had always been recognized that some countries were far more developed than others, until the 1950s there was little awareness of the existence of any North-South division within the international system. A decisive factor in the ultimate recognition of such a division was decolonization and its repercussions on institutions. Decolonization created in the former metropolises a need to contribute to the solution of the economic problems faced by the emerging nations; they wished to maintain an economic presence in their former colonies both because of their "cold war" fear that the latter might fall into the communist sphere of influence and because of humanitarian demands of conscience.[2] In 1964, a major step taken at the institutional level, within the United Nations, led to a decisive recognition among both groups of countries of a rich-poor or North-South division in international systems. This institutionalization of the dichotomy was the creation of the U.N. Conference on Trade and Development (UNCTAD), which subsequently became the forum of a North-South relationship more closely resembling a confrontation than a dialogue.

"Nonaligned," "Third World," and "Group of 77" became the identifications of the group of nations of the world's Southern segment, which soon understood that their problem was not limited to a lower level of development measured in terms of *welfare*; above all, it measured their international marginality in terms of *power*. Many factors contributed to this new awareness until the North-South division gradually acquired the form of the classical dichotomy between great and small powers, in which the standard of difference is not geographical size or population but the ability to mobilize the sources of power necessary to influence the vital decisions of the existing international system.

---

[2]Demands of conscience are important to the extent that they influence public opinion, as illustrated by the case of American public opinion regarding Vietnam.

This awareness was perhaps strongest in those countries which understood that the solution of their development problem did not depend exclusively on their ability to achieve a higher level of welfare but rather on their ability to attain the measure of power necessary to determine autonomously both the *kind* of welfare and life style that they wanted and the *methods* to be used to achieve these goals. This recognition brought them face to face with the problem of dependence characterizing their global and regional linkages and limiting, to a greater or lesser extent, their capacity to control the domestic effects of external factors or to exert real influence over their own external relations. Countries such as Brazil, Argentina, Mexico, Venezuela, Colombia, Peru, and Chile—to mention only a few in Latin America—have objective reasons for aspiring to a greater measure of true international participation than they enjoy at present.[3] What they desire is more power to influence major decisions affecting the structure and functioning of international systems, in particular the financial and commercial negotiations that shape the international economic system. Their major problem therefore relates to their ability 1) to initiate at the domestic level and ensure at the international level policies that will mobilize or increase their resources; and 2) to use these resources to strengthen their bargaining capacity to attain the measure of autonomy necessary to determine the type of welfare they wish to achieve.

Major Changes in the International System

Countries in the Southern segment perceive at least three trends—all related to the changes taking place in the international system—that play a part in shaping an understanding of the real significance of the North-South dichotomy. These trends are: 1) increased "permissiveness" or freedom of maneuver within the international system due to the transition from an era of nuclear confrontation to one of industrial and technological confrontation; 2) a tendency on the part of the great powers to freeze the existing world power structure in self-defense, to maintain the nuclear status quo; and 3) the emergence of an altogether new type of international relations—transnational relations—in which the entities involved, the multinational corporations, are often far more powerful than many nations.

The *first* of these trends, increased permissiveness, clearly affects the freedom of nations to develop new strategies to maximize international power. During the period of nuclear confrontation that followed World War II, the international system was characterized by bipolarity and

---

[3]It should be pointed out that once the integration variable is introduced, practically all Latin American countries consider themselves to be in this position.

strong ideological differences among the major powers. Most nations were aligned with one or the other ideological bloc. Within each bloc, countries were stratified according to their relative importance from the point of view of nuclear strategy. Any attempt to split off from either bloc was severely punished (e.g., Hungary, Cuba). The least indication on the part of any "member" of a bloc of intent to form a relationship with a country in the opposite bloc was rejected by each of the super-powers.[4] In the 1960s, as a result of the proliferation of nuclear power and the danger of total destruction of the contenders in case of war, this situation became more flexible. Although the possibility of nuclear confrontation remained latent, a new era of industrial and technological confrontations began. This new era, which brought a multipolarity in relations among the major powers and a softening of the ideological conflict, was characterized by the diplomacy of Henry Kissinger, by former President Nixon's trip to Peking, by the policy of détente between the Soviet Union and the United States, and by an open confrontation of the Western powers through their corporations. The superpowers came to view the rest of the world less as a place where they had to search for allies in the event of a nuclear conflict or had to prevent the infiltration of the enemy at any price, and more as a place in which markets could be found and increasingly scarce raw materials obtained. Thus, among the major powers, the rules of the game and the standards used to define friends and enemies changed considerably—first, because of the relative shift of forces from the military to the economic domain, and second, because there now were several actors on the stage instead of only two principals.

In this situation, countries which could offer markets and raw materials began to be able to exploit the advantages derived from their contacts with the more industrial powers and to diversify the sources of the supply of external resources needed for the development of their own countries. Thus "poor" countries discovered that they must become "rich" in terms of power—perhaps not global power but at least influence in some specific areas of decision making. Countries immediately or potentially capable of providing large markets—or establishing such markets through integration—might become "rich." The cases of Brazil and the countries in the Andean Group illustrated such potential. Countries possessing scarce raw materials such as oil, copper, or high-protein food likewise might become "rich." Any of these factors could provide the countries of the South with a basis for planning their strategies, either jointly or independently, to acquire greater power and thereby an increased role in decisions relating to international systems. Such strategies would have

---

[4]For example, the attempts to alter relations with the United States made by Presidents Quadros and Goulart in Brazil and Frondizi in Argentina.

to take into consideration both the obvious global disadvantage of the Southern countries and their specific advantages in those areas in which the industrialized powers are vulnerable.[5]

For the developing countries, the *second* major trend mentioned— attempts by rich nations to freeze the existing world power structure— constitutes an external danger and a challenge to their very survival as independent, and even important, parts of the international system. This challenge is manifest in the "Kissinger approach" to the organization of the international system—namely, a strong tendency to maintain the existing international balance of power. The present multipolar division of economic power is not contradictory to such an approach, and, if appropriately controlled, may even be made to serve it. The nuclear confrontation was brought under control thanks to the nuclear parity of the United States and the Soviet Union. The danger presented by today's economic multipolarity is the possibility of its transformation into nuclear multipolarity, which would of course threaten international security. This makes it essential that the "rules of the game" of international industrial and technological competition preclude a new, multipolar nuclear race and confrontation. From the point of view of the nuclear powers, the maintenance of peace appears to be linked to the nonproliferation of nuclear power and to the establishment of a close understanding among the powers already possessing nuclear arms. From within, such an alliance may be seen as a means to ensure not only global security but also a rational distribution of increasingly scarce world resources as well as of the benefits of technological progress.

It may well be that the rigid international stratification of power required to prevent the widespread dissemination of nuclear technology is also seen to require the imposition of barriers to the dissemination of nonnuclear technology—or at least to the creation of the capacity to *generate* advanced technology. If so, the division of technological activity within international corporations may well serve these objectives. Thus from the point of view of the "Kissinger approach" to international political stability, the role of multinational corporations in the global division of technological activity may be acceptable.

But in every oligarchical structure, problems arise not for those who withhold power, but for those from whom it is withheld. Moreover, the validity of the structure is often questionable even if it does promise to provide increasing overall welfare. It cannot be denied that the freezing of the existing world power structure and the division of technological activity may provide mankind with material gains. But history indicates that mankind and nations have never been motivated solely by a search

---

[5]*Las nuevas estructuras del comercio internacional*, 2 Vols. (Mexico City: Fondo de Cultura Económica, 1974).

for material welfare. Even if this were so, the question of the *kind* of welfare to which they aspire would remain unanswered. There are clear indications that Latin America, in any case, neither aspires to the kind of welfare achieved by the highly industrialized nations nor is willing to pay the individual and social costs of its achievement. (We need only recall the two great wars, or the costs of the Soviet model of industrialization.)

It is very doubtful that the new "concert-of-nations" approach to the organization of the international system will be accepted in practice by the world's Southern sector. Moreover, the freezing of the world power structure is contrary to the dictates of history: experiments of this type—whether at the national or international level—generally have not succeeded over the long term.

The *third* global trend, the emergence of a new type of transnational relations, is closely related to the two trends involving powerful non-governmental entities already discussed. Transnational interactions at the nongovernmental level are not new; they have always coexisted with international governmental relations. Tourism, multinational enterprises, international churches, political and labor groups that are part of international movements, and influential newspapers and books with an international circulation are all well-known aspects of international life. Revolutionary improvements in the fields of transportation and communications, the prosperity achieved by many countries, and the fact that war is waged only in "marginal" areas far away from industrial centers also have wrought substantial changes in transnational relations. What is new, however, is the relative importance and independence that transnational nongovernmental actors have acquired in relations among governments.

The large international corporations dealing in goods or services which increasingly are becoming principal agents in the international transfer of resources (whether of capital, goods, or technology) have become important links between the different entities of the international global system. Due to the volume and type of resources they can mobilize and control, they are acquiring so much power to influence national and international affairs that it would be difficult to understand international politics while persisting to ignore their existence and continuing to act on the basis of the myth that governments have a monopoly over political issues. The recent case of ITT's (International Telephone and Telegraph) involvement in U.S. domestic politics and policies, as well as in the U.S. relationship with Chile, provides only one conspicuous example of this trend.

The current international debates concerning the restructuring of the monetary system, the dollar crisis, the regulation of world trade, the barriers to trade in products exported by developing countries, and the form and conditions of transfer of technology to these countries can no longer ignore the confrontations taking place among the large Japanese, North American, and European corporations.

It is not my intention to attempt to prove that the entire structure of contemporary international relations can be understood in the light of conflicts among powerful nongovernmental actors, but only to point to the emergence of a new kind of international politics, in which governmental and nongovernmental actions are closely linked. Moreover, important events are occasionally strongly influenced by the conduct of the nongovernmental actors unrestrained by the governments.[6]

In "transnational" politics, the activities of national actors (governments or business enterprises) are oriented toward other national entities in order to obtain reactions favorable to the achievement of their objectives. They assume, in some cases, the character of "inside" actors of a national political system and participate directly in the exercise of internal political authority. Examples of "penetrative linkages" of this kind[7] are the subsidiaries of international corporations such as ITT, IBM, or General Motors, political parties, and labor unions. The loyalties of such inside actors within a national political system are divided, being slanted in part toward a foreign decision-making center that is closely linked to the host nation.[8]

The importance of "transnational" relations and the existence of a sphere of "transnational politics" challenges both the theory of international relations—usually limited to inter*governmental* relations—and the very concept of what constitutes the foreign policy of a country. It seems unrealistic to go on believing that a country's foreign policy is formulated and discharged exclusively by the traditional agency—the ministry of foreign affairs. Concurrently with the activities in what may be called the diplomatic arena, the foreign policy of a country is also implemented through a wide range of activities carried out by different national agencies (including public corporations) as well as through internal activities that have a decisive effect on the pattern of a country's foreign

---

[6]See Karl Kaiser, "Transnational Politics: Toward a Theory of Multinational Politics," *International Organization*, Vol. 25, No. 4 (Autumn 1971), pp. 790 ff.

[7]See James Rosenau, "Toward the Study of National-International Linkages," in J. Rosenau, ed., *Linkages Politics* (New York: Free Press, 1969), pp. 44 ff.

[8]Much remains to be investigated in this field. But it seems clear that at least where Latin American countries are concerned, foreign linkage through penetration has increased and diversified as a result of the postwar process of industrialization and the use of financial and technological resources obtained from foreign corporations and through the installation of their subsidiaries. The concept of import substitution has greatly encouraged the process of foreign economic penetration, since it created the need and the conditions for its development. The principal international corporations came to Latin America not only because of the region's investment opportunities and the fact that conditions in their own economies stimulated expansion, but also because the Latin American countries—intent upon rapid industrialization and availability of modern consumer goods—offered these corporations the most favorable conditions imaginable for the import of their technological resources.

relations. The latter activities are generally manifestations of a country's linkages with external nongovernmental decision centers.

From the point of view of the Southern countries, the formulation of national policies relating to these internal manifestations of external policies is crucial. For countries whose economic systems require outside resources in order to develop and function, it is important to ascertain that domestic subsidiaries of transnational activities in fact express desired kinds of linkages with the international system and that they are financed and operated according to established conditions. This of course requires the formulation and administration of foreign investment regulations—including those affecting the forms of technology transfer and other aspects of foreign-controlled companies (for example, access to loans, or the authorization to operate in specific sectors of the economy, such as banking).

Bearing in mind these complex relationships, let us briefly resume our attempt to clarify the scope of the existing North-South dichotomy. The profound difference between the countries of the world's Northern and Southern segments obviously is more than a question of greater or smaller riches, greater or lesser welfare, or greater or lesser industrial development. The most important differentiating characteristic is a country's capacity to *generate technology*, which allows it to play a specific role in the international transfer of resources and, as a result, to belong to the group of great powers in an international system characterized by industrial and technological competition. Industrialization based on the import of technology may lead to an increase in welfare, but only industrialization supported by the technological *maturity* of a society makes it possible to acquire the ability to influence actively the most vital international decisions. Thus the central issue implicit in the North-South dichotomy is that of *real political participation in the international system.*

It is true that the unequal distribution of power has been the basis of all international systems. But this distribution previously was always founded on *quantitative* differences in existing and potential capacities. What varied from country to country was the volume of "offer" power, understood to be the reserve productive capacity and the possibility and will to mobilize it. It is a well-known fact, however, that the stratification of power is now *qualitative* as well as quantitative. Greater power is now attained by qualitative superiority in nonnuclear as well as nuclear scientific and technological areas.

In the production sectors essential for the development of a national economic system, the developed countries of the world's North are now the almost exclusive possessors of the technologies and the scientific infrastructure needed to continue the process of technological innovation; moreover, they control the means and conditions of transfer of this technology and of the products related to its use to the countries of the world's South. Obviously, this does not hinder the latter from achieving industrial development, nor from competing as exporters of manufactured products in the world market. But it does mean that the ability of these countries to achieve industrial development and to play an important role as exporters of manufactures depends to a large extent on technologies that they can obtain from the industrialized countries. This dependence may condition the *type* of industrial development to which they can aspire and may in fact compel them to accept a development model not suitable to the combination of resources they possess, or to the predominant values of their societies. It may also condition these countries' patterns of external linkage.

Even if one agrees with A. F. Organski's vision that we are progressing from a historical period of industrialized, semi-industrialized, and pre-industrialized countries toward a foreseeable era in which all countries shall be industrialized,[9] there are reasons to fear that when this future is reached, the North-South division of labor will still persist—reflecting a continuation of the patterns of technology generation and industrial production that characterize these two groups of countries today. Fear of the continuation of this dichotomy compels some countries to question systematically every attempt to consolidate the existing power structure. They thus try to a) maximize their participation in vital decisions (for example, those relating to the regulation of the international monetary and commercial systems) as well as to b) prevent, by all possible means, the imposition of behaviour patterns (for example, those relating to birth control or environmental protection policies) that might be instrumental in permanently freezing the present power structure.

But let us be realistic. The countries that perceive the trend toward a freezing of the present dichotomy in the international system and are questioning this trend do not necessarily do so because they consider such a dichotomy to be necessarily "good" or "bad." They do so to avoid remaining permanently powerless relative to the major Northern countries.

A misunderstanding of this fundamental concern frequently leads to errors in the analysis of the conduct of developing countries in forums such as UNCTAD. The Southern segment is not homogeneous, and the common interests of the countries that compose it are few. All these countries invoke international justice: some because they believe or wish to believe in it, others because they find it useful in their efforts to acquire a place among the industrial countries.

The great powers are aware of these distinctions—and of a certain amount of competitiveness among the developing countries—and there-

---

[9]See A. F. Organski, *World Politics* (New York: Alfred A. Knopf, Inc., 1968), pp. 338-96.

fore are rather indifferent to UNCTAD debates and recommendations. Certainly the New Delhi (1968) and Santiago (1972) sessions of UNCTAD provide ample proof of the limits of understanding among developing countries. The existing differences of views among the developing countries have made it relatively easy for some observers to maintain that the economic policies of the great powers need not take the developing countries into account. These observers conclude that given the great untapped potential of markets in the world's Northern sector, and given the continuing discovery of new sources of natural resource wealth in these countries and in "stable" countries (such as Australia), the industrialized nations may be able to dispense with and definitely "marginalize" those developing countries which do not accept their conditions and demands. There are others, however, who argue that the dynamics of oligopolistic competition between the large corporations in industrialized countries compel them to search for and value all possible markets which the competitor may penetrate. And indeed, the conduct of the large corporations in recent years appears to substantiate this assumption, suggesting that in coming years, competition between the great powers for all markets and resources will intensify.

The present multipolar distribution of economic power among the great powers of course limits the margin of maneuverability of a country of the world's Southern segment to prevent the existing North-South division from becoming permanent and to achieve a more viable position of power in the international system. Nevertheless, it is feasible for developing countries—especially those whose resource endowments or other characteristics give credibility to their aspirations for greater international influence—to pursue the dual objective of maximizing their welfare and power and obtaining from abroad financial, technological, and managerial resources of importance for their industrial development. To achieve these aims, developing countries must take advantage of the effects of the present industrial and technological confrontation among the developed countries to maximize their bargaining position in such a way that their use of outside resources does not make them more dependent. At least some of the developing countries can effectively counter the present trend toward the freezing of the North-South dichotomy by making certain that their use of foreign resources does not hinder the development of their own technological capacity to allow them to play a part similar to that of the existing great powers in the international system of transfer of resources.

In summary, a number of important facts must not be ignored by those who analyze contemporary international life and clearly must be taken into consideration at the decision-making level:

(a) Productive resources valuable to developing countries are in the possession of economic groups or enterprises in developed countries that are engaged in industrial and technological competition;

(b) The owners of these resources value the markets provided by developing countries because of oligopolistic competition and the needs of big corporations;

(c) The ideological and nuclear confrontation has become less intense, increasing bargaining leverage on other bases; and

(d) At least some of the developing countries have become aware of these realities and are prepared to act accordingly.

The terms of the existing North-South relationship can only be changed through firm action by those developing countries which fully understand the international situation. One of the major areas in which these countries can take effective action is in their decisions governing the operation of international corporations within their economies.

Multinational Enterprises Viewed from the South

Much empirical knowledge already has been accumulated on multinational corporations, their importance to the international economy, and their impact on both home countries and host countries. Progress has also been made in studying the significance of these enterprises in the international system.[10] It is not necessary to dwell here on well-known facts, or to start defining already well-known concepts. There is some measure of agreement that this type of corporation may become a significant dynamic force in the growth of the international economy. Differences of opinion emerge, however, when attempts are made to identify the principal *beneficiaries* of the existence and activity of this type of enterprise.[11] Are they the "exporters" of multinational corporations? The host countries? All of humanity? A segment of humanity? These are the broad considerations that prompt the following reflections on the presence of international corporations in the world's Southern segment. The emphasis in these remarks is less on the *welfare* effects of these corporations than on their impact in terms of *power*—since, as already argued, this is the only perspective that can clarify the present behavior of the Southern countries toward the great powers.

---

[10]See especially U.N. Department of Economic and Social Affairs, *Multinational Corporations in World Development* (New York: Praeger Publishers, Inc., 1974), which includes a particularly useful bibliography and statistical appendix; and Commission des Communautés Européennes, *Les entreprises multinationales dans le contexte des reglements communautaires*, DOC. COM (73), Brussels, November 7, 1973.

[11]See Constantine V. Vaitsos, *Transfer of Resources and Preservation of Monopoly Rents*, Center of International Affairs, Harvard University Economic Development Report No. 168, 1970, as well as the same author's *Intercountry Income Distribution and Transnational Enterprises* (Oxford: Oxford University Press, 1974).

The "nationalistic" policies of many host countries toward the presence of international corporations[12] are based not only on the fear that these corporations may hamper material progress, but also on apprehensions of a political nature. There is likewise doubt that the massive presence of subsidiaries of foreign corporations in a country has impact on economic relations alone.[13] The political concern about the role of these subsidiaries relates to the perception of a strong trend toward a penetrative linkage pattern,[14] whereby the political systems of great powers influence the as yet unconsolidated political systems of the Southern countries. As already emphasized, there is also considerable anxiety that the current pattern of technological innovation will permanently freeze North-South relations in their present form, thus barring many developing countries from participating in the principal decisions which affect the structure and function of the international system.

For the developing countries, the most disturbing aspects of the involvement of multinational corporations in their economies are the following:[15]

(a) The subsidiaries of foreign corporations have a strong impact on some extractive or industrial sectors as well as on some services (banking and international transportation) in which no effective counterweight mechanism exists;[16]

---

[12]It can be argued that almost all of these "nationalistic" policies are legal practices and instruments that have precedents in the highly industrialized countries, including the United States. See references to such legislation and practices in Commission des Communautés Européennes, *Les entreprises multinationales , op. cit.*

[13]See Vaitsos, *Transfer of Resources*, op. cit.

[14]It must be kept in mind that most Southern countries generally are new countries that have not yet consolidated their national integration processes or built up stable political systems. Seen from this point of view, "nationalism" is an inevitable power force. The problem is one of reconciling "nationalistic" requirements with the need to link up with the existing international system and its transmission of goods and ideas.

[15]Latin American perspectives on these issues have been provided by José Mindlin (of the Federation of Industries of the State of Sao Paulo), in "Capital estrangeiro e empresas multinacionais," mimeographed, Sao Paulo, October 1973; by Theophilo Azeredo Santos (President of the Latin American Bank Federation), in "Empresas internacionais e multinacionais," mimeographed, Rio de Janeiro, October 1973; and by José Campillo Sainz (Under-Secretary for Industries of Mexico), in *Summary of the Hearings Before the Group of Eminent Persons to Study the Impact of Multinational Corporations on Development*, U.N. Pub. Sales No. E.74.II.A.9 (New York: United Nations, 1974), pp. 22–33.

[16]The problem of the gravitation of foreign enterprises toward a relatively developed economic system is illustrated by the case of Argentina, where, in 1970, 64 of the 120 largest enterprises (in terms of sales volume) were partly or wholly foreign-controlled branches of foreign companies, and 31 of the foreign-controlled branches were of U.S. origin. The sales of these foreign enterprises amounted to $3,154 million. In contrast, the number of Argentine enterprises was 42, and their total sales amounted to $1,365 million. The remainder consisted of state-controlled companies—a total of 14, the most important of which provided services (such as railroad transport), with total sales amounting to $1,936 million (*Cuestionario*, No. 8, December 1973). The same problem exists on a lesser scale in Europe, where (as pointed out in the memorandum of the Commission mentioned in note 10) it is apparent in the lack of a suitable counterweight power to the presence of foreign corporations. It can be argued that the weaker the counterweight power in terms of state-controlled or national

(b) Through their participation in the host economy and their transfer of productive resources,[17] international corporations tend to become important channels for the transfer of consumption patterns and values that may affect a country's style of life;

(c) The transfer of technology through international corporations is not always beneficial to a local economy and may in some cases even hamper the development of a country's own technology;

(d) By operating in high-profit sectors, international corporations impede local entrepreneurs or, what is even worse, contribute to their displacement (through the purchase of enterprises).[18]

Some of these reasons for concern are clearly political in nature and not necessarily valid from a purely economic point of view. This explains the existence of certain differences in estimates of the significance of the role of international corporations. But the important factor is that the poli-

---

enterprises, the greater the propensity toward nationalistic reactions—once awareness develops of the relative importance of the foreign corporation. It also can be argued that industrial concentration is an idiosyncrasy of all capitalist economic systems, and that the same might happen in the United States. However, the problem in developing countries in general is that the concentration is primarily one of subsidiaries of *foreign* corporations. Furthermore, the weakness of the private sectors in these countries compels their governments to participate directly in production— at least in the basic sectors of their economies—in order to create the necessary counterweight power. This trend is apparent in almost all Latin American countries.

[17]Foreign enterprise participation in the export of manufactured products is high. According to a report of the Fundación de Investigaciones Latinoamericanas (FIEL), based on a study made by the Institute for Latin American Integration and issued in Buenos Aires in 1973, branches of foreign corporations in 1969 accounted for 73 per cent of Argentina's total exports of manufactured products, which that year amounted to $254.2 million. A part of these exports is generated by the internal commerce of multinational enterprises (branch to branch, or branch to company headquarters). From the economic point of view, it could be maintained that this is a positive result, although account must be taken of the problem of transfer prices for "internal commerce." But from a political standpoint, a problem arises in that decisions regarding exports are made with a view to benefiting the foreign company, and not necessarily the host country. The fact that the branch is subject to the laws of its own country also may create a problem in the event that export controls are imposed. This recently occurred in the Argentine automobile industry when U.S. branches attempted to prevent the export of cars to Cuba—leading to an energetic intervention by the Argentine Government (press conference given by President Perón on December 20, 1973). However, the fact that these branches finally agreed to export to Cuba shows that the government of a country such as Argentina can usually ensure that an international corporation will behave in a manner compatible with the government's policies.

[18]This factor greatly irritates national industries. As Brazilian businessman José Mindlin has stated in this connection: "The complementary character of the foreign firm seems to me, however, to be a basic requisite of a Brazilian economic development policy. Furthermore, foreign investment will be truly useful only if it is channelled toward sectors which require dynamic technology or if such investment fills gaps in our growth strategy. The penetration into the national market by foreign firms does not contribute to the interests of the country; moreover, it is a counter-incentive to efforts made by national entrepreneurs. Consequently, the purchase of national firms by foreign ones should be discouraged although it should not be prohibited in any absolute way inasmuch as it can be useful in certain cases and also because the freedom of entrepreneurial decisions should be respected although it should be subordinate to the general interest." ("Foreign Capital in Multinational Firms," mimeographed, Sao Paulo, October 1973).

ticians of countries will always tend to visualize the problem from the point of view of internal or external power. Certainly those Latin American countries that have in the past few years achieved important changes in their foreign investment and technology transfer policies have acted on the basis of their interpretation of their long-term political as well as economic national interests.[19] It is significant that in most cases, these Latin American countries have acted on the basic premise that foreign resources are needed by national economies. Their action implies rejection of a completely closed model of development and a positive assessment of the role that international corporations can play in national economies as long as they observe preestablished conditions. Moreover, the general tendency of the leadership in these countries is to consider the international corporation as neither "good" nor "evil" in itself but rather as an agent for the transfer of scarce resources.[20]

The Need for Control at the National Level

This brings the consideration of the role of international corporations back to the national plane. The problem involved is one of conforming the standards of behavior of the foreign economic agents to the particular development objectives of each country.[21] Obviously, in order to achieve this aim, each country must first define its national development goals and the type of development model it desires. Only thus can national interest be determined, and only thus is it possible to develop a strategy to ensure that the international corporations' operations in a country conform to that country's needs.

The following points are important components of national strategies to obtain necessary external resources from international corporations on the best possible conditions:

---

[19]The most interesting legislative actions on this subject are: Decision 24 of the Cartagena Agreement and the new laws on foreign investment and transfer of technology of Mexico and Argentina. For an analysis of new trends of Latin American foreign investment policies, see Constantine V. Vaitsos, "The Changing Policies of Latin American Governments Toward Economic Development and Direct Foreign Investments," Junta del Acuerdo de Cartagena, Doc. J/AJ, 36/Rev.1, April 26, 1973. See Chapter 5 of this volume by Constantine Vaitsos. See also Ricardo French Davis, "La inversión extranjera en América Latina: tendencias recientes y perspectivas," *Trimestre Económico* (Mexico), January-March 1973, pp. 173 ff., and two recent studies on the legal aspects of multinational enterprises in Latin America: Félix Peña, "Empresas binaciónales y multinaciónales Latinoamericanas: ideas en torno a algunos de sus aspectos jurídicos," *Derecho de la integración,* No. 13 (July 1973), pp. 11 ff., and Eduardo White, *Empresas multinacionales Latinoamericanas* (Mexico City: Fondo de Cultura Económica, 1973).

[20]As was apparent, for example, in public statements made by General Geisel (subsequently President of Brazil) on September 18, 1973, and by President Peron of Argentina on December 20, 1973.

[21]See particularly the statement by Campillo Sainz in *Summary of the Hearings Before the Group of Eminent Persons,* op. cit.

1. *Relations with international corporations should be integrated into plans for the overall development of the national economy and for the establishment of external linkages.*

2. *A thorough assessment should be obtained of the volume and type of external resources required for development and of the sectors and activities for which they are needed.*[22]

3. *Alternative sources of external resources should be explored to increase the nation's bargaining power.*[23]

4. *National administrative structures must be adequate to the task of implementing the chosen strategy and controlling its results.*

Each of the above points offers a tremendous range of options. Precedents of how to implement these options easily can be found in international experience, which abounds with all types of legal and administrative instruments for controlling external resources.

Once awareness of the need for this type of strategy is achieved, two points must be considered. First, the more attractions a national economy can offer a foreign investor, the more likely is the success of a country's strategy to deal with international corporations. This of course poses the problem of the minimum acceptable size of the internal market or, conversely, of the easiest form of expanding this market through economic integration. Fundamentally, the country should reassess the value of its economy to market-hungry international corporations and, for this purpose, attempt to profit in the greatest possible measure from its inalienable right to grant access to its market. Second, the organization of a permanent capacity to review the behavior of foreign corporations in any country and the effect of this behavior on national aims is as important as the strategy itself. An analysis of the general behavior of these corporations cannot be dispensed with; it is the best way to obtain a complete picture of the ways corporations will try to offset the strategies of host nations.

The above points deliberately imply a preference for the establishment of a *national* system of control of international corporations. Such a system could, of course, also be implemented at the regional level by nations that envisage a process of integration and therefore choose to establish a collective policy of foreign investment and technology transfer.[24] A country's participation in an integration scheme not only increases its bargaining power by expanding its market, but also facilitates—where

---

[22]This point and note 24 are considered in the legal texts cited in note 19.

[23]International experience abounds on this subject. Foreign resources may be obtained through direct investment or through contracts; the selection of one or the other depends on the particular situation. In this regard, the measures adopted by the Andean Group, particularly in the field of technology, are important.

[24]On control systems, see Francisco Orrego Vicuña, "El control de las empresas multinacionales," *Foro Internacional*, Vol. 14, No. 1 (July-September 1973), pp. 106 ff.

regional investment plans are involved—the conclusion of agreements between a group of nations and the multinational enterprises interested in operating in a specific sector. It also facilitates the establishment of production systems that are integrated on a multinational level and that contemplate the interests of all parties involved.[25]

What does the support of control at the national level imply about the importance of an *international* system of control? Various proposals made so far with respect to this type of control have not provided a convincing answer to the question of who will supervise the controllers. Two alternatives have been suggested: 1) that those who control do so in a democratic form and that all countries participate in such action, or 2) that the control system reflect the existing international stratification and in fact be directed by the great powers. It is very likely that the first of these alternatives would be ineffective. As for the second, it is certain that it would not benefit the interests of the developing countries.

The greatest barrier to an effective international system of control is the fact that it would be difficult to define its aims or the interests it should defend. Should control be exerted on behalf of a supposed international public interest? If so, who can define such public interest? The great powers? All nations? If a system of control is to be useful, the rationale for its existence must be well known and acceptable; for the present, it appears that such a definition can only be provided at the national level or, in cases of integration, perhaps at the regional level.

However, proposals for an international system of control of multinational corporations are not without some redeeming features. An international system could serve an important information-gathering function which cannot be provided at the national level. Although the continuous collection and publication of data on existing corporations, their organizational structure, and their techniques of operation would be no substitute for national controls in this field, it could be an extremely valuable aid to countries which had decided to introduce national strategies of control. Such information would be highly useful not only to developing countries, but also to those nations which "export" the multinational corporations.

Greater international access to information on the activities of multinational corporations as well as on existing governmental controls in this field and the motives behind them might serve yet another purpose. It might lessen the criticism often leveled at developing-country actions by developed-country interests which insist on economic rationality as the only ac-

---

[25]See Jack N. Behrman, "Sharing International Production through the Multinational Enterprise and Sectoral Integration," *Law and Policy in International Business*, Vol. 4, No. 1 (1972). The Andean Group is the only integrated system that has achieved definite progress in the programming of sectors of industrial development in its approval of a program of the machine and machine tool industry and the preparation of programs for the petrochemical and automobile industries.

ceptable criterion for justifying what are essentially political-economic decisions. Censure of this kind frequently has been used to weaken the position—international as well as domestic—of those who have assumed the political responsibility for facing up to the problems of international corporations in political power terms. There is much scope for action to improve mutual understanding in this area, and much that could be done by those groups in industrialized countries which are concerned about the state of North-South relations. Their actions might show that the policies of developing countries are not "irrational," as is sometimes claimed in industrial nations; in fact they generally are based on governmental policy precedents provided by the industrialized countries themselves.

The Usefulness of Confrontation and Dialogue

The problems that international corporations pose for the Southern countries can only be clearly understood in the political context of the North-South dichotomy. These corporations are so linked with international political as well as economic systems that no analysis or strategy that attempts to isolate them from the dynamics of these systems can be valid.

North-South relations can only be modified if the Southern countries understand that it is their responsibility to defend their own interests, whether jointly, or individually, or both. To achieve this aim, they must not be afraid to develop a strategy of confrontation, provided it is rational and cognizant of the limits imposed by their weaker position. Not all countries in the Southern segment will do this. Obviously, however, those who wish to make the attempt cannot wait for those who refuse to make history.

But confrontation does not preclude a North-South dialogue. On the contrary, it is one of the preconditions of such a dialogue—provided there is recognition that the countries of the Southern segment aspire to power to direct their own national development within the international system. Moreover, confrontation does not preclude recognition that both sides of the dialogue possess certain ideals. What it does require, however, is rejection of the naive belief that countries act on an exclusively idealistic basis. True dialogue between the Northern and Southern countries can begin only when—without excluding idealism—positions are stated in terms of reciprocal interests.

The anomalies in North-South relations must be eliminated. One of the most flagrant of these incongruities is the invocation of forgotten international principles to justify threats of military action against countries in the South that develop an aggressive strategy with respect to sovereignty over their raw materials. Another is developed-country censure of foreign investment or technology policies similar to the very policies that long have been applied by the industrialized countries themselves. Yet the political analyst cannot deny that such contradictions do characterize the behavior of both sides of the North-South relationship, and that they are a reality that must be taken into account in drawing up policies to strengthen the bargaining power of the Southern countries and to make the international economic order more responsive to their needs.

Chapter 5

Foreign Investment and Productive Knowledge

Constantine V. Vaitsos

In the highly hypothetical world of Robinson Crusoe—the case in which an individual confronts nature alone—only technical problems need be considered in attempting to maximize one's interests, given the resources available and the circumstances dictated by the environment. In the far more perplexing world of social interchange, however, a) participants pursue different objectives, b) no individual controls all the variables that have a bearing on his interests, and c) both individual actions and their results are affected by the actions of others. Furthermore, in the absence of absolute (dictatorial) rule or of a binding agreement that weights the objectives pursued, all participants seek to maximize their interests at the same time.[1]

These characteristics of social interchange apply to the particular case of foreign direct investment in developing countries—in the manufacturing, service, or extractive sectors—in a complex bargaining setting. The following three factors, whose implications can be analyzed from a political and/or economic perspective, are important components of that bargaining setting.

1. *Foreign direct investment approximates the case of bilateral monopoly[2] or oligopoly situations.* Its final returns and their distribution depend on the relative strength and exercise of bargaining *power* among the parties involved. The results obtained are "legitimate" only in terms of the prevailing power configurations and do not obey normative rules or necessarily reflect "adequate" solutions for existing development or growth requirements.

---

[1]See John Von Neumann and Oskar Morgenstern, *Theory of Games and Economic Behavior* (Princeton, N.J.: Princeton University Press, 1944), Chapter 1.
[2]See A. L. Bowley, "On Bilateral Monopoly," *Economic Journal*, December 1928.

2. *The bargaining situation that the participants confront represents what is referred to as a "non-zero-sum game" situation,* or one which includes a combination of distributable and nondistributable elements leading to interactions of conflict and collaboration. In such cases, the *distribution* of gains has an impact on the *size* of the total benefits that can be obtained by *both* participants. This accentuates the type of interaction that exists between conflict and collaboration in a way that is absent in zero-sum-game situations, in which what one participant gains another loses.[3] Furthermore, in view of some key characteristics of foreign direct investment, the areas of conflict and collaboration shift over time (e.g., skills and knowledge do not need to be reacquired once they are mastered by individuals in developing countries, nor are they lost while they are used).

3. *Given the spread of transnational enterprises around the world, the parent firms have the option of establishing policies on the basis of international multiplant production activities.* This clearly increases their degree of freedom in confronting particular conflict situations. Furthermore, these firms, unlike the individual host governments, aim to achieve maximum benefits at the *global* rather than the national level. (Obviously these firms are not pursuing activities for the general welfare but are attempting to enhance their own private benefit through worldwide activities.) Finally, *the objectives of the various participants differ* not only with respect to geographical spread, but also with respect to substance—that is, national development goals compete with corporate performance goals. These characteristics—namely, international multiplant activities, geographically divergent interests, and differences in objectives—increase the elements of conflict in the bargaining process.

The structure of relationships described above contrasts sharply with the emphasis of traditional economic analysis on relative national factor endowments and the mutual benefits deriving from international factor flows. Such analysis often has served as a convenient instrument for rationalizing national or private interests as they are expressed in the positions of governments on private foreign direct investment by their nationals. Economic "laws" (with their impeccable professional reasoning) have not only served "to depersonalize [and] create a determinate system in which everybody is absolved of all responsibility: they have also been used to prove the existence of a harmony of interests."[4] Yet the environment in which we live includes imperfect world markets, barriers to trade and resource flows, market sharing and oligopolistic transnational enterprises, and costly and inequitably distributed productive knowledge. In such an environment, "there is no hidden hand which assures all countries of

---

[3]See T. Schelling, *The Strategy of Conflict* (Oxford: Oxford University Press, 1963).
[4]T. Balogh, "Fact and Fancy in International Economic Relations," *World Development*, Vol. 1, No. 1 and 2 (February 1973), p. 76.

optimizing their dynamic comparative advantage, let alone being assured of an equitable distribution of the [resulting] benefits."[5]

Official Policy and Investment Flows

It has been suggested that "official policy has a rather limited direct role in determining the volume of private investment abroad."[6] Yet surely the broad term "official policy" includes not only investment insurance guarantees and exemptions from restraints on capital flows but also a host of other elements of a political and/or economic nature that have proven to be highly significant in determining the form of foreign direct investment. For example, available statistics indicate that in many developing nations, foreign investment is very closely linked to old colonial ties, special political relations, and spheres of economic influence. Table 1 presents the percentage shares of selected European countries in the total foreign investment in selected developing countries. These percentage shares, together with the information presented in Table 2, which covers U.S. investments, indicate a marked division of the Third World into areas of economic influence. Moreover, the United Kingdom accounts for 20 per cent and France for 8 per cent of all foreign direct investment in developing countries; the U.S. share in the book value of total direct investment in the Third World in 1967 was about 50 per cent.

Tables 1 and 2 do not distinguish between investment in the manufacturing and service sectors and investment in extractive activities. Given its strategic importance, the extractive sector (which represents about 50 per cent of the reported book value of foreign investment in developing countries) is much more strongly linked to old colonial ties (in the case of European nations) and to strong political and military influence (in the case of the United States). However, even investment in the manufacturing and service sectors clearly reflects overall political and economic links and other historical ties.[7]

In the postwar era, two major changes have occurred. During the 1950s and early 1960s, the worldwide political and economic presence and power of the United States resulted in an increasing participation of U.S. private interests in areas that previously were almost exclusively under

---

[5]J. H. Dunning, "Multinational Enterprises and Trade Flows in Less Developed Countries," paper presented at the Cambridge Conference on Development, 1972, OSC Document No. C72/10, p. 3.

[6]*Reassessing North-South Economic Relations, A Tripartite Report by Thirteen Experts from the European Community, Japan, and North America* (Washington, D.C.: The Brookings Institution, 1972), p. 21.

[7]See Constantine V. Vaitsos, "Power, Knowledge and Development Policy: Relations between Transnational Enterprises and Developing Countries," in G. K. Helleiner, ed., *Disillusion and Disorder: The New International Economics of Development*, forthcoming.

Table 1. European Direct Investment in Selected Developing Countries, End 1967 (book value, expressed as percentage of total investment reported)

Investment by United Kingdom in: Africa		Investment by France in:		Investment by Belgium in: Africa		Investment by Italy in: Africa	
Swaziland	96.6	Africa		Zaire	87.8	Somalia	83.3
Malawi	92.7	Niger	95.7	Rwanda	86.8	Tunisia	28.5
Botswana	88.0	Central African Rep.	91.8	Burundi	84.5	Dahomey	25.7
Rhodesia	83.3	Senegal	87.4				
Zambia	79.6	Chad	80.4				
Kenya	78.8	Mali	76.9				
Sudan	74.9	Cameroon	75.1				
Ghana	59.1	Gabon	73.4				
Nigeria	53.8	Algeria	71.7				
Asia		Asia					
Sri Lanka	95.1	New Caledonia	91.4				
Burma	92.8	Khmer Republic	88.2				
Malaysia	74.3	French Polynesia	72.7				
India	64.6	Rep. of Vietnam	65.7				
Pakistan	59.5						
Latin America		Latin America					
British Honduras (Belize)	70.2	French Guyana	100.0				
		French Antilles	71.7				

SOURCE: Stock of Private Direct Investment by DAC Countries in Developing Countries, End 1967 (Paris: Organisation for Economic Cooperation and Development, 1972), as analyzed and cited in Department of Economic and Social Affairs, Multinational Corporations in World Development (New York: United Nations, 1973).

Table 2.   U.S. Direct Investment in Selected
Developing Countries, End 1967
(book value, expressed as percentage of total investment reported)

Liberia	57.8
South Korea	92.3
Philippines	88.4
Indonesia	73.2
Bahrein	91.8
Libyan Arab Republic	77.7
Jordan	75.0
Israel	59.8
Kuwait	54.4
Afghanistan	54.2
Honduras	97.7
Chile	91.3
Panama	90.8
Costa Rica	89.3
Colombia	86.2
Guatemala	84.4
Peru	84.4
Bolivia	82.9
Dominican Republic	81.1
Mexico	76.4
Venezuela	73.0

SOURCE: *Stock of Private Direct Investment by DAC Countries in Developing Coun-tries, End 1967* (Paris: Organisation for Economic Co-operation and Development, 1972), as analyzed and cited in Department of Economic and Social Affairs, *Multinational Corpora-tions in World Development* (New York: United Nations, 1973).

European or Japanese influence.[8] In the late 1960s and early 1970s—with their postwar recovery completed and their economic expansion well under way—Western Europe and Japan made inroads in some areas where the U.S. presence previously had been predominant.[9] However, the figures and trends shown in Tables 1 and 2 need to be qualified by the fact that only a

[8]For comments on the shift of relative standing in Saudi Arabia from British to U.S. oil companies, see R. S. Barnet, *Roots of War: The Men and Institutions behind U.S. Foreign Policy* (Baltimore: Penguin Books, 1971), pp. 199 ff.
[9]Until 1966, European direct investments in Colombia amounted to about 16 per cent; in the 1967–1970 period these investments increased to 25.4 per cent, with a high corresponding decrease of U.S. investment. See Constantine V. Vaitsos, "Policies on Foreign Direct Investments and Economic Development in Latin America," *Journal of World Trade Law*, January 1974.

few countries—Mexico, Brazil, Argentina, Venezuela, some Caribbean islands, one Asian country (India), and one African country (Nigeria)—accounted for 43 per cent of the total foreign investment reported by the Third World in 1967. Thirteen other countries (mostly in the Middle East and in Latin America) accounted for another 30 per cent.[10]

In addition to being a reflection of the history of political-military-economic influence, official policy affects foreign investment through the rules applied by multilateral lending agencies,[11] retaliatory acts in trade relations,[12] links with foreign aid policies, and direct diplomatic pressure.[13] Given the international framework of relative political power and its effects on developing countries, these practices are only the more conspicuous exercises of official policy on matters affecting the flow and composition of foreign investment.

Prior to World War II, industrialists—individually or in groups—were able to affect directly the official foreign policy decisions of their governments relating to the various areas, both geographic and substantive, that enhanced their own private interests. In more recent times, however, the determination of foreign policy has rested more clearly in the hands of the state, while firms have exercised their influence directly (by lobbying) or indirectly (through the conduct of their business) on the content and direction of policy. The extent of that influence depends on the presence and strength of any other developed-country interests in the same area. Quite often, however, company representatives feel that "an activist foreign policy by their home government may do them more harm than good."[14] In other cases, relations between governments are clouded as a result of the specific interests of private investors.

The influence of transnational enterprises obviously does not take place only through official channels. For example, as J. A. Mayobre has observed, when Latin American countries have tried to modify to their advantage the conditions under which extractive industries operate in their countries, propaganda campaigns have been launched against their efforts, resistance has arisen in foreign banking circles, and attempts have been made to distort their image abroad—all of which has resulted in an adverse

---

[10]U.N. Department of Economic and Social Affairs, *Multinational Corporations in World Development* (New York: Praeger Publishers, Inc., 1974), p. 19.

[11]See *Reassessing North-South Economic Relations*, op. cit., p. 20.

[12]It has been suggested that Japan's recent liberalization of its foreign investment regulations was related to U.S. indications of a hardening prospect for Japanese exports to the U.S. market. See the recommendation by Jack N. Behrman on trade pressures on developing countries linked to the treatment applied by the latter to foreign investors in his chapter, "U.S. Private Investment in the Developing World," in Robert E. Hunter and the staff of the Overseas Development Council, *The United States and the Developing World: Agenda for Action, 1973* (Washington, D.C.: Overseas Development Council, 1973), p. 40.

[13]For the cases of Peru, Colombia, and other Andean countries, see Vaitsos, "Policies on Foreign Direct Investments," op. cit.

[14]Barnet, *Roots of War*, op. cit., pp. 182–86.

climate for foreign cooperation with national development.[15] Similar cases have been noted in the manufacturing and service sectors.[16] In the face of such pressures, the interests of developing countries can be safeguarded only if they can amass countervailing powers.

Development Assistance versus National and Private Investment Interests

Transnational enterprises pursue their foreign investments for three main reasons: a) to take advantage of sales potential or to avoid barriers to imports in the host countries; b) to take advantage of cost opportunities (particularly low-wage labor) in the host economies that are critical to the competitive position of their products in world markets; and c) to secure access to foreign sources of critical inputs, such as mineral resources. Although their rhetoric and diplomacy emphasize that their operations constitute a form of foreign assistance, this factor is not reflected in their decisions concerning the commitment of resources abroad.[17]

A recent study by the U.S. Senate[18] indicates that in the late 1960s, the United States obtained significant overall benefits (although there were important variations in the benefits obtained by different industries) from the worldwide operations of U.S.-based transnational enterprises. Such firms, whose share of total U.S. exports of manufactured goods amounted to 62 per cent, showed an overall direct increase of $3.4 billion in net exports (exports minus imports) to the rest of the world for the 1966–1970 period. Over the same period, "nontransnational" firms experienced a negative net trade balance of $3.6 billion. Even when the *indirect* effect of the trans-

---

[15]José Antonio Mayobre, "Política sobre inversión extranjera en materia de recursos naturales: El régimen del petróleo y su futuro," in K. H. Stanzick and H. H. Godoy, eds., *Inversiones extranjeras y transferencia de technología en América Latina* (Santiago: ILDIS, 1972), p. 278.

[16]See, for example, M. S. Wionczek, "La reacción norteamericana ante el tratado común a los capitales extranjeros en el grupo andino," *Comercio Exterior*, May 1971, pp. 406–8.

[17]As Jack N. Behrman has pointed out: "Since the end of World War II, the U.S. Government has asserted that a major element of its programs for assistance to developing countries would be reliance on the contributions of private foreign investment . . . In fact, however, the U.S. private investment flow, excluding the extractive sector, has only been significant for those few countries which are beginning to emerge from the ranks of the underdeveloped." See Behrman, "U.S. Private Investment in the Developing World," op. cit., p. 39. In this connection it is also interesting to note that in 1943, a U.S. Assistant Secretary of State observed that the only alternative to a continuing search abroad for investment outlets and markets for U.S. goods would be "to turn our country into an armed camp, police the seven seas, tighten our belts, and live by the ration books for the next century or so." Statement of former Assistant Secretary of State W. Clayton in *Foreign Commerce Weekly*, November 20, 1943, p. 11, quoted in D. Horowitz, ed., *Corporations and the Cold War* (New York: Monthly Review Press, 1969), p. 149.

[18]U.S. Senate, Committee on Finance, *Implications of Multinational Firms for World Trade and Investment and for U.S. Trade and Labor* (Washington, D.C.: U.S. Government Printing Office, 1973).

nationals on net exports (the most likely substitution of the products of foreign affiliates for U.S. exports to foreign markets) is taken into account, net exports to the world indicate a net gain of $400 million over the same years.[19]

In terms of the basic balance of payments (that is, the balance on current account and on long-term capital movements), U.S.-based transnational firms improved their position by $2.8 billion in 1966–1970. During the same period, the basic balance of nontransnationals deteriorated by $3.3 billion. The U.S. account as a whole also deteriorated[20] during this period. The U.S. Senate study indicated that its most consistent conclusion was that, in their transactions with the United States, the U.S.-based transnationals "exert a uniformly large, negative impact on the current accounts of balances of payments of the host countries (conversely, of course, they have a favorable impact on the corresponding account of the U.S. balance of payments)."[21] While the conclusion is correct for the U.S. economy, for the host country the appropriate question at this level of analysis is: what would have happened in the absence of that U.S. investment? Yet, as will be discussed later, in a non-zero-sum bargaining situation, in which both parties might have an interest, this "opportunity cost" question is not the only relevant one to ask.

A further fact that bears on the situation is that only about 15 per cent of the funds needed to finance the worldwide activities of U.S.-based transnational firms originated in the United States.[22] Even this 15 per cent is an overestimate, in view of the common practices of capitalizing intangible elements of overseas investment, using secondhand machinery, and revaluing assets, none of which constitute an additional financial investment for the U.S. firms. The remaining funds were provided by the local savings of the host economies (including local borrowing, depreciation allowances, and reinvested profits) and other non-U.S. sources of finance. In this sense, the term "foreign investment" is a misnomer; a more accurate term would be "foreign-*controlled* investments or firms."

The developing countries, for their part, in 1968 accounted for about one third of the book value of all foreign investment outside the centrally planned economies. This contrasts with their share of the global GNP (one sixth) and their participation in world exports (one fifth), again excluding the centrally planned economies.[23]

---

[19]Ibid., p. 5.
[20]Ibid., p. 7.
[21]Ibid., p. 29.
[22]Ibid., p. 38.
[23]Half of the foreign direct investment in the Third World was in the extractive industries, about one third in manufacturing, and the rest in banking, commerce, public services, tourism, etc. See U.N., *Multinational Corporations in World Development*, op. cit., p. 16.

There are at least two different perspectives from which the economic effects of foreign investment on the developing countries can be evaluated. The first involves analysis of different economic indicators of the impact of foreign investment (e.g., income effects, balance-of-payments effects, employment, etc.) on the host developing countries alone. The second requires analysis of the *total* benefits obtained from such investment and the way they are distributed among *all* participants.

One of the most complete intercountry and interindustry attempts to measure the full income effects of foreign subsidiaries[24] in the 1960s was the study of 156 manufacturing firms in six developing countries undertaken for the U.N. Conference on Trade and Development (UNCTAD) by a team of Oxford economists. The team concluded that "on a fairly reasonable set of assumptions nearly 40 per cent of the firms in the six countries taken together have negative effects on the overall social income of the host economies."[25] For another 30 per cent of the firms studied, the full social, rather than private, income generated for the host economy (including government revenues) amounted to less than 10 per cent of their sales[26] —that is, less than the margins usually obtained by wholesalers or distributors.

Some of the negative effects could have been reduced or even avoided by correcting certain host-government policies, such as the high level of protection of foreign affiliates—although such policies are not independent of the terms set by such firms as conditions for their entry into the country. In other cases, even with more appropriate government policies, the full effects still could be negative. Not all investments are in the interest of the host economy. In such cases, developing countries need to have an evaluating and regulatory capability and the political will to refuse the entry of such investments in the first place. "The leap from the sensible proposition that some trade [or some investment] can potentially make everyone better off as compared with no trade [or no investment] to the conviction that more trade [or more investment] is always likely to do just that, is taken with remarkable ease."[27] The rationalization of one's own interests or

---

[24]The full effects include 1) net (after payments abroad of dividends, royalties, interests, etc.) and direct income effects of the activities of foreign investors; 2) indirect effects through imports, investment, etc., induced by the operations of foreign investment; and 3) the use of scarce local resources by foreign enterprises, thereby forgoing income contributions elsewhere in the local economy.

[25]See P. P. Streeten and S. Lall, *Evaluation of Methods and Main Findings of the UNCTAD Study of Private Overseas Investment in Selected Less-Developed Countries,* U.N. Doc. No. TD/B/C.3/111. The team used the Little-Mirrlees project evaluation methodology as described in I. M. D. Little and J. A. Mirrlees, *Manual of Industrial Project Analysis in Developing Countries* (Paris: Organisation for Economic Co-operation and Development, 1969).

[26]Streeten and Lall, *Evaluation of Methods,* op. cit., p. 62.

[27]For a discussion of the case of trade, see Carlos F. Díaz-Alejandro, "Trade Policies and Economic Development" (Discussion Paper No. 180), Economic Growth Center, Yale University, June 1973, p. 5.

conventional wisdom in the area of foreign investments often results in such "leaps." (As various Brazilian economists increasingly are finding, maximum foreign investment flows do not mean maximum benefits for Brazil.)

In other cases, however, host countries can enhance their growth prospects as a result of the activities of foreign firms. Because of their size and particularly their accumulation of human capital and productive knowledge, transnational enterprises hold certain distinct advantages that can be ascribed to their total organization rather than to the specific activities of any of their branches or subsidiaries. Such advantages include:

> the ability to attract and deploy high-caliber personnel, worldwide procurement facilities and marketing networks, a financial reputation that can be used to obtain large quantities of capital, and immediate access to the parent company's accumulated and continually expanding store of research and development.[28]

As already noted, however, resort to such advantages requires *access* to host-country markets (for example, import-substitution opportunities) or access to host-country resources (i.e., natural resources or low-wage labor). The *distribution* of the resulting benefits will depend on diverse types of knowledge as well as on the availability and use of bargaining power, given the industry's characteristics and the type of activity involved. The application of cost-benefit analysis to the host country alone—which is a common practice—omits any appreciation of the returns to the foreign investors. Research conducted in the 1960s in Latin America revealed that the average effective profitability (as distinct from the declared one, which omits transfer pricing considerations) of foreign manufacturing subsidiaries ranged up to 40 per cent.[29] Given this level of profitability, foreign firms might well be interested in investing in or selling inputs under alternative types of ownership and production structures—such as licensing agreements, joint ventures, or coproduction schemes—under which a greater share of benefits would accrue to the host economies.

In the extractive industries—after a long and turbulent history of relations between host countries and foreign investors—significant redistributive steps were taken at the end of the 1960s that improved the relative position of host developing countries in agreements with foreign investors.[30]

---

[28]Peter P. Gabriel, "The Multinational Corporation on the Defensive (If Not at Bay)," *Fortune*, January 1972, p. 120.

[29]See Shane Hunt, "Evaluating Direct Foreign Investment in Latin America," in Luigi R. Einaudi, ed., *Latin America in the 1970s* (Santa Monica: RAND Corporation, 1972).

[30]For example, the Braden Company in Chile was paying taxes that amounted to less than 1 per cent of gross sales value over 1913–1924 and less than 6 per cent for 1930–1939, but reached 64 per cent by 1953. See M. Mamalakis, "Contribution of Copper to Chilean Economic Development, 1920–1967: Profile of a Foreign-Owned Export Sector," in R. F. Mikesell, ed., *Foreign Investment in the Petroleum and Mineral Industries* (Baltimore: published for Resources for the Future by Johns Hopkins Press, 1971), pp. 387–420.

In some cases these gains were achieved through participation in ownership or production schemes or through changes in tax structure within certain price ranges that were set in markets controlled by transnational enterprises and affected by developed-country government policies. For example, before the Teheran negotiations of 1971, the principal oil producing countries earned approximately $1 per barrel of refined oil in terms of royalties and taxes. In contrast, tax collectors in the Western European oil importing countries averaged gains of about $4.50 on each barrel sold in Europe for about $8.00.[31]

In the 1970s, in the context of the special market demand for energy and limited (economically viable) alternative sources of energy, the actions taken by the oil producers have led to an unprecedented redistribution of income. Given preexisting price structures in the world oil market, a redistribution on such a scale could be achieved only through price changes, not merely through changes in fiscal rates or ownership structures. Furthermore, a sine qua non of such major shifts in market power was coordinated producer action, which, in the case of the major Middle Eastern oil producers, required the highest political authorities to cement the necessary commitments for joint action.

While this occasion marked the first major and highly effective coordinated action by Third World countries in their economic relations with Western countries, individual developing countries often have been at the receiving end of the results of similar actions taken by the industrialized world. Such actions have taken the forms of a) official policies affecting access to multilateral or private lending agencies (e.g., the experiences of Peru and Chile in the late 1960s and early 1970s), b) coordinated company action blocking the ability of Third World countries to sell their own products (Iran in 1951, Iraq in 1972) or to buy certain goods and services abroad (e.g., the movie distributors' boycott of Colombia in 1969 because of royalty renegotiation disputes on film rights).

The economics of the manufacturing and service sectors of developing countries is quite distinct from that of the extractive industries. Market characteristics, share in total demand for products, and risk factors differ markedly from those in the natural resources sector. Nevertheless, some broad characteristics and knowledge of the operations of vertically and internationally integrated firms in these sectors—and their effects with respect to transfer pricing, market segmentation (i.e., division of markets through restrictive business practices), market access, and labor relations —are comparable to those which mark the extractive industries. In these areas, the developing countries had attained, as of the 1960s, a level of understanding of the manufacturing sector comparable to their understanding of the extractive industry in the first half of this century. Common action in this sector still is quite limited, however—the Andean Pact being a

---

[31]See *Fortune*, March 1971, p. 30.

notable exception. Consequently, in manufacturing and services, benefits to the Third World should be expected to accrue largely from a variety of actions that at this stage need to be undertaken primarily within and among the developing countries.

Inappropriateness of Products and Technology[32]

Foreign investors in the manufacturing sector have catered primarily to high-income consumers. Their original markets in rich industrialized countries and the technological implications deriving from this stage of operation, as well as the degree of standardization they employ to achieve production efficiency, often are unrelated to the basic human needs and to the financial means of the majority of the population in the Third World.[33] The basic health, nutrition, and housing requirements of low-income earners are not areas to which such firms tend to dedicate their resources. So far such companies have indicated either that they are not interested in or not equipped to enter these areas of activity. Their lack of interest stems essentially from a belief that their private returns—unlike the benefits to society derived from better health and education, for example—might not be very large. Their inability to meet such basic human needs is related to the complexity and diversity of social organization, cultural attitudes, and a variety of other factors inherent in economic backwardness. These factors create situations which are not subject to standardization or to uniform consumption patterns—a norm of behavior which is explicit or implicit in many of the activities of transnational firms and which is inappropriate in such situations.

Thus to a great extent, the efforts necessary to satisfy the basic human needs of the majority of the population in developing countries are outside the realm of activity of foreign investors—at least in the case of the manufacturing sector. Rather, they are subject to the policies and efforts of governments and other economic actors at the *national* level. International assistance and commitment are needed for such purposes, but these have to come through channels other than transnational enterprises.

This does not mean that foreign firms do not have a direct bearing on the national policies of poor countries; it merely means that the influence of foreign investors is often negative. First, directly or indirectly, foreign investors attract scarce local technological capabilities and other resources

---

[32]An earlier version of this section appeared in the summary notes of the presentation by Constantine V. Vaitsos before the U.N. Group of Eminent Persons. See *Summary of the Hearings Before the Group of Eminent Persons to Study the Impact of Multinational Corporations on Development*, U.N. Pub. Sales No. E.74.II.A.9 (New York: United Nations, 1974), pp. 396–404.

[33]See F. Stewart, "Technology and Employment in LDCs," paper presented at the New Delhi Conference on Technology and Employment, sponsored by the Ford Foundation, March 1973.

into areas that do not represent the basic needs of the developing countries. This constitutes a domestic "brain drain" of an importance equal to or greater than the international one. Second, governmental efforts to pursue policies and introduce structural changes which imply a more equitable income distribution can have a negative effect on at least the short-term interests of foreign investors. Such changes also affect local interest groups associated with the transnational enterprises. As a result, these groups may constitute an impediment to the introduction of necessary changes to promote greater equity and growth in the Third World.

Another area of major concern relates to the appropriateness of the techniques of production used. The technology developed and employed by transnational enterprises in their worldwide operations stems from research and development (R and D) activities in the industrialized world and is concentrated mainly in the home countries of such firms. (For example, in 1966, U.S.-based transnationals undertook about 97 per cent of their global R and D activities in the United States.[34] As a result of a) high absolute savings levels, b) accumulated capital stock, c) relatively high labor costs, and d) large-scale production of goods and services, technological development in the high-income countries has been directed toward increasingly capital-biased production processes. The application of these largely unadapted processes by foreign-owned subsidiaries and national firms in developing countries can lead not only to inappropriate relative factor utilization but also to absolute direct labor displacement.[35] Such labor displacement can and does take place even under conditions of expanding production. Thus the resulting technological orientation accentuates existing problems of unequal income distribution—both within a country and internationally—and counteracts basic developmental needs related to the enhancement of employment opportunities in the Third World.

A "Code of Conduct" for Transnational Enterprises

The subject of an international code of conduct for foreign investors and suppliers of "know-how" has now been with us for some time. In the mid-1960s, specific proposals were presented on this subject by various economists. Lately the subject has obtained considerable prominence in view of its explicit consideration during the U.N. hearings before the Group of Eminent Persons on the Role of Multinational Corporations. In addition, specific resolutions in support of the adoption of such a code have been passed by

---

[34]See K. L. R. Pavitt, "The Multinational Enterprise and the Transfer of Technology," in J. H. Dunning, ed., *The Multinational Enterprise* (London: Allen and Unwinn, 1971).
[35]See Constantine V. Vaitsos, "Employment Effects of Foreign Direct Investments," paper presented at the New Delhi Conference on Technology and Employment, sponsored by the Ford Foundation, March 1973.

UNCTAD, by conferences such as Pugwash,[36] and by private-sector representatives such as the International Chamber of Commerce.

These "codes"—which are yet to be drafted—will tend to be of a general nature, establishing broad criteria that already have been incorporated in the legislation of certain developing countries and in the industrialized world (e.g., criteria against restrictive business practices). They also will contain some of the principles that have been included in countless resolutions passed by U.N. bodies and Third World meetings, but that up to now have not had any major repercussions on actual business conduct—on account of the power relations and relative knowledge (or ignorance) among participants about the foreign investment process. The codes also will highlight certain problem areas, and in this sense their effect will be to foster the interests of developing countries. They could, however, also constitute a conservative force, since a general and widely accepted code could have such a low common denominator that it would actually retard certain necessary changes in the Third World.

If such codes of conduct are approved, they probably will not differentiate among the various industries (with the possible exception of the extractive versus the manufacturing and service sectors), despite the significant differences among them in terms of their structure, conduct, and performance. Neither are they likely to differentiate sufficiently among the host developing countries, which—as a result of their divergent size, level of overall development, political orientation, development objectives, and past history with foreign firms and expertise in dealing with them—have quite different needs in their operations with foreign suppliers of factors of production. Furthermore, such codes will certainly not differentiate among firms, despite their varied effects on host economies as a result of differences in size, links with other economic interests (e.g., banking institutions that are related to or even control manufacturing firms, and vice versa), corporate behavior (i.e., first entrants versus imitators), market spread, and product specialization.

Despite all these qualifications, international codes of conduct are likely to be approved in the future. But the entities that will be affected least by such international action (as distinct from national or regional legislation or actions by countries owning similar resources) will be the transnational enterprises themselves. This is why the *transnational enterprises will be among the strongest supporters of international codes of conduct*—for reasons quite different from those of other supporters.

As is discussed below, the basic behavior of transnational firms will not be affected significantly by these codes, given the transnational character of such firms and their corporate objectives.

---

[36]See "Pugwash Conferences on Science and World Affairs, Draft Code of Conduct on Transfer of Technology," *World Development*, Vol. 2, No. 4 and 5 (April-May, 1974), pp. 77–82.

1. *Income distribution and interaffiliate sales and purchases.* Although transnational enterprises are the product of market economies, they at present constitute one of the most important *non*market forces in world economic relations. This is the result of a) the increasing role of central and long-run planning and control in the management of these firms as they confront oligopolistic markets, b) their ability to generate demand for their own products and to influence their economic environment, and c) the increasing share of world trade and production exchanged among firms that are affiliated and therefore able to bypass market considerations.

Broadly indicative figures suggest that about one third of U.S. trade in manufactured products is accounted for by sales among affiliates controlled by U.S.-based parent firms.[37] In many host countries (developing as well as developed)—and in specific sectors—the percentages of interaffiliate trade are even higher. For example, in the late 1960s, about half of the exports of U.S. subsidiaries based in the United Kingdom went to their affiliates. In Canada the figure was 75 per cent in 1969.[38]

Such a structure of production and trade control by parent firms divorces the decisions and consequences relating to the location of production from those relating to the valorization of the product through administrative price setting, and this in turn affects the generation and distribution of income both within and between countries.

The pricing of goods and services exchanged among affiliates is a critically important element of business behavior closely related to such diverse factors as a) global tax minimization or tax avoidance, b) reduction of tariff payments for goods imported into a host country and effects on the tariffs of goods produced in a host country, c) market control and price setting that impedes entry by other firms, d) hedging against changes in currency values, and e) reduction of the risk of host-government reactions, trade union pressures, and antitrust and other government actions in response to high rates of profitability.

No code of conduct can deal adequately with transfer pricing, which is complex and critical for the enterprises. Calling for "just" or "market equivalent" prices runs into problems because of the many highly diversified components and parts that are traded. Even more serious questions arise with respect to international participation in covering company overheads. For example, what is the "just" price that a host country should pay for the training or R and D expenses of Swiss pharmacologists, Japanese auto engineers, or U.S. electronics specialists whose costs are charged by the parent firms in selling to or buying from their foreign subsidiaries? Or what is a "fair" price that a host country should pay to cover part of the expenses of foreign firms lobbying in the home country for the application of eco-

---

[37]See S. Lall, "Transfer Pricing by Multinational Manufacturing Firms," *Oxford Economic Papers*, 1973.
[38]U.N., *Multinational Corporations in World Development*, op. cit., p. 54.

nomic sanctions in case of nationalization of their assets abroad?

The resolution of such problems requires *multiple* actions that include market price lists for standardized and "freely" traded goods, administrative rules for handling diversified products (for example, the "depletion allowance" practices of the automotive industry), and, most of all, hard bargaining between buyers and sellers.

2. *Worldwide activities and market segmentation.* The international spread of transnational enterprises is undoubtedly one of the major dynamic forces in world trade—given their enormous procurement and selling capabilities and their worldwide sourcing and production. Yet the same worldwide expansion and the creation of links among affiliated firms could result (and in many cases has resulted) in market segmentation, which in previous decades was considered to be one aspect of cartel agreements among independent firms and which today is undertaken through the control of subsidiaries located abroad.

Research on technology-licensing contracts between parent and subsidiary firms has revealed the very frequent existence of export-prohibiting clauses, price-fixing arrangements, and other restrictive business practices.[39] An international code of conduct that would discourage such explicit contractual limitations might, however, leave untouched some very important *implicit* restrictive business practices that can be achieved through ownership or control—such as export limitations or prohibitions, which do not have to be written into contracts to be applicable among affiliates.

Host countries have found that some of the more effective means of promoting exports, untying sources of inputs, etc., include direct negotiations with foreign investors, offers of certain incentives or cost advantages (as in the case of exports), and the direct screening of imports (as in the case of tied purchases).

3. *The location of productive activities and investment and the selection of products and techniques.* Whether they are countries or firms, economic units tend to ensure their own participation and maintain their comparative advantages in a changing world through production and the accumulation of knowledge and other resources. Neither fiscal compensation among countries (as in the case of the East African Association) nor charity can constitute the basis for economic advancement. In this context, the major economic effects of transnational firms thus need to be examined by analyzing what they do, for whom, and where.

Transnational enterprises select their products and techniques and locate their activities on the basis of their own global objectives and the constraints placed on their use of resources by economic, legal, and political factors. Specific governmental actions or competitors' activities can, in varying degrees, affect all of these parameters of the firm's decision-making

---

[39]See Constantine V. Vaitsos, *Intercountry Income Distribution and Transnational Enterprises* (Oxford: Oxford University Press, 1974).

process. However, apart from the possibility of raising some legal issues and introducing stricter disclosure requirements, an international code of conduct is not likely to have a major impact on their decisions.

In conclusion, then, the adoption of an international "code of behavior" for transnational firms most probably will have only minor benefits beyond what has been or could be achieved by other actions; on the negative side, it could even constitute a conservative force in the face of needed changes, and it could, if made a major focus of work by the international community, divert attention from other, higher-priority actions.

International Insurance Schemes for the Assets of Foreign Investors, Subrogation Rights, and the Resolution of Conflicts

Several industrialized countries have established official insurance schemes that cover their nationals' investments abroad with respect to the risks of expropriation, war, remission possibilities, and related issues.[40] Some of these schemes have been linked to the foreign aid agencies and national economic interests (e.g., exports or balances of payments) of the *insuring* countries. A major disadvantage of such arrangements has been their direct linkage with and subrogation of the property rights of private companies by the insuring governments, which has involved both the insuring and the host governments in conflicts over investors' properties. As a result, such insurance schemes constitute latent cases for retaliation through measures such as the Hickenlooper Amendment to the U.S. Foreign Assitance Act, which calls for the cessation of bilateral assistance to countries involved in certain investment disputes with U.S. firms.

Although developing countries have shown an interest in the internationalization of insurance schemes (see the voting record of UNCTAD meetings on this subject),[41] they have expressed serious reservations about the way in which they would be applied. Industrialized countries, too, have registered certain objections, despite initiatives by the World Bank and the Organisation for Economic Co-operation and Development (OECD)—since a multilateral insurance scheme might reduce their influence and special links with certain developing nations, or since they might not wish to participate in the risks of the nationals of other countries.[42]

---

[40]The following countries have such insurance schemes: Australia, Canada, Denmark, Holland, Japan, Norway, Portugal, Sweden, Switzerland, the United States, and West Germany.

[41]See Center for Latin American Monetary Studies (CEMLA), "Proyecto del BIRF de creación de un organismo internacional de seguros sobre las inversiones extranjeras," *Boletín Mensual*, Vol. 17, Nos. 3 and 4 (March and April 1971), p. 105.

[42]In the late 1960s, France, West Germany, Japan, and the United Kingdom indicated that they were not interested in the World Bank project in this area. Also, in December 1969 the President of France recommended that the other members of the European Community adopt a common insurance mechanism for investments in the Third World under the auspices of the Community.

The advantage of multilateral—as compared to bilateral—insurance schemes for Third World countries will depend greatly on the solution of some critical elements involved in their application. Most important among these are the questions of 1) who in fact controls these multilateral insurance schemes and with what authority, 2) how the subrogation of investors' property rights is handled, and 3) what the functions of arbitration and the role of national and international courts are in the resolution of conflicts.

1. *The mandate and control of multilateral insurance schemes.* The proposals advanced by various developed countries on the control of the multilateral insurance organizations have generally placed developing countries in a minority position. For example, the U.S. position on the World Bank's proposal for a multilateral insurance scheme stipulated, in a memorandum of September 8, 1970, that voting participation in decision-making bodies of the proposed organization should be linked to the financial participation of the member countries—on the pattern of the vote-distribution systems of the World Bank itself and the International Development Association (IDA).[43] On the matter of the mandate of the international insurance organization, important questions arise as to whether it would include not only the judiciary functions of interpretation but also legislative ones. The latter would imply the creation of a supranational legislative authority controlled by a majority vote of the developed countries. Some of its provisions might well be in conflict with national legislative and constitutional requirements.

2. *Subrogation of property rights.* In cases of conflict, the property rights of the insured are generally subrogated—under existing legislation in the industrialized countries—by the insuring government or state organization.[44] In sharp contrast, as of 1971, the members of the Andean Pact agreed in their common treatment of foreign investment not to accept the subrogation of the property rights of foreign investors by their home governments.[45]

At the multilateral level, added complications arise for developing countries if conflicts and subrogation of properties of private investors are linked with international institutions (such as the World Bank) whose other functions in the process of aiding economic development thus might be seriously biased. This is particularly so if bilateral conflicts could result in diplomatic pressures exerted by individual governments.

3. *Arbitration and the international resolution of controversies.* The process of resolving conflicts or controversies at the international level has itself proved to be a matter of conflict in North-South economic relations. Developed countries have maintained that differences between states and nationals of other states should be resolved by *international* mechanisms

---

[43]See CEMLA, "Proyecto del BIRF," op. cit., p. 153.
[44]By the end of 1969, 87 countries (77 of which are developing) had accepted such provisions in bilateral insurance agreements with the United States. See CEMLA, "Proyecto del BIRF," op. cit., p. 157.
[45]See Decision 24, Article 51, of the Commission of the Andean Pact.

and courts.[46] Third World countries, particularly the Latin American nations, disagree with this position for legal reasons and because of their past experiences with such mechanisms. Legally, the recommendation or application of the international resolution of controversies bypasses or dispenses with the competence of the national laws and courts of the state involved in the conflict. As a result,

> a private investor, by virtue of being foreign, is given the right to make claims against a sovereign state outside of the latter's national territory, dispensing with the national tribunals. This disposition is contrary to the traditional legal norms of . . . [various] countries and, in fact, establishes a privilege in favor of a foreign investor, putting the national ones in an inferior position.[47]

Historical evidence has also indicated that "international tribunals [rarely] have ruled favorably on attempts to reopen general negotiations based on the contention of changed conditions."[48] Thus developing countries contend that international courts, both because of their composition and because of limited precedents, cannot be expected to defend Third World interests adequately. The existing power structure of international relations and its effects on the interpretation of the law have prevented resort to the *rebus sic stantibus* clause in favor of the developing countries. However, this clause, which holds that agreements are binding only so long as conditions have not substantially changed, has been applied in labor disputes within developed countries, in the renegotiation of contracts between private firms and their states, and in the renegotiation of treaties among nation states.

It is for these reasons that developing countries are proposing or adopting positions such as the following on the jurisprudence of international law: "Acts which do not recognize the exclusive jurisdiction of the courts of the country which nationalizes foreign assets . . . constitute a violation of the sovereignty of such a country."[49]

---

[46]See, for example, "Agreement on Resolution of Differences between States and Nationals of Other States," which entered into effect on October 14, 1944. All major capital-exporting countries, and many African and Asian developing countries, but none of the Latin American countries (with the exception of Jamaica and Trinidad and Tobago), are participants of the Agreement. Similar provisions were included in the World Bank project on insurance of foreign investors' assets.

[47]Félix Ruiz (Chilean Governor to the IBRD), speech delivered at the Annual Meeting of the Boards of Governors of the IBRD and IMF, Tokyo, Japan, September 7-11, 1964. This speech represented the Latin American position in rejecting adherence to the proposed mechanisms for the international settlement of disputes between states and the nationals of other states. This position has its roots in the Calvo Doctrine on the sovereignty of states involved in investment disputes.

[48]See L. T. Wells, Jr., "The Evolution of Concession Agreements," paper presented at the Harvard Development Advisory Service Conference, Sorrento, Italy, 1968, p. 22.

[49]Resolution passed during the meeting of the copper exporting countries (CIPEC) in 1972, as reported in *El Mercurio* (Santiago), December 2, 1972.

Conclusions

Power and knowledge are determining factors in the operations of foreign-controlled enterprises in their host countries. Generally, foreign direct investment constitutes a relatively small, and in many cases decreasing, part of the overall economic relations among the affiliates of transnational enterprises. The volume and command of resources (generated by their economic environment as well as from within the firms), accumulated and continuously expanding knowledge, official policies of the home governments,[50] collusion with host-government representatives, orientation and control of private or public multilateral lending agencies, and the panoply of the existing legal framework (for example, the international patent system) are among the elements that strongly augment the relative power of transnational enterprises in their relations with the Third World countries. The power of the developing countries is further diluted by their number and the relatively small size of their economies, their diverging objectives and policies, and their limited knowledge.

The international economic repercussions of some of the developing countries' strengths (as in the case of mineral resources) can take place through their own self-reliance and coordinated action, given sufficient knowledge and adeptness in responding to market, risk, and political factors. National repercussions (as in the case of the manufacturing and service sectors) also can be affected progressively through enhanced knowledge, political will, and certain types of coordinated action. For the Third World, both external power relations and internal political and economic structural characteristics are critical.

The economic environment within which transnational enterprises operate is one of *interdependence*, which in numerous cases requires collaboration and compromise in economic and other relations for the benefit of all the participants. Yet this environment at the same time includes aspects that make it possible for nations to pursue divergent interests and objectives, leading to conflicts which, if resolved one-sidedly, can only accentuate dependence and inequalities. The rhetoric of "oneness of interests"—which is different from true interdependence—has too often been used as a rationalization for subordination.

---

[50]Some of these policies do, however, protect the overall interests of the developed countries and thus limit or restrict the operations of transnational enterprises.

Chapter 6

Population Policy from the Southern Perspective

Krishna Roy

During the long period when most of today's Third World countries were still under the direct rule of one or another Western power, there was not much scope for any rational regional population policy except for the mainly racially oriented one that suited colonial political and economic policy. National progress and power were identified with the rapid increase and Europeanization of the population. This ideology was associated with economies almost entirely oriented toward raw-material exports and dominated by land-owning commercial elites convinced of the ethnic inferiority of the masses of the population. During this period populations were very small in relation to territory; rates of natural increase were low (with high fertility and high mortality); and urbanization was limited. Large numbers of Europeans wanted to emigrate, and the countries able to attract them forged ahead both economically and in terms of political stability. Population increase through European immigration meant that most of the increment could be incorporated directly into the labor force at the modest skill levels called for by existing systems of production, with the costs of upbringing already covered by the country of origin. This situation prevailed until the 1920s in Latin America and until the 1950s in many African countries, and it still persists in many Asian countries today.

The Evolution of Population Policy

Although many of the countries in these three regions won their political independence and began to change their policies and practices to fit their new circumstances, attitudes favorable to population increase and a lack of concern about the geographical or urban-rural distribution of the population nevertheless often continued unquestioned. At the same time, however, more emphasis was placed on the need to raise the quality of life of the population through education and other social measures. Accelerating urbanization was looked upon with optimism as a stimulus to development through the concentration of consumer demand and occupational skills. These views were associated with the following trends: the rise of nationalism and the defense of indigenous cultural traits against English, European, and North American cultural intrusions; the rapid growth of a politically articulate urban middle class; a shift of emphasis from export-oriented economic patterns toward the development of import-substitution industries offering new job opportunities in the cities; and a widening acceptance of development policies relying on industrialization, international financial and technical cooperation, formal long-term planning, and socio-economic structural reform.

More recently, concern over population policy has greatly intensified in the face of growing scarcity of resources essential to meeting the needs of multiplying millions and the increasing threat of environmental pollution. However, the nature of this concern varies from country to country. For the sake of perspective, it is interesting to note that population policies historically have been tied to social and political ideologies and have shifted from one base to another. As only a handful of examples, it is worth recalling Plato's elitist tendencies to justify a limited population; the mercantilists' interest in cheap labor and its commercial exploitation for the benefit of the state; Malthus's rationalization of conservative economic policies; John Stuart Mill's acceptance of birth control as part of social liberalism and individual rights; Marx's subordination of population growth to the proper economic organization of the means of production; the championing of access to birth control by Margaret Sanger and her followers as an important part of the women's rights movement earlier in this century; and the advocacy of the right to obtain an abortion as part of the platform of the women's liberation movement in the 1970s. A quarter of a century ago there was concern about a declining population in the Western world—as there now is in many Eastern European countries. And not long before then, the world witnessed spurious *Lebensraum* arguments used to justify the military adventures of the Axis powers and equally spurious arguments concerning genetic deterioration used to justify eugenic proposals. Thus circumstances —whether political or social—have greatly influenced population policy. Within a quarter century, we have moved from a concern about population decline in the developed countries to a concern about high population growth rates in the developing countries. A relatively new but very important aspect of international thinking about population-related problems is the growing anxiety about affluence and overconsumption in many of the rich countries as these trends continue to contribute to global resource depletion and environmental deterioration.

96

The Urgency of Population Planning

The censuses of 1960 awakened the world to the reality of the population explosion. In many cases, particularly in Latin America, these censuses showed that the population was considerably larger than had been expected and that it was increasing at an unprecedented rate. As part of the resulting demographic concern, there was a resurgence of Malthusian fears, and books and articles joined in such prophecies of doom. While it can be argued that some of these forecasts and warnings were overly pessimistic, it was nevertheless clear that the high rate of world population growth had become a problem demanding careful and extensive study and effective solutions.

The adoption of a national population policy by all the countries of the world, and particularly by those of the South, has become increasingly urgent as the years go by—all the more so because of the past and present implications of population growth, in the developing countries in particular, in terms of a) economic growth rates, b) the waste of human life implicit in high fertility and relatively high mortality rates, c) unemployment, d) inadequate health and education services, and e) disparities in per capita GNP. More important, the differences characterizing the historical transition of demographic growth in the countries of the North and in those of the South have made the situation worse for the developing world. In the North, high-growth instability was transformed into low-growth stability over a period of *100 to 150 years.* In the South, there has been a demographic transition from a high-growth instability to a high-growth stability within a matter of *two to three decades*—with the disastrous implications of continually exploding population growth rates among the poorer segments of the world's population. Whereas it took until about the year 1830 for world population to reach the level of 1 billion, it took only another hundred years, until around 1930, to add the second billion. By this time, with mortality declining in the more industrialized nations, the world growth rate had doubled from 0.5 per cent to approximately 1.0 per cent per year. And by 1960, only 30 years later, world population had reached the 3 billion mark and the growth rate had nearly doubled again to about 1.8 per cent per year. At present, the world population is estimated to be close to 3.8 billion and is growing at slightly over 2.0 per cent per year. At this rate, it may be expected to reach 4 billion by the end of 1975 and 5 billion before 1985.

The Political Sensitivity of Population Policies

In the context of changing and conflicting concepts of the nature of the population problem in the late 1960s—the second half of the First U.N. Development Decade—many sought to delimit population policy and to determine more definitely its place within the continually widening range of influences that the state exercises on the economy. While it is possible (though not very useful) to include all social and economic development programs under population policy, it is logical—and in fact imperative—to include population policy in economic development programs. At the same time, the range of activities open to the public sector for direct intervention in demographic change is narrow—particularly in the context of developing economies with traditional values. Public activities that have the greatest actual or potential influence on demographic variables are often discarded for political considerations, in which case this influence becomes secondary or is disregarded altogether.

Since the early 1960s, developed-country and developing-country interpretations of the role of population change have become increasingly divergent, conflicting, and ideologically "charged." In the developing countries, opinion on population policy is closely related to the following conditions and developments:

(a) The partial frustration of the hopes invested in the global development objectives of the First U.N. Development Decade;
(b) Accelerated growth in the numbers of persons who annually reach working age (as a result of faster population growth since the 1940s);
(c) The rapidly increasing visibility and spread of urban marginality (the problems posed for and by those urban poor who live at the very margin of survival, lacking work—and consequently food and shelter);
(d) Structural unemployment and underutilization of human resources;
(e) A widening gap between aspirations for social services and their availability; and
(f) The relatively sudden extension to the developing countries of a worldwide campaign insisting on the catastrophic consequences of continued population expansion and on family planning as the only remedy.

The two extreme positions between the North and some of the countries of the South stem from the fact that whereas the North accepts and puts into practice the view that the attainment of a zero population growth rate in the shortest possible time is essential and that family planning as now defined and practiced must continue, a number of the countries in the South believe that the way in which family planning is being introduced means that the national authorities are abdicating their control over national policy to international organizations and governments acting for the furtherance of their own interests. However, the widely disparate economic and social conditions of the developing countries are reflected in the varying stages of program planning and development in the area of population policy.

General Objectives of a Population Policy

Population policy, since it deals with people, potentially covers an extremely broad and complex range of human affairs—including some factors which are consequences of population change and others which are its determinants. Its main general aims, however, should be to:

(a) Contribute to the enhancement of human welfare and human rights at the level of the family and the individual;

(b) Influence population growth, age distribution, and geographic distribution so as to make them as compatible as possible with accelerated development as well as with a more equitable distribution of the fruits of development; and

(c) Enhance understanding of demographic trends among political leaders, planners, and the general public in order to ensure that population trends are more adequately taken into account in all areas of policy and planning.

Beyond these broad aims, however, national strategies have to be different because of the varying natures of the countries concerned.

Clearly the scope of a realistic and operational population policy should be limited to measures intended to influence population growth, size, composition, and distribution, with the provision that such a population policy must be integrated into an overall development policy. Such a policy first of all should involve an adequate understanding of the implications of the demographic variables and the constraints that they impose on economic development; and second, should make certain that the measures selected to affect these variables are mutually supportive and compatible.

Typical Population Positions of Some Poor Countries

A number of different (and to some extent overlapping) positions on population policy and economic development and the relationship of the two have taken shape in the developing world. *First*, there are those countries which identify development with higher rates of increase in production and consumption. Thus in Hong Kong, India, and some countries of the Middle East, it is assumed that this goal can be attained if the developmental policies of the previous decades are pursued vigorously and if international cooperation through aid and trade becomes more generous and dependable. This view assumes that only when a high economic growth rate is reached can the ever-increasing unemployed "marginal" population in rural areas as well as in the cities be productively employed and its full participation in the social order be achieved. Any reduction in the population will alleviate the pressure for nonproductive uses of public resources, reduce the likelihood of violence, and give the national authorities more time and greater flexibility to assign resources to high-priority developmental tasks. (Many of the opponents of this position see the reduction of the population growth rate itself as an alternative to the higher-growth-rate approach to development.)

A *second* position—one adopted by Argentina, for example—is that the strategy mentioned above can result only in pseudo-development and threatens perpetual dependence on external sources. They believe that development necessarily involves a revolutionary transformation of power and an independence from external bonds. According to this position, it is dependence on foreign aid that is mainly responsible for the continued growth of a "marginal" population. As long as existing institutions remain intact, any measures of population control, if effective, will in fact alleviate tensions, and thus only prolong the survival of economic and social structures that should instead disappear as soon as possible to make way for the building up of a new world social order not only in the South but also in the North. (To its opponents, this position seems to advocate misery as a means of instituting social reform and a new order.)

A *third* point of view—held by countries such as Colombia, Costa Rica, Burma, and Mali—emphasizes the rights of the family to have access to means of limiting the number of children irrespective of the implications for development or for public policy regarding population increase. Its proponents recognize the need for economic development, but they doubt the ability of the public authorities to apply population policies based on ambitious development plans, and they are not willing to settle for fragmentary governmental measures with regard to the immediate needs of families. Some advocates of this position limit their support to a certain range of family planning techniques considered morally acceptable while others are prepared to support the free availability of all methods, including abortion.

A *fourth* position—attributable to Zaire and Chile among others—accepts the *human rights argument* and also considers lower rates of population growth highly desirable, yet its proponents feel that a) both the developmental urgency and the appropriate content of policies for demographic rationalization differ widely according to the circumstances of specific countries; that b) the relevance of such policies to the alleviation of pressures arising from marginalization is questionable—whether such alleviation is viewed as desirable or not; and that c) the capacity of the state to control population growth during the foreseeable future through the techniques now being advocated will probably be of much less importance than the changes in family life and cultural attitudes brought about by ongoing social and economic changes. Those who hold this position assume that in the short term the developmental effects of such policies will be limited and more important to the welfare of families than to solving the resource-allocation problems faced by the state, but that attention cannot be limited to the short term.

A *fifth* position—one taken by countries such as Taiwan and the Philippines—considers population growth control to be essential for ensuring the success of developmental efforts. In countries which accept this view, family planning takes place on a national scale through very intensive measures and huge budgetary allocations for this purpose.

The five positions described so far all favor population growth control—although in varying degrees—but there are at least five other developing-country positions which take the opposing view. Those who oppose population control generally either ignore the population problem altogether or deny its importance in order to minimize the "distraction" of public attention from problem areas believed to be more urgent and more susceptible to planned action.

In this confusion of real problems, ideas, and polemics, the position taken in the South by the main acceptors of external sources of development aid and advice has produced, on the one hand, a sometimes grudging acceptance of population control as one item in a "package" of financial aid and, on the other, an automatic rejection of the desirability of population control by those who are primarily preoccupied with the dangers of dependence on external aid.

A *sixth* developing-country position—one which seemingly at least acknowledges the population problem—is exemplified by some of the signatories of the 1967 Declaration of Chiefs of State (representing more than a third of the world's population), which combined a strong affirmation of the danger of rapid population increase with explicit support of family planning. Although the Declaration was signed by thirty countries—of which some two thirds were developing and one third developed countries—its signatories have generally continued their earlier policies either of accepting or of rejecting population control. Thus expressed intentions have not always been translated into effective policies. Moreover, very few governments of the developing world have as yet fixed quantitative objectives for changes in demographic variables. In practice, most have followed laissez-faire policies combined with varying degrees of public support for family planning activities. Migration policy, once the only active component in national population policies, has received very little attention except in some Caribbean countries and more recently in mainland China. Hence population policy has come to be identified more and more with receptivity to family planning.

Among those who specifically oppose family planning, a *seventh* and mainly political position derives its substance from the relationship of national size to international power. There is continuing feeling among many political leaders in Asia, Africa, and Latin America that a small country cannot attain a position of international influence. This belief tends to obscure the demographic facts (such as population density and resource availability) and to contribute to a posture of complacency about, or even a sanctioning of, population increases. Strong feelings of nationalism support this attitude and undoubtedly influence the priority and emphasis attached to the population question.

An *eighth* position is held by countries which are against population growth control because they perceive a need for military manpower. This is true of Peru, for example, which is surrounded along a major part of its border by Brazil, whose policies it considers to be expansionist and therefore threatening. This has been one of the reasons for holding back the development of an effective national population policy. Thus demographic realities may be forgotten in a military regime which does not recognize that even an ambitious pro-natalist policy started now would have absolutely no effect on the availability of military manpower for at least fifteen years and that the effect during even the following ten years would be negligible. Nor have frequent statements of the importance of military quality rather than quantity eliminated this justification of opposing population control in many countries of the South.

A *ninth* position is held by those who oppose population control out of strong ethnic awareness. Some ethnic-group leaders have voiced the concern that family planning would reduce their group's relative size and influence. Ethnic awareness at least partially accounts for the reluctance of national leaders to speak out forcefully and frequently in favor of family planning— even in those countries where a national policy and a national family planning program already exist.

A *tenth* position is held by those who defer population control measures in favor of what they consider to be competing economic priorities. The immediate economic situation is such that the diversion of scarce resources to long-term development projects—of which they see population planning as one—is easily rejected for more immediate needs.

In addition to the positions enumerated above that have the effect of obstructing efforts to limit population growth, there are certain physical obstacles to the adoption of a rational policy on population growth and size. First, many countries of the South *lack reliable vital statistics.* For example, the official birth rate reported in 1965 in the Philippines was 27 per thousand, whereas other estimates suggested it to be around 45. Second, difficulties arise from what may be termed *low visibility.* The consequences of rapid population growth are not readily apparent to the casual observer. Infants remain at home; do not consume much rice, meat, or potatoes; and become "visible" only when and if they enter school. It takes at least fifteen years for a new generation of infants to enter the labor market. Moreover, the impact of a successful population program on the economy may not become obvious for a number of years. Significant changes in the labor force will not become apparent until thirty years or more after the program has started. For example, a 10 per cent reduction in the rate of natural increase every five years would have no effect on the labor force for twenty years and would result in only about an 8 per cent difference in the size of the labor force at the end of thirty years.

These attitudes and difficulties have all influenced the adoption of a population program and the chances of its success in many of the countries of the South.

Progress Toward Population Policies in the Developing World

The 1960s saw a rapid growth of research programs and policies in the population field. A myriad of efforts was mounted by government agencies and private national and international organizations in an attempt to understand more completely the nature of the population explosion and ultimately to control it. What have these programs achieved thus far? How have fertility and mortality patterns changed, both in response to direct family planning and health assistance and in response to other indirect social and economic factors, such as increasing income levels and urbanization? The following data from the latest censuses undertaken in a number of developing countries in Africa, Asia, and Latin America should be helpful in at least partially answering these questions.

Africa. Living on a continent that has a quarter of the earth's surface and less than one tenth of its people, many Africans find it difficult to believe that for them, too, population growth poses a significant problem. Yet population growth without commensurate economic development and expansion of social services has already created severe problems.

Africa's birth rate of 47 per thousand per year is the highest in the world, and its population of an estimated 363 million in 1972 could, at the current growth rate, double in less than 27 years. The mortality rate of 21 per thousand is the highest of any region, although it is declining with the expansion of health and sanitation facilities. The rate of population growth, which was only 1.47 per cent in 1920, is now 2.6 per cent per year. Nearly half the population is composed of children under 15 years of age, who need to be fed, clothed, housed, educated, and eventually employed.

The economic and social development needed to support a growing population has been slow to come. With an average per capita gross national product of $184, Africa has many people living on the edge of subsistence, some in remote rural areas, others caught up in the vortex of urbanization that has touched many parts of the continent. Africa's urban population is growing at the rate of 5 per cent annually. Thus many countries on the continent are having a difficult time meeting the economic and social needs of both rural and city dwellers. For example, the absolute rate of growth of gross national product in the less developed countries of Africa between

1960 and 1969 was 4.2 per cent, but population growth reduced this favorable rate to only 1.8 per cent per capita. Moreover, recent census results have indicated that the rate of population growth may well be even higher than previously estimated.

Africa's *potential* agricultural and industrial resources are impressively large. However, very large long-term investments of capital will be required to realize this still untapped potential. Diffficult agricultural conditions further complicate Africa's population problems. In many cases, food production has not kept pace with population growth. A U.S. Department of Agriculture survey of thirty African countries shows that in thirteen of them the index of per capita agricultural production has actually declined since the period 1961–1965. The situation has of course reached disaster proportions in the vast regions of Africa that have been suffering from severe drought conditions almost continuously since 1972.

On the positive side, African awareness of the implications of rapid population growth is increasing. So is the readiness to go from awareness to action. Some countries have expanded and accelerated their existing population programs. In other countries, the pressure of population growth on already serious problems of economic and social development has encouraged the adoption of various measures designed to lower population growth rates, to space births to benefit the health of mother and child, and to improve the quality of life for all the people. A few countries formerly opposed to family planning are now showing an interest or are asking for aid. Governments of black African countries on the whole either support family planning programs or permit such efforts to exist under private auspices.

Despite this seeming support for family planning, however, only about 22 per cent of Africa's population lives in countries that have *official* policies to reduce the growth rate of population, 40 per cent lives in countries with policies set for other than demographic reasons, and 38 per cent in countries that have no population policy whatsoever.

Asia. In Asia, these percentages are very different, with 91 per cent of the population living under some government-established population policies, 4 per cent under policies established for nondemographic reasons, and only 5 per cent in countries having no population policies at all. However, the widely disparate economic and social conditions in the countries of this region are reflected in the varying stages of population planning and development.

In East Asia, notable progress has been made during the past few years in initiating and expanding family planning programs designed to reduce population growth rates. Eight East Asian countries comprising a population of more than a quarter billion currently either have national programs or support the efforts of private groups in this field. In Taiwan, where voluntary efforts and government action have reinforced one another, the birth rate, which in 1956 was 45 per thousand, today is down to 28 per thousand. Over the same period, the birth rate declined from 48 to 22 per thousand in Singapore, from 45 to 31 in South Korea, and from 40 to 20 in Hong Kong. Malaysia, which currently has a birth rate of 36 per thousand and an annual population growth rate of nearly 3 per cent, hopes to reduce its growth rate to 2 per cent by 1985.

Population programs in East Asia have encountered little religious opposition. Even in the Philippines, an official program to reduce the population growth rate got under way in late 1969, and the Catholic Church there is developing its own program to encourage responsible parenthood. Growing levels of literacy and urbanization have boosted these programs. There are, however, still several obstacles to family planning programs, including communications difficulties in countries with several languages and/or large rural populations, socio-cultural attitudes which promote large families, and discontinuance of contraceptive practices for various reasons.

In contrast to other East Asian countries, Indonesia, the Philippines, and Thailand have birth rates ranging between 42 and 44 per thousand. The population of the Philippines is growing at a rate of 3.4 per cent annually —the highest rate in East Asia—while the per capita gross national product is growing at only 2.6 per cent. Thus some countries in the region are barely able to maintain their current standards of living, with little or no added income for economic and social development. Most of Asia's governments recognize this problem and are seeking to improve the quality of life by planning population growth so as to support economic and social progress.

Perhaps the most difficult challenge to family planning in East Asia is yet to come. Since birth increased substantially after World War II, an exceptionally large number of young people will be reaching marriageable age within the next few years. This is particularly true of Hong Kong, Singapore, and Taiwan. For this reason, family planning efforts are directed more and more toward younger age groups.

In the countries of the Near East and South Asia, birth rates exceed 40 per thousand—more than double the U.S. birthrate—while none of the countries of this region has reached a stage of economic or social development that would tend to push birth rates downward. Total population in the region is now estimated at about 882 million and, if present trends continue, it will double by the end of the century. With the growing awareness of the impact of population growth on social and economic development, countries in the region are beginning to expand or initiate population programs to slow the present rapid growth rates. Nevertheless, traditional patterns largely continue to prevail and to erode the hard-won rewards of economic development. While the governments of various countries are committed to long-term social and economic development, their significantly different stages of development clearly affect their attempts to cope with population growth.

Latin America. The population in tropical Latin America (including the Caribbean) is experiencing the most rapid growth in the world. And here as in other areas there is a rising concern about the consequences of such growth and an emerging determination to do something about it. This is apparent in the development of private family-planning organizations and in the extension of family planning through public health services. Of Latin America's twenty-nine countries, less than a fourth have official population programs; about half have population programs for other than demographic reasons, and about a third have no such programs at all.

At almost 3 per cent a year, the population growth rate is moving Latin America toward a population of 756 million by the year 2000 compared with the current population of 291 million. The problem of population is most severe in the cities, where the growth rate is approximately 7 per cent per year. If continued, this would result in the doubling of urban population in only 10 years. Already the accelerated rate of urban growth—largely due to the migration of rural population to the cities—has led to overcrowded slum conditions, inadequate social services, and increased unemployment.

Latin American economies are growing at respectable rates, but these gains are offset significantly by high population growth rates. For example, the rate of increase in per capita income in Latin America has slowed substantially in recent years. In 1969–70, Latin America's gross national product grew at an average annual rate of 7.6 per cent. However, because of the high rate of population growth, the increase in GNP per capita amounted to only about half the rate (3.5 per cent). Another dimension of the population problem that also hinders economic growth in Latin America is the large proportion of young people. Over 40 per cent of the Latin Americans are under 15 years of age, compared to only 25–30 per cent in developed countries.

Official attitudes toward the population problem vary widely among the Latin American countries. In general, family planning is a sensitive political issue. A few governments are negative toward slowing down population growth, a few others are giving increasingly active support, and many are neutral—permitting private groups to offer family planning services while not getting directly involved themselves.

Nevertheless, acceptance of family planning is growing throughout Latin America. This is in part a result of the high incidence of induced abortions, which is viewed as a serious health problem. Working through maternal and child health programs, government public health services are able to offer family planning as a substitute for this hazardous means of limiting family size. The declining birth rates of a few areas are a hopeful sign. Chile's birth rate fell from 37 per thousand in 1963 to 28 per thousand in 1970. Costa Rica's birth rate during the same period declined from 45 to 33 per thousand. El Salvador, Guatemala, Panama, and the English-speaking countries of the Caribbean showed downward trends during the 1960s, as did the city of Sao Paulo, Brazil. In reporting to a 1971 session of the U.N. Economic and Social Council, the U.N. Economic Commission for Latin America suggested that a plausible reason for these declines may have been the result of individual initiative rather than governmental policy; during this period large numbers of persons already wanted—and therefore sought—more reliable methods of controlling their fertility.

In summary, some 74 per cent of the population of the developing world lives in countries with population policies, 13 per cent lives in countries that have population programs for nondemographic reasons, and the remaining 13 per cent in countries where there are no population programs at all. This stands in glaring contrast with the countries of the developed world, which all have population policies in operation. In fact, the contrast between the developed and developing nations with respect to population policy is even sharper, since the above-mentioned figure of 74 per cent refers primarily to people living in countries with family planning programs but not necessarily with population policies, and hence is considerably inflated.

Certainly some developing countries have moved beyond merely resorting to family planning and legalized abortion by also adopting measures such as a higher legal age for marriage; greater educational, recreational, and employment opportunities for women; bonus payments for periods of nonpregnancy; tax incentives to discourage large families; tax penalties for too many children; societal tolerance of deviant sexual behavior; and compulsory sterilization after a certain number of children. Even in those countries where population policies as such do not exist, governments are increasingly adopting or supporting family planning programs—both in recognition of the health-related values of controlling family size and in order to cope with their high rates of population growth.

Conclusions

Clearly, neither family planning programs nor population policy programs offer an *alternative* to economic development plans in the South. Whatever the population growth rate, without economic development there can be no real advance toward meeting socio-political aspirations; but without lower population growth rates, economic development may prove to be too slow. The fact that family planning programs are not only compatible with economic development but also an integral part of the institutional changes required if countries are to develop rapidly and effectively still goes largely unrecognized in most countries of the South.

Regional differences are striking in this respect. In Asia, which includes the world's most populous nations and has a very high population density, a large majority of the people live in countries whose governments are committed to a reduction in the population growth rate because of the economic exigencies of their situations. In Africa and Latin America, on the other hand, the two continents with the highest growth rates, less than half of the governments are committed to a reduction in their national population growth rates. In Africa, this lack of official interest in curbing population growth can be attributed to the newness of the states, to political and ethnic rivalries, and to the absence of reliable data on population size and growth. In Latin America, the influence of the Roman Catholic Church tends to discourage official expression of interest in reducing rates of population growth. In both Africa and Latin America, policy makers also may be influenced by the existence of vast stretches of sparsely populated, inhospitable regions that make for low *average* national population densities even though large proportions of the population in fact live under conditions of high density.

In general, when Asian governments do consider the population question, their official pronouncements usually encompass an anti-natalist policy and a family planning program; in Africa, their policies are likely to be generally aimed at a higher population growth rate but accompanied by slowly developing programs; while in Latin America the emphasis tends to be on family planning programs in the interests of maternal and child health and the reduction of resort to abortion.

Thus while the developing world is still uncertain whether population policies to reduce growth rates are good or bad, the developed world for the most part has launched its policies and can now cope fairly effectively with population problems. The largest numerical increases are taking place in those developing countries where annual population growth rates are anywhere from 2.1 per cent to 4.0 per cent.

Tables 1 and 2 show the sharp contrast between natural rates of population increase and per capita income in developed and developing countries and clearly indicate the scope of the problem confronting the developing countries, if the population growth rates for the rest of this century go unchecked. The critical question is: Can the world's limited resource endowment withstand both the increasing levels of affluence and consumption by a small minority of economically prosperous nations (which for the most part have launched population policies) and the complete divorce between economic reality and population policy found in many of the world's developing countries? Since the answer obviously is "no," what way is there out of this predicament?

A less aggressive attitude on the part of the developed countries in persuading the developing countries could do much to encourage the adoption of national population policies in these countries. In this respect, moral persuasion is preferable to economic coercion and penalties such as

Table 1. Annual Rate of Population Increase, 1971

Annual Rate of Natural Population Increase, 1971 (percentages)	72 Developing Countries	16 Developed Countries
Less than 0.51%	0	4
0.51 – 1.0	0	8
1.1 – 1.5	2	4
1.6 – 2.0	8	0
2.1 – 2.5	21	0
2.6 – 3.0	18	0
3.1 – 3.5	19	0
3.6 – 4.0	1	0
n.a.	3	0
Total	72	16

denial of foreign aid unless a country reduces its population growth rate by a specified date. Such compulsion does more harm than good in that it creates a sense of veritable hatred for the rich among the poor—whatever justification the North provides for its action in economic terms. Aid for economic projects and aid for population programs should be provided without making the one a precondition for the other. In a world partnership between the rich and the poor, the relatively rich and comfortable North cannot

Table 2. Per Capita Income, 1970-71

Per Capita Income, 1970-71	72 Developing Countries				16 Developed Countries
	All Developing Areas	Africa	Asia	Latin America	
Under $100	12	6	5	1	0
$100 – $299	25	14	6	5	0
$300 – $499	15	1	8	6	0
$500 – $749	5	0	0	5	0
$750 – $999	4	1	1	2	0
$1,000 – $1,499	2	0	1	1	1
$1,500 – $1,999	1	0	0	1	1
$2,000 and over	0	0	0	0	10
Unavailable	8	0	7	1	4
Total	72	22	28	22	16

indefinitely flout the misery and need that characterize the life of the majority of people "on the other side of the fence" in the developing countries.

One can imagine a scenario of Southern retaliation in which that part of the developing world which has essential raw materials will—as it already has—take advantage of its temporary market-determined superiority. Admittedly, such action would be not only to the detriment of the developed world but also to the even graver disadvantage of those parts of the developing world that do not themselves produce the essential commodity in question.

The population policies of the North and South are, in fact, more or less carefully reasoned derivatives of complex historical, ideological, political, social, and economic considerations. Owing to great differences between the North and the South with respect to these factors, it cannot be expected that they would adopt similar policies. The adoption of similar policies, or at least mutual understanding, can best be brought about by better dialogue and communication about the fundamental differences of approach and the great variety of factors that shape the population policies of the North and the South.

Chapter 7

An African Experiment in Grass Roots Development

Soumana Traoré

In their struggles for freedom and decolonization, African leaders took on the solution of political and economic development problems simultaneously. They did so, however, in the midst of a confusion of possible approaches, a diversity of objectives, and varying degrees of motivation and drive. Some leaders became aware of the complex sociological realities of development and wanted to introduce radical changes; others remained completely ignorant of socio-economic development problems.

Furthermore, once African leaders began to comprehend the specific requirements of economic development, they quickly realized that Africa for a long time would continue to need capital and technical aid from the industrialized countries. To obtain the necessary foreign exchange, African countries would need stable and advantageous prices for their raw-material exports—even if this meant acceptance of bilateral agreements.

Yet many African leaders were also fully aware that economic and technical aid, however helpful it might be, could only be a temporary measure that could not solve a serious, essentially *social* problem: underdeveloped nations urgently need new organizational structures, not just capital. The beginnings of a solution to this problem might have been found by referring to foreign models, for example, to Soviet or Chinese experience, or to the ideas of socialist theorists. But here we must consider the African personality. What sort of African person do Africans want to create?

Rather than choose between the Eastern and Western models, Africans must take into account their own specific realities and aspirations. In the area of economic options—which of course influence political options—several experiments have been attempted, with varying degrees of success. These have ranged from capitalism to scientific socialism and have included many attempts to synthesize these two concepts into what has been called "African socialism" or "Africanism."

Current Practices and Policies

Regardless of the type of political-economic system they chose, all African countries have encountered a multitude of problems that are largely external in origin. These problems generally stem from the fact that the rich countries continue to consider the poor countries mainly as cheap sources of primary commodities and as ready markets for their manufactured goods. So far, investments in underdeveloped countries have been left up to private enterprises—generally financial or industrial groups whose headquarters are located in wealthy countries. Indeed, many firms operating in Africa are branches more closely linked to their home offices than to the host-country economy.

It is true that the wealthy countries grant aid and furnish private capital to the poor countries. However, if the financing they provide is tied to the purchase of luxury products or equipment (often at prices higher than those prevalent in world markets), do they not merely subsidize rich-country industries? If foreign investment, whatever its volume, does not take into account the human factor and the sociological characteristics of the local milieu, is it not a waste of money and effort for the public sector of the home country and perhaps a negative investment from the perspective of the public sector of the host country? In any case, under such conditions, relations between wealthy countries and poor countries can only be to the disadvantage of Third World countries. As long as the means of implementing development objectives remain concentrated in the hands of the capital- and technology-rich countries, this situation will prevail. What is even more serious is that rich countries, to obtain the maximum safeguards for their capital investment, model the development of the countries in which they intervene after the pattern of their own growth—so much so that the very sovereignty of the states receiving aid is seriously compromised. This situation creates virtually eternal bonds of economic and political dependence and tends to produce social upsets on both sides when even the slightest change occurs in the relationship. In these circumstances, if rich countries continue to impose restrictive conditions on aid and private investment that are incompatible with the development of poor countries, the latter will be justified in assuming a skeptical attitude toward foreign capital.

The economies of most of the underdeveloped African countries (except for the oil producing African countries, whose special situation is not taken up in this chapter) depend on their primary products, especially agricultural commodities. Indeed, agricultural products represent 50 per cent to 100 per cent of the total exports of these countries. Since the

112

world output and prices of these commodities fluctuate greatly, not even the support sometimes granted commodity exports by wealthy countries ensures their producers a stable income.

The economic orientation inherited from the colonial period and the constraints of project financing make foreign exchange earnings dependent upon increasing the volume of exports of primary products. Unfortunately, the consumption of several primary commodities has been declining in certain industrialized countries. These consumption decreases have been due to product substitution and to the production of synthetics. However, the recent oil crisis has improved the prospects of most primary products; a stronger case can be made for higher prices and greater price stability for primary products in a period of growing resource scarcity and growing producer cooperation. While OPEC-style cartelization may not be duplicable, the situation encountered by OPEC presages similar demand-supply situations for other essential and possibly nonreplenishable commodities. Another interesting development applies to the case of one product—cotton—whose prospects relative to its formerly strong competitor, synthetics, recently have improved dramatically because of steep cost increases in the energy-intensive production of synthetic fibers. Analogous "side effects" may affect the prospects of other major commodities.

At the same time, a variety of factors resulting in increasing costs in industrialized countries are raising the costs of the imports of Third World countries, leading to a deterioration in their terms of trade. Thus even if the recent oil crisis and the price increases of a number of other primary commodities enable certain countries of the Third World to mobilize more resources for their development, the eventual increases in the prices of their imports from industrialized countries and resulting payments difficulties may. bring about another test of the adequacy of the present system for all countries. Indeed, such a test of the traditional pattern of trade relations between rich and poor nations may be desirable.

Within a framework of appropriate strategies and administrative structures, income from agricultural exports can help to create the basis for real national development. What is of central importance is the exercise of national options. The best strategies and administrative mechanisms will be needed to determine by whom, for whom, and how development operations should be conducted. In Africa, this will be particularly difficult to achieve, because in most countries 90 per cent of the population consists of a still illiterate peasantry. Thus officials can be recruited only from a thin stratum of educated persons. The resulting concentration of the nation's trained persons in government—together with the absence of political dissent—has given an aura of special importance to the public sector. Moreover, for reasons inherent in colonialism, those African officials for whom the colonial state represented the oppressor did not always do their best to shape and implement development policy in the public interest. Indeed, even after independence, broad-based development did not always receive their wholehearted support. "Doing the least for the most" still is the motto of many administrators—despite the incompatibility of this attitude with the requirements of agencies created to promote national development.

It must also be emphasized that, in a subsistence economy, the establishment of a public office along Western lines serves only to widen the gap that has always existed between government workers and peasants. In most African countries, the salary of a minor administrative official is greater than the income of an entire family of peasants. This situation reaches its most scandalous proportions when government officials become more concerned with luxurious villas and automobiles than with the progress of the poor majority of the population in their countries. Such consumption practices bind the poor country even more to foreign influences. Many younger officials become discouraged soon after entering this system of relationships. They are generally highly motivated at the end of their studies, but become less so after a few years of official service. Many of those who want to be "successful" are driven to playing political games to achieve their objectives and stray far from aims acquired in development-oriented educational programs.

Thus in addition to the problems created by the external economic pressures mentioned earlier, the new states of Africa must cope with no less important pressures resulting from *domestic* bottlenecks. It is not surprising that the gap is becoming wider not only between the wealthy countries and the poor countries but also between the controlling classes and the masses *within* underdeveloped countries.

An Alternative Approach

If international efforts are to exert a positive force on the development of the poor countries, it is necessary that these efforts be integrated with dynamic national structures. Developing countries must abandon the development approaches that were set for them long ago by other, economically more powerful nations and must take a new route—one that will not be easy but that will be more in line with their own aspirations and will receive greater support from their peoples. The nature of this new approach—a "third alternative" different from either communism or capitalism—will depend on the internal sociological features of each state and on the human factor, which is the backbone of any social development program. This brief essay cannot pretend to provide a solution for the problems confronting the Third World, but it nevertheless may help prepare the ground for a development approach that will take into account both the African personality and existing international pressures.

The essential points which justify this "third" approach are: a) an appreciation of the actual conditions in a country and the failure of present approaches; and b) the objectives of development—which differ from country to country and between social classes. The needs of the Lobi peasant are at present still different from, say, those of a program director of a radio station, although each may have the same keen interest in finding solutions to his problems and each may muster the same amount of effort to reach his objectives. Therefore the aim should be to seek a combination of their different objectives that will allow each to achieve at least some of his goals.

Since rural activities are so important in African countries, the new approach suggested in this paper will be based on an analysis of some rural projects. International constraints on rural projects result from both the form and the terms of external financing, which shape projects in many ways. Most development projects involve the production of commodities that are traded in world markets. However, unfavorable terms of trade may in fact hurt the producers. Obtaining adequate financing may depend on the management of the project by a team of expatriate technicians or by a foreign private concern. In these circumstances, serious problems frequently arise in the relationship of foreign technicians introducing imported technology to a host-country staff in the local social and economic environment. For example, obstacles of a psychological nature may arise because of differences between foreigners and nationals in terms of their respective incomes and responsibilities.

When foreign private firms manage development projects, the flexibility of their structures and the wages they give their workers often allow them to achieve good results. Yet host-country policy choices will be influenced by a desire to derive the greatest benefit from these projects once a loan from abroad has been acquired. Therefore the public sector generally reserves the right to collect the profits through its agents. This may lead to a monopoly situation in marketing or processing—the production phases in which profits tend to be greatest.

On the other hand the bureaucratic red tape that often affects the work of state agencies; the low salaries of public employees compared to the sums they handle; and the priorities that guide decisions concerning the use of state funds often make public-sector operations less effective than private operations. Frequently, this inefficiency of the public sector adversely affects the volume of exports or increases the cost of finished products; at the same time, the state's monopoly may handicap or even eliminate traditional local traders, who might be more efficient under competitive circumstances.

It would be difficult, however, to base the financing of domestic development on the profits of such traditional private traders. Few among them possess the requisite financial means and analytical capability for making successful medium- or long-term domestic investments. Furthermore, both traditional traders and expatriate trading concerns often transmit their profits abroad. Seeking immediate profits, they either do not recognize—or mistakenly assign little importance to—the long-term consequences of the continued impoverishment of unorganized producers.

In light of all of these obstacles to the development process, it may be useful to enumerate a number of principles that could be applied to encouraging development under the conditions prevailing in African countries:

(1) Give the producer the profit from the value added through the marketing and processing of products in order to reduce the impact of a deterioration in the terms of trade and thus avoid a decrease in production;

(2) Mobilize domestic savings to bring into play dynamic local forces for generating profits and employment, making it possible to set the foundations for domestic development; and

(3) Utilize the abilities of domestic technicians where their efforts can best be used and justly rewarded.

The aim should be the creation of structures in which organized producers form new relationships with the businessmen that handle the financing—with the cooperation and under the direction of trained technicians whose experience has been acquired in the course of the enterprise.

Organizing the Producers

Once it has been decided that producer organizations are a valid developmental mechanism, how can they best be geared to effective action? The most efficient tool to encourage producers to organize themselves is the provision of personal incentives. Pools of producers cannot and must not be organized unless the organization established enables each member to derive an individual profit based on a percentage of total production. The best approach is suggested by the elementary motivation principle of finding solutions to those problems which are felt and defined by the group. In many instances, the failure of cooperatives in underdeveloped countries could have been avoided by the use of economic incentives appropriate to the modern environment into which the producers have been plunged. The expectation that participants will behave like saints and act without a personal incentive is an unrealistic foundation for cooperative action.

Once they are organized, rural producer groups represent a force with which not only traditional merchants but even modern enterprises are obliged to deal. Rural populations constitute both the market and the source of supply. Under these conditions, it would seem possible to ask the merchants to provide some of the financing for the purchase of equipment for the processing of rural produce. An incentive for the individual merchant would be the desire to avoid the risk of his eventual elimination from the marketing network by state agencies or even by cooperatives.

According to their capacity to comprehend the overall situation and act appropriately, local leaders can gain the trust of local communities and play an important catalytic role. If their own success is linked to that of the cooperative enterprises, conditions favorable to the development of private enterprise will be created. Although development, too, is based on individual self-interest—which is after all the main motivation of human actions—it must seek to consolidate the bonds between classes by emphasizing their interdependence.

One African Experiment

The experiment conducted by the Precooperative Village Pools in the territorial jurisdiction of the Regional Development Agency of Bougouriba, Upper Volta, illustrates several of the issues considered in this chapter.

Priorities defined by a large number of rural inhabitants were the starting point of the experiment. First priority was assigned to the creation of networks of producers of consumer goods. Prior to the experiment's introduction, the great number of intermediaries between the urban wholesalers and rural consumers had raised the cost of manufactured products. The creation of the Precooperative Village Pools was intended to check this trend. The Pools managed to unite rural persons of all classes, who, by means of paying a "subscription" to the Pool, were able to place large orders while bypassing most of the intermediaries in the traditional commercial chain.

Between 1966 and 1972, twenty-five Precooperative Village Pools were formed, regrouping 4,900 producers, or 14 per cent of the heads of rural families of the region. Each Pool controlled a sales shop for essential goods such as salt, sugar, or soap. The working capital of the shops was created on the basis of subscriptions of CFA Francs 500 (representing nearly one tenth of the annual monetary income of most of the producers). The volume of business for all shops grew from CFA Francs 701,725 in 1967 to CFA Francs 30,000,000 in 1973.

Although the profits realized at present do not exceed 10 per cent of the turnover, the local merchants nevertheless have lowered their prices and have created at the producers' level demands which they themselves can satisfy, thereby benefiting the development of agricultural production.

An "Engine of Growth"

The Precooperative Village Pools are veritable "engines of growth" in terms of their capacity to stimulate agricultural development. Their members are sensitized to the problems of improving their own existence and consequently are interested in undertaking profit-yielding efforts. For example, since 1968, the shops of the Pools have marketed factors of production such as fertilizers, insecticides, and hoes. Furthermore, in the course of 1972, the membership of the Precooperative Village Pools rose markedly—from 3,049 to 4,900—largely because of the availability of cattle-vaccination and rice-marketing programs initiated by one of the Pools.

In 1972–73, after a promotional campaign, the Precooperative Village Pools that were charged with the initial collection of peanuts and millet for sale succeeded in controlling more than 50 per cent of the amounts of these commodities marketed in the region. This effective marketing campaign enabled the members to make a considerable profit.

The Processing of Agricultural Products

The participation of Precooperative Village Pools in the collection of crops for sale forced some private merchants to abandon the collection of peanuts altogether at the time of the 1972–73 harvest. But to consolidate the gains of that year, to encourage the growth of the membership in the Precooperative Village Pools, and to increase the Pools' possibilities for profit, further processing tasks were assigned to the Pools in 1973–74.

The participation of all social strata in this development process will be achieved at the regional level by the institution of two rice-husking units (representing an investment of 15 million CFA Francs) under the sponsorship of an association combining the Precooperative Village Pools, the local merchants, and an organization interested in promoting the participation of *local private-sector technicians* in the project and in helping orient development efforts along productive lines.

Conclusions

Caution and patience are among the major reasons behind the success of the Precooperative Village Pools program. Project promotion in a rural environment is a very demanding art that requires a great deal of time—especially when one wants to include the maximum number of the project's participants in the decisions to be taken. Moreover, a few reservations must be cited regarding the reality of popular participation in development. The requirements of commercial and industrial operations may conflict with the objective of the prompt integration of the Precooperative Village Pools—and of the producers themselves—into new organizational structures. Should popular participation be sacrificed to the accumulation of profit? This is very difficult to answer conclusively, but the success of the organizational structure described in this chapter brightens the outlook for African development strategies that are *sensitive to the needs of people* while at the same time aiming to achieve a rate of return on investment.

The fundamental objective remains the development of the human being. However, the poor outlook for the development of Africa's countries in the face of external international pressures requires us to proceed quickly. Hopefully, this race against time will give rise to a new network of "national capitalist" enterprises that will thrive even while ensuring socio-economic development in the rural sector. It is very important, however, that these enterprises from the very start provide for the channelling of a more equitable share of their profits to the majority of the population, which at present benefits only marginally from the distribution of the gains from international trade.

Chapter 8

Ocean Issues on the International Agenda

Bension Varon

For ten weeks in 1974, some 5,000 officials from 148 nations met in Caracas, Venezuela, to participate in what has been described as the largest international conference in history: the first substantive session of the Third U.N. Conference on the Law of the Sea.[1] The problems considered by the Conference are competing for attention with the host of other issues that must be dealt with at the international level: the relatively new issues of energy management, food shortages, global inflation, reform of the monetary system, political and military détente, unfettered trade relations, orderly and equitable exploitation of natural resources, and the role of multinational corporations, as well as the longer recognized problems of environmental protection, population control, and the development of the "have not" nations. On this overwhelming agenda, the exploitation, sharing, and management of the oceans would seem to deserve no more than a back seat in the order of priorities, given the relatively noncontentious history of traditional ocean use. Why then is there a sense of urgency about these issues? One reason is the growing perception of the oceans as a great potential source of wealth and the development of new means to exploit this potential; another is that in this international debate the participants are numerous and many of their claims relate to the broader agenda of issues raised by developing nations.

The Evolution of Ocean Issues

Historically, the attitude governing the use of the oceans has been one of laissez faire. Although the oceans have been relied upon for centuries as

---

[1] The Third Law of the Sea Conference has met for three sessions: the first formal procedural session in New York (December 1973), the first substantive session in Caracas (June–August 1974), and the second substantive session in Geneva (March–May 1975). A fourth session is scheduled to take place in New York in March 1976.

avenues for trade and travel, as a food source of seeming inexhaustibility, as a natural bastion against enemies, as an expedient to colonization (though never colonized), they have not—in contrast to land—been the object of much contention among nations. Wars have been fought on them and for their control, but the end objective thus far always has been domination of the *lands* to which they give access.

Twentieth-century technology and ever increasing food and resource requirements have changed all this. The oceans must now yield a large portion of the protein necessary to support population levels of unprecedented magnitude. Without proper management, however, fish stocks are in danger of such critical depletion that they may become a "nonrenewable" resource. At the same time, rapidly growing energy requirements have extended petroleum exploitation beyond land-based sources and to the ocean beds. The quest for new sources of other raw materials has led to opening up the vast storehouses of nonfuel minerals on the ocean floor. These new developments—coupled with the use of the oceans for both waste disposal and the dramatically increased transport of potentially polluting substances such as fuels and chemicals—require that the old laissez faire attitudes be abandoned and that a new era of international management take their place. From a scientific viewpoint, environmental concerns alone have long dictated speedy and forceful action toward an international agreement. But the new worldwide concern about access to both existing and new sources of nonrenewable resources has intensified and further politicized the issues of ocean sharing and management; it has likewise strengthened the demand that any new international management scheme take into account the special development problems of the poor countries.

The politics of ocean exploitation and management are predicated on definitions of what rights and privileges already exist or are to be stipulated in connection with the use of the oceans. By time-honored tradition, the oceans are held to be the common heritage of mankind, as reflected in the operative principle of international waters: while nations claim *territorial* waters as a matter of right, their use of *international* waters is by tradition a privilege based on their geography, economic power, and economic requirements. A new international principle currently under consideration is that of the coastal-state "economic zone"; if accepted, it would extend the economic jurisdiction and dominion of coastal states over parts of the oceans far beyond present territorial limits, thus enlarging their resource base—and at the same time enabling them to exercise tighter control against the damages of pollution. A major exception to coastal-state jurisdiction in the zone would be the right of free passage through coastal waters and straits. But the wealth and promise of the oceans extend far beyond any proposed economic zone. For example, mineral resources, such as manganese nodules (potato-shaped formations with concentrations of copper, cobalt, manganese, and nickel), lie on the ocean floor far from shore. Their exploitation as well as the management of fish stocks and the results of scientific research conducted in the oceans must be shared; these "hunting grounds" are held in common, but a powerful "hunter" could still easily make a mockery of the concept of the "common heritage" if he chose to ignore it.

Clearly, some operational framework for safeguarding the interests of all nations must be formulated. This task transcends the domain of routine diplomacy; new subject areas must be covered, and while the burdens of past mistakes therefore are lacking, so are past precedents and operational guidelines. What is certain is that those developing nations whose needs for resources and capital are the greatest will keep urging that the principle of *equitable* sharing and participation be the cornerstone of any agreement.

As will be more fully argued later, the only viable framework for action under these givens is an international approach. Its success depends on whether or not the movers and thinkers with the power to translate their concerns into action are sufficiently involved with the problem of ocean management to take action. What precisely is at stake, and why is action now necessary?

The oceans contain enormous resources of energy, food, and raw materials. Judiciously exploited, these resources can make a significant difference in the survival and quality of life of an overpopulated world. In contrast, harvesting them recklessly and selfishly will mean inefficiency and waste, inequitable distribution of costs and benefits, and possibly permanent damage to the resources themselves. Although energy and food are the resources of most immediate interest—because of current concern over the availability of these essential goods—the question of access to manganese nodules is at the heart of both the optimism and the controversy about the potential of the oceans for a number of reasons:

1. Mining the ocean bottom at depths of 12,000–18,000 feet, where most nodules of commercial value occur, is an unprecedented activity, and the true volume and ultimate use and benefits of these resources still are unknown. It is, however, already known that the nodules are an economic resource of great potential value, as demonstrated by the fact that today about thirty companies and consortia from the United States, Japan, and Western Europe are actively engaged in their exploration and development, and in equipment construction for this purpose. The Soviet Union and the Eastern European countries also are keenly interested in this resource.

2. Except for some concentrations within 200 miles of the shores of Mexico and of several Pacific islands, most nodules are found in international waters, and their exploitation is hampered by jurisdictional problems. While their recovery is bound to be restricted to the technologically advanced nations in the foreseeable future, their benefits should be shared by all.

3. The controversy over the exploitation of manganese nodules coincides with fears of resource shortages (either physical or imposed) and dissatisfaction with the traditional arrangements between host countries and foreign-based corporations. The nodules issue is an extension of the broader natural-resource development issue. In dealing with the latter, unless one takes the oceans into account, one is not addressing the problem fully.

4. For more than two years, draft legislation has been before the U.S. Congress that would enable U.S. companies to begin seabed mining operations, although the desire to proceed with exploitation expeditiously is not restricted to U.S. firms. The choice facing the international community is not whether to exploit these resources, but whether to proceed with exploitation in an orderly manner that would accommodate the needs and interests of all, or to do so in a way that would favor only a few—namely, the technologically advanced nations.

While large-scale mining of the seabed is thought to lie in the distant future, technological progress and the need to solve potentially explosive social and economic problems quickly have shortened the time available to decide under what form of jurisdiction and control seabed mining or "harvesting" is to take place. Over $150 million of investment and nearly ten years of research and development have resulted in such rapid progress in the deep-ocean mining of manganese nodules that, as early as 1972, the United Nations Secretariat concluded that the major problem in this field was no longer technical but primarily legal and political.[2]

The race among the rich countries to harvest the mineral wealth of the seabed is spurred on by the following considerations: a) manganese, copper, nickel, and cobalt are important industrial raw materials; b) most of the developed countries are seriously deficient in these metals and rely on imports for the bulk of their requirements; and c) developing a secure source of supply which would not be open to OPEC-type cartelization ranks high among the priorities of the rich countries.

Moreover, ocean issues generally place rich and poor countries in an adversary position, since in many instances their immediate interests appear to conflict. Developing countries feel they cannot remain passive players. Some already are among the largest suppliers of the minerals found in the oceans. A few, for example, Zaire and Zambia, are large exporters of two or more of these minerals and are heavily dependent on exports of these minerals as a source of income; countries in this category are particularly— and justifiably—fearful that unless seabed mining is properly regulated, it may eventually displace their output or depress their revenues and thereby

---

[2]United Nations, *Projections of Natural Resources Reserves, Supply and Future Demand*, U.N. Doc. No. E/C.70/40/Add.2, December 5, 1972.

thwart their development efforts. The possibility of an international development fund created out of seabed-mining revenues does not especially excite them, since what they are more keenly interested in is *participating* in the action rather than receiving handouts. This position not only unites land-based mineral producers in the developing world, but also links them more closely with other developing countries, which see the problem posed by seabed mining as a test case for the equitable solution of international problems involving, for example, the distribution of the benefits of technology. The long and painful history of receiving the short end of the economic stick makes the developing countries as a group particularly anxious not to be cut off from the benefits of this new economic frontier. The developed countries, on the other hand, feel compelled to plan a long-term response to changing realities; their projected oil import bills of unprecedented magnitude, for instance, provide strong impetus for cutting down outlays for other natural resources and for seeking guaranteed access to those natural resources.

The Resources at Stake

In addition to nodules (both manganese and phosphorus), the oceans contain other minerals, some already exploited, such as those in the form of unconsolidated deposits (e.g., sand, gravel, tin, gold, raw materials for titanium, phosphorite, and possibly chromite), consolidated deposits (e.g., coal, with access currently being gained from shafts on land), metalliferous muds and brines (such as those of the Red Sea, which contain extraordinarily rich concentrations of iron), and of course oil—the earth's most sought-after mineral product. Estimates prepared for the United Nations indicate that the oceans may contain at least 170 billion barrels of proven oil reserves and 2.3 trillion barrels of exploitable resources. (Moreover, some experts suggest that these estimates may be highly conservative, since they do not take into account fully the enormous potential of Argentina's vast continental shelf.)

It is a curious fact that despite this potential, oil has not been a significant factor in debate or in negotiation. The facts that nearly 90 per cent of these resources are believed to occur within 200 miles from shore and that most of the oil in international waters occurs at depths not exploitable with current technology do not explain the secondary position of oil in the oceans debate—given the inevitably speculative nature of information on the location and magnitude of oil resources, the dynamism of technology, and the strong incentive not to exclude oil from the balance sheet of interests. The reason for the conspicuous omission may stem from the very importance of oil, which gives rich and poor countries alike a strong impetus to extend ownership or control over the area 200 miles from shore, even in cases where the true potential is not known and even though coastal countries may not possess the technology to exploit it. Another explanation may lie in the structure of the oil industry and in the nationalistic nature of policy making in this field. In the pre-OPEC era, when consuming nations had easy access to oil, all actions were more or less unilateral—nations were in business for themselves. Although post-OPEC realities suggest that consumers' access to oil sources is circumscribed and that new multilateral approaches are now in order, the old habit of unilateral action—and careful safeguarding of all pertinent data—is hard to break.

In addition to their potential mineral wealth, the oceans already yield an annual fish catch of about 70 million tons, valued at nearly $10 billion. Fisheries also now pose a number of complex issues, the most urgent of which are conservation and the sharing of exploitation and benefits. Although there is growing and legitimate concern about the conservation of specific species, a hopeful aspect of the fisheries problem is that fish are currently a renewable resource and hence nations are not just engaged in a holding action; with proper management and technology, the resource base can be increased significantly. The maximum sustainable fish yield from the oceans is probably twice as great as the current annual catch—and this is without the antarctic krill, which can yield up to 100 million tons of protein a year on a sustainable basis. As with other ocean resources, the situation is not yet one of crisis—bilateral disputes notwithstanding—but rather a challenge of averting a protein-resource crisis.

Moreover, although many of the diverse uses of ocean space are age-old, they have become the subject of fresh controversy in recent years because ocean space stands to be carved up politically under any new form of agreement. The extension of territorial waters to 12 miles, for example, would transform 116 straits, many of them on major trade routes, into national arteries. Military uses, no matter how controversial, are non-negotiable. In the cases of transport, trade routes and therefore trade costs are at stake. The principle of free passage is inviolable, if world trade is not to be disrupted. With regard to scientific research in the oceans (as in outer space), there are some precedents for cooperation and regulation; the basic principle to be established in this area is some kind of "open door" policy on sharing the knowledge acquired.

The Complexity of the Issues

Dealing with this range of problems to every country's satisfaction is a difficult and probably impossible task for three reasons:

1. The diverse uses of the oceans interrelate and interconnect. For example, waste disposal interferes with fishing and recreation, mining

can upset ocean ecology, shipping may increase the hazard of pollution.

2. Geography and geomorphology do not lend themselves to precise measurement or to the drawing up of visible or identifiable boundaries according to uniform criteria. The depth and breadth of the continental shelf—which has always figured prominently in new definitions of zones subject to political or economic control—cannot be ascertained with equal confidence in every case. On account of geological variations, coastal length alone gives little indication of the actual area and value of the seabed—either in terms of the various proposed limits of national jurisdiction (such as the continental shelf or the continental margin) or in terms of miles from shore.

3. Countries cannot be neatly categorized into interest groups that hold together on all ocean issues—since their positions are shaped by a variety of factors such as development level, geography, patterns of consumption, trade and output, political and economic alliances, and expectations.

Indeed, national expectations are affected less by differences in goals than by differences in how far countries look ahead. To illustrate this with reference to seabed mining, it should first be emphasized that land-based resources of the four important minerals that are found in the manganese nodules are ample for the next thirty years. There is no evidence that obtaining these minerals from the oceans, even at lower prices, would measurably benefit the economic well-being of the developed countries in the immediate future—nor, even if this were the case, that any significant portion of these benefits would flow to the developing countries. Since there are no demonstrable *immediate* large benefits to be derived from seabed mining, one can argue that there is no urgency to institute arrangements that might well fall short of being acceptable to all parties. However, a long-run perspective significantly alters the question. If technological obstacles to large-scale nodule mining are overcome (and if no new obstacles arise), ocean resources can offer strong and lasting cost advantages to today's industrialized countries as well as to tomorrow's large consumers among the currently underdeveloped countries. Since the availability of *high-grade* nodules will not decline rapidly, the exploitation of nodules is expected to have a horizontal cost curve (long-run supply curve) for many decades—offering a distinct advantage over the steeply rising cost curve of land-based resources. Consequently, in the long run, the interests of rich and poor countries will tend to converge. But in the absence of equitable regulation based on informed and intelligent judgment, the present, short-term diversity of national interests may lead to nothing but conflict.

126

The Beginnings of an International Approach

Since the genesis of the ocean debate in the postwar period, most countries, developed and developing, have resolved to deal with the problem of regulating the uses and abuses of the oceans multilaterally—under the auspices of the United Nations—and to draw up a convention for this purpose. What progress has been made so far?

The Third Conference on the Law of the Sea represents the culmination of efforts originating in the First Conference held in Geneva in 1958. The 1958 Conference led to the adoption of four conventions, with more than one hundred articles embodying such principles as the freedom of the high seas, rights of innocent passage through territorial waters and international straits, rights of vessels of all states to fish the high seas, rights of coastal states to the continental shelf, rights of landlocked states concerning access to the sea, and comprehensive provisions for settling fishing disputes and conservation matters through the offices of an independent commission. These conventions have been ratified by fewer than half of the nations of the world and have had little impact. In 1960, the Second Conference on the Law of the Sea was convened to deal with two principal problems left unresolved by the First Conference—the breadth of the territorial sea and fishery limits. However, the Second Conference failed to adopt any substantive new proposals.

In 1968, international discussions in this field gained a new momentum when the U.N. General Assembly established the Committee on the Peaceful Uses of the Seabed and the Ocean Floor Beyond the Limits of National Jurisdiction, which later came to be known as the Seabed Committee. A year later, in December 1969, the General Assembly adopted a resolution declaring a moratorium on all exploitation of deep seabed resources, pending the establishment of a deep seabed regime. Finally, in 1970, two other important resolutions were adopted. One consisted of a Declaration of Principles Governing the Seabed and Ocean Floor, which affirmed that the ocean floor beyond the limits of national jurisdiction and its resources are "the common heritage of mankind"; the other called for the convocation of the Third Law of the Sea Conference in 1973 (later postponed until 1974) and entrusted the Seabed Committee with all the preparatory work as well as the tasks of drafting treaty articles and an agenda for the session.

The work of the Third Law of the Sea Conference is divided among three committees: Committee I deals with the proposed international regime for the seabed, addressing itself in particular to the question of who should be given the right to mine the seabed and under what conditions; Committee III handles the subjects of scientific research, marine pollution, and transfer of technology; and Committee II covers all other matters concerning the law of the sea—such as the definition of legal and economic boundaries and rights or duties, the regime of straits and archipelagos, the settlement of disputes, and the rights of landlocked countries. Each committee has before it a set of draft articles together with the key positions on every article that have emerged from earlier discussions.

The Caracas Session

The Caracas meeting of the Conference did not succeed in adopting an international convention or in approving a set of articles on the issues dealt with by any of its three committees. The first five weeks of the session were taken up by approving rules of procedure, settling disputes over credentials, and speeches—some of which were peripheral to the issues involved, and were intended largely for consumption "at home." Serious negotiations were never really launched; instead, the three committees spent several weeks reading the draft articles with a view to narrowing down their differences on each. But even this proved difficult despite attempts to call on the parties with opposing views to take the lead in compromising. The Conference Chairman, Ambassador H. Shirley Amerasinghe of Sri Lanka, reflected the lingering pessimism—as well as the genuine disappointment of many—when he remarked to the press toward the end of the Caracas session that it might take three more such conferences to achieve concrete results. Indeed, Ambassador Amerasinghe almost was proven right (although he was hardly likely to have derived any comfort from the fact), since the Conference ended by calling for another eight-week session to begin in Geneva on March 17, 1975, and that session, too, closed with the decision to reconvene for another eight weeks in New York in March 1976. In short, all the major ocean issues still remain on the international agenda.

So little was accomplished at the Caracas session that any attempt to summarize its results seems pointless; it is perhaps more appropriate for the future course of international negotiations in this field to speculate about the reasons behind its failure. First, ocean issues have many interconnected aspects; for example, no disposition of rights in a zone could be made without first defining the zone itself. Second, the economic potential of the oceans thus far has been estimated more in terms of "maybe's" than of definite empirical data. Consequently, newly independent countries which did not participate in the earlier stages of the debate have found it especially difficult to evolve a position on the issues. Third, after the initial flush of good will and group solidarity, countries are ultimately bound to take a stand on the basis of purely national interest—a process requiring time and care.

The most optimistic interpretation of the Caracas session of the Conference is to conclude that differences among nations at least were clearly identified, which should facilitate progress in the future. A more cynical assessment is that the substantive failure of the Conference was preordained, given the deterioration of the world economic situation and the present unfavorable climate for international cooperation. On a more specific plane, environmentalists, oceanographers, and social activists have been dismayed about the degree of support that the concept of the 200-mile limit received at the Caracas session. Those who object to this view perceive it as an attempt at de jure colonization of the oceans that will make it impossible to control pollution, expand scientific research, or internationalize the wealth of the oceans.

The Geneva Session and Beyond

The six-month period between the Caracas and Geneva sessions was one of mixed expectations. Some encouraging signs were provided by a series of meetings of selected groups of countries; these meetings were designed to narrow down differences in order to facilitate negotiations in Geneva. Notable among these efforts were the working group established by the Group of 77, which met in January and February 1975, and the so-called Evensen Group of 15 developed and developing countries—organized by Ambassador Jens Evensen of Norway—which met informally several times with the objective of reconciling differences in matters falling under the purview of Committee II. On the negative side, the much-publicized Hughes/ C.I.A. affair cast a dark shadow over Geneva, as did the initiative of Deepsea Ventures, Inc.—the U.S. company furthest ahead in the commercial development of manganese nodules—in filing a "claim" with the U.S. State Department and legal authorities for an area of about 60,000 sq. km. in the Pacific Ocean and seeking U.S. diplomatic protection. Ironically, news of the Deepsea Ventures initiative was received with considerable glee by those frustrated by the slow progress of negotiations and prone to place the blame on the Third World. Clearly, on the eve of the Geneva session, the pessimists were in the majority. A *New York Times* editorial of March 17 stated that "the Law of the Sea Conference which reconvenes in Geneva today offers the last chance that the international community can anticipate to organize for orderly use and exploitation, for the benefit of all mankind, the more than two thirds of this planet that is covered by water."

The Geneva session opened with less fanfare than the Caracas one and started its work in a more businesslike fashion, with informal negotiating groups meeting from the very first day and plenary meetings held to a minimum. Yet real progress eluded the negotiators despite these more auspicious beginnings. The major achievement of the session was a compromise designed to salvage the world opinion of the Conference and keep the spirit of negotiation alive. The form of this compromise was the draft-

129

ing of a single negotiating text for consideration at the March 1976 session in New York. This was no more than a calculated procedural step. The document itself—115 pages long and comprising 304 draft articles—at best is no more than an informal working paper that does not bind any country to anything. It was drafted by the committee chairmen acting "on their individual responsibility," and it "is not a negotiated or consensus text."

Nevertheless, keeping alive the spirit of negotiation is an achievement that should not be belittled. A single negotiating text is a step forward that may facilitate the resolution of differences by permitting voting on individual draft articles—something that has not been possible so far, since countries had before them four or more alternative formulations for each article. Nevertheless, the international community is not much closer to an international agreement than before. The emerging consensus on the concepts of 12-mile territorial waters and 200-mile economic zones is dwarfed by remaining differences concerning navigation, fisheries, the power of the proposed international seabed authority, and other issues. National differences on these issues generally are not related to developed- or developing-country status. It has become increasingly clear that geography alone is a potent factor that determines how different groups of developing countries (for example, the landlocked states and coastal states) perceive their national interests. Reconciling these differences requires tedious appraisal of national interests as much as systematic and informal multilateral negotiations. Although the hiatus of nearly a year between the March 1975 Geneva session and the forthcoming one in New York in March 1976 is designed to give countries sufficient time to do just that, one can argue that the hiatus is perhaps too long in view of the pressure of countries possessing the technology to "go it alone" and begin exploiting mineral riches of the oceans.

Admittedly, instituting a system of government for the oceans is an awesome undertaking fraught with obvious difficulties. Yet failure to come to an agreement in this area would further undermine confidence in the feasibility of international action to bring about peaceful political and economic relations in other areas as well. The failure will be even greater, however, if a large-scale agreement at a future session can be realized only by abandoning the principle of internationalism embodied in the perception of the oceans as "the common heritage of mankind." At present it seems that the principle has been virtually abandoned—perhaps irrevocably.

If developing countries find it hard to compromise on this vital principle, it is because their goal—development—depends on both national and international efforts. Both their inflexibility and their procrastination flow from the realization that their stake in this issue is extraordinarily important and that the best possible arrangement is one that reduces the odds against the attainment of their development goals. Responsible decisions by the industrialized nations should be sympathetic to this concern. On the other hand, a development like seabed mining can be initiated only by those with the necessary equipment and know-how—if need be, unilaterally. Extremely slow progress in reaching a general agreement makes this outcome increasingly certain. Thus a balance may have to be struck between the ideal of cooperation and the realities of global power relations.

Reality indeed is pressing upon what was thought to be the business of the future, and discussion of the issues has to focus on the specific national or regional interests. Time to work out a broad international agreement is running out; therefore agreement should come soon, at least on the most critical specific issues—mining, fishing, and navigation—before the behavior patterns of individual nations become established and entrenched. It is dangerous to maintain that since the concert of nations cannot agree on everything it can agree on nothing.

Part III

Toward a
North-South Bargain

Chapter 9

The Developing World's "Challenge" in Perspective

Guy F. Erb

"Power always impinges on weakness," Reinhold Niebuhr observed some years ago in describing the domination and dependence resulting from the impingement of the industrialized countries of the West on less developed countries.[1] The aphorism still holds, but its dispassion is a long remove from the exasperation most African, Asian, and Latin American leaders feel with the continuing impasse on reforms that might make "international" economic systems serve their interests at least as well as they serve those of the industrial world. Attempts by these leaders to obtain greater economic power and a more balanced interdependence with the developed world will pose major challenges for American and other developed-country policy makers in the years ahead.

A strong and growing body of opinion underlies the international actions and statements of their representatives. In the developing nations, a consensus for change has formed around the perception that their dependent situation can be altered by both domestic and international reform. The essays by individuals from developing countries included in this volume document that consensus. This chapter sets out the background and current setting of the debates and conflicts between rich and poor nations and some policy options for decision makers in both groups of countries.

A Changing World

In a single generation, over seventy countries have gained their independence. These countries, which now number well over a hundred, have

---

[1]Reinhold Niebuhr, "Power and Ideology in National and International Affairs," in W. T. R. Fox, ed., *Theoretical Aspects of International Relations* (Notre Dame: University Press, 1959), p. 114.

swelled the membership of the United Nations and other international agencies. Although most of them still are weak relative to developed nations, they no longer are passive actors in the world economy, and industrialized countries can no longer ignore their interests without regard for the consequences.

Much of the current contention between developed and developing countries stems from the continuance of rich-country control of production, investment, and trade and from the reluctance of developed-country policy makers to alter approaches based, at best, on a trilateral consensus reached by Western Europe, North America, and Japan. The economic recovery and sustained growth of Western Europe and Japan after World War II, and the continuing strength of the economy of the United States, allowed the industrialized countries to dominate the international economic policy-making framework. The economic advances achieved by developing countries have not yet involved them fully in international decision making, but they have begun to add economic strength to the political independence of many developing nations. Nevertheless, most developing countries are still considered as militarily insignificant, and their ability to wield important economic leverage is questioned. Yet individual countries—and in some cases groups of developing nations—are shifting toward export-oriented trade policies, placing more demands on foreign investors seeking to do business in their markets, and changing in their favor the contractual arrangements that govern the exploration for, and development of, natural resources. Other issues which also have contributed to a greater pluralism in international economic relations include the legal and illegal migration of many millions from developing to industrialized nations as well as the differing environmental priorities that have already resulted in the movement of some mineral-processing and petroleum-refining operations to developing areas.

The changes which are altering the patterns of the post-World War II international economic systems are well illustrated by the exports of manufactures from developing countries. The value of these exports grew at 15 per cent annually between 1958–1960 and 1969–1971. The boom years of 1972 and 1973 saw additional annual increases in value in excess of 30 per cent. Moreover, manufactured exports accounted for over one half of the total increase in the *volume* of exports from developing countries in 1973.[2] The expansion and diversification of trade achieved by a considerable number of developing nations have brought gains to both rich and poor nations; at the same time, however, they have sparked disputes over the restrictions sometimes placed by industrialized countries on imports of manufactured goods from developing countries and over relations between developing

---

[2]General Agreement on Tariffs and Trade (GATT), *International Trade 1973/74* (Geneva), 1974, p. 104.

countries and the foreign companies that carry out much of the new production and trade.

Dramatic evidence of change was also provided in 1973–74 by the actions of members of the Organization of Petroleum Exporting Countries (OPEC) as well as of other suppliers of raw materials during and after the boom in commodity prices. Those developing nations that have significant energy resources have demonstrably increased their influence on the world economy; other producers of raw materials are also attempting individually and collectively to overcome the long-standing instability of earnings from raw-material exports and the overwhelming concentration of processing industries in developed areas. Less conspicuous but equally or even more important in the long run is the shift in attitudes within the developing world that has become apparent in their actions relating to the exploitation of their natural resources, to new trade in manufactured goods, and to the activities of multinational companies operating within their borders. Other factors that are changing the setting of North-South relations include domestic demands for change in inequitable *internal* social systems in developing countries, the increasing legal and economic skills in the official and private sectors of these nations, the increasing concern of many countries (both rich and poor) about reliable access to needed food and resources, and the determination of suppliers to obtain a greater proportion of the final price of their processed raw materials. At the same time that these developments are shifting negotiating power between developed and developing countries, resistance by developed-country labor and industrial interests to changes in the customary patterns of employment and production is complicating the formulation of policies in industrialized countries whose responsiveness on these issues could significantly affect development progress.

Outside the economic sphere, other changes that have added elements of uncertainty to international relations are the reaction of developing countries against their use as proxies in disputes between East and West and the rapid spread of armaments and nuclear technology. Furthermore, the internal pressures that accompany social change or its suppression in the developing world have proven capable of catalyzing events that directly affect the investments or the citizens of industrialized nations situated in developing countries—such as the 1974 demonstrations in Thailand against the economic presence of Japan in that country, or the acts of terrorism against foreigners in some African and Latin American countries.

Despite the major changes that are taking place in the developing world, however, at least three quarters of global income, investment, and services—and nearly all research—remain concentrated in the upper quarter of the world's population. Instability of income still confronts producers of primary commodities, who have seen the prices of their imports of manufactured goods rise steadily in spite of a widespread recession. Moreover, the poorest countries remain at the margin of the world economy. And *within* most developing nations, economic growth—although substantial—has not noticeably improved the lot of the poor majority, since upper-income classes continue to dominate internal economic structures.

The Political Climate

The present U.S. response to the initiatives of developing countries that aim at changing global economic relationships is greatly influenced by the view that no lasting challenge to the international economic order can be mounted by developing countries. According to this view, developing countries—through their economic growth and the spill-over of benefits to them from economic growth in the industrialized world—can make steady economic advances within the present international economic system. Trade and monetary policies and continued resource transfers from developed to developing areas are thus justified primarily on moral grounds, rather than by a perception that the long-run economic interests of industrialized nations can be seriously affected by events in the Third World. Attempts to maximize all nations' gains from economic growth and development through cooperative policies are seen as unnecessary, given the limited political-economic strength of developing countries.

As is to be expected in this period of transition away from a period of relatively unchallenged economic dominance by industrialized nations, there are factors which seem mutually contradictory: for every instance of economic or political power exercised by the poor nations, examples can be cited of their persistent poverty and political-economic weakness. Thus changes in developing countries should be neither overdramatized nor ignored, but assessed a) in relation to the specific areas where individual or collective actions by developing countries may have a significant impact and b) in the context of the political, economic, and social evolution that is prompting these countries to seek greater political and economic autonomy.

This striving for autonomy is the current manifestation of the long struggle for national self-determination that began with the earliest independence efforts. It is a bond that unites developing countries and is a growing force for change in international relations that will persist even though developing countries may experience setbacks with respect to particular political or economic issues. In the current context, for example, whether or not exporters of raw materials succeed in forming viable groups of producer countries, they and others will continue their drive for economic advancement and a corresponding increase in their influence over international economic events. The international financial and monetary institutions, investment relations, and the growing imports of manufactured goods from developing nations offer other areas where pressure points may be found to influence industrialized nations.

In recent years, there has been much talk of "interdependence" between rich and poor nations. Certainly many nations—both industrialized and underdeveloped—currently face grave economic and social problems brought on by the energy, food, and fertilizer crises and by the recession in developed countries. And certainly the rapid expansion of industrialized economies prior to the recession heightened awareness in developed-country capitals of the developed world's import dependence on raw-material exports. But as developing-country leaders have pointed out, such "interdependence" is not new. They have heard many times before that within an open world economy all nations can gain from the developed countries' needs for the resources of the Third World and that developing countries are increasingly important as markets for rich-country exports. They also have heard that greater resource transfers from rich to poor are morally right—even while they have seen the stagnation of official development assistance. The advocacy of such views in liberal economic circles in developed countries is a familiar part of the inconclusive debate that has long characterized North-South encounters. From the point of view of the developing countries, these elements of interdependence are mere slogans that have not led to an equitable international distribution of the gains from economic growth.

Dependency Theory and Changing Attitudes. Persistence into the post-colonial period of great disparities of wealth and power and the obstacles facing developing countries attempting to alter their relationship with the industrialized world has led to a profound reaction by Africans, Asians, and Latin Americans against the dependency of their countries. This movement has found expression—first in Latin America and the Caribbean but increasingly in other developing regions as well—in the theory of dependency that attributes the underdevelopment of Third World economies to the predominance of external influences transmitted to poor countries by the international capitalist system.[3] Dependency theory emphasizes the international power relationships that underlie the functioning of the world economy. It sees internal inequities as largely a result of the impact of external factors. Consumption patterns, for example, are viewed as

---

[3]For a range of the views encompassed by dependency theory, see Norman Girvan, ed., *Dependence and Underdevelopment in the New World and the Old*, a special issue of *Social and Economic Studies*, Vol. 22, No. 1, March 1973, Institute of Social and Economic Research, University of the West Indies, Jamaica. This collection includes essays by Norman Girvan, Anibal Pinto and Jan Kñakal, Havelock Brewster, Andrés Bianchi, Celso Furtado, Osvaldo Sunkel, and Samir Amin. Other sources include: J. D. Cockcoft, Andres Gunder Frank, and Dale Johnson, *Dependence and Underdevelopment* (New York: Doubleday, 1972); Andres Gunder Frank, *Latin America: Underdevelopment or Revolution* (New York: Monthly Review Press, 1969); Helio Jaguaribe, Theotonio dos Santos, ed., *La dependencia político-economica de America Latina* (Mexico: Siglo XXI, 1970); Fernando H. Cardoso, *Cuestiones de sociología del desarrollo de America Latina* (Santiago: Editorial Universitaria, 1968); and Susanne Bodenheimer, "Dependency and Imperialism: The Roots of Latin American Underdevelopment," in K. T. Fann and D. C. Hodges, *Readings in U.S. Imperialism* (Boston: Porter Sargent, 1971).

stemming from high technology, production of luxury goods, and from the creation of a class in developing nations that identifies with foreign interests rather than with its own society's needs.

Dependency theory tends to exaggerate the role of external influences and consequently downplays the internal obstacles to the development of more equitable domestic economic, social, and political systems. A lessening of dependence on the industrialized world requires not only the achievement of better international bargains but also improved management of local resources and significant social and economic changes *within* developing countries.[4] Such changes are essential for the political viability of those developing-country regimes that do not depend on force to stay in power; in the long run change will occur even in those cases. The relationship between more equitable national development and the international capability of a developing nation's government to affect its economic destiny is increasingly recognized by developing-country commentators—although much of the debate between rich and poor nations still focuses on the problems posed by external influences on developing economies. Ironically, some in the Third World are turning their attention to domestic barriers to change and development and consequently are abandoning the overreliance of dependency theory on external influences just as the theory is attracting more attention in developed countries.[5]

Dependency theory clearly has contributed to the increased awareness of developing-country leaders of the relative strengths and weaknesses of their position and has certainly heightened their desire for greater autonomy in international economic affairs. It is one of the most important factors that has contributed to the growing sense of self-reliance that is prompting developing nations to seek more influence over their political and economic destinies.

Paternalism or Partnership? Although *domestic* institutional and other reforms clearly are critical for the advancement of developing countries, external factors confronting individual developing countries nevertheless can either help or hinder the introduction of changes in their societies. Shifts in international political and economic power that might offer developing-country leaders an opportunity to respond to domestic pressures for more equity can be either facilitated or impeded by industrialized nations. Presently, however, interests in developed countries continue to resist the changes in patterns of trade, investment, and production that are likely to result in shifting patterns of international power.

---

[4]On this see Peter L. Berger, *Pyramids of Sacrifice: Political Ethics and Social Change* (New York: Basic Books, 1974), pp. 217–221.

[5]See José Luis de Imaz, "Adios a la teoría de la dependencia? Una perspectiva desde la Argentina," *Estudios Internacionales* (Buenos Aires), No. 28 (October-December 1974), pp. 49–75.

This resistance traditionally has been accompanied by strong paternalistic tendencies in relations with developing countries. In the 1920s, industrially advanced countries envisaged a system of tutelage for underdeveloped areas within an international *legal* order. This attitude has its contemporary forms. Recently, for example, a group of European commentators defined the international economic order as "the institutions established in the late 1940s to manage the world economy."[6] Apparently assuming that the Bretton Woods institutions still contribute to "order" by adequately meeting the aspirations of their members, the group ignored the objections by developing nations to the preponderant voice that weighted voting in the World Bank and International Monetary Fund gives to developed nations and the traditional concentration of the General Agreement on Tariffs and Trade (GATT) on developed-country concerns.

In another recent analysis, a possible approach was proposed in which the advanced countries would act as "steerers" and "pace setters" in many areas of world economic management.[7] This study recognized that there would be cases in which the ability of rich countries to lead would be limited but argued that their "high degree of economic interdependence and interaction" would impel them to participate in codes and regulations that developing countries as well as communist countries would be unable or unwilling to accept. The overall objective would be the establishment of a global economic system within which the key-country subsystems would operate.

But past examples of "key-country" actions—such as decision making on monetary affairs in the "Group of Ten" and even in a "Group of Five," or mutual support among developed countries for restrictive approaches to international trade in fibers and textiles—do not offer grounds for optimism that such advanced-country groupings would be consistent with a global system genuinely attempting to meet the needs of Africa, Asia, and Latin America as well as of the industrialized world. Moreover, no small group of advanced countries, whatever its intent, would meet the demands of developing countries for a greater share in the international decision-making process.

These demands are often difficult for representatives of industrialized countries to comprehend. The objective of greater participation in decision making may stem primarily from a sense of being left out: detailed proposals for alternative decision-making structures may not have been proposed. In responding to the demands, therefore, the central issue is the seriousness

---

[6]Trade Policy Research Centre (London), "Reform of the International Commercial System," *Bellagio Memorandum*, p. 8. (1973).

[7]Miriam Camps, *The Management of Interdependence: A Preliminary View* (New York: Council on Foreign Relations, 1974), pp. 18–19, 44–46, 58, 90–91.

with which developed countries take into account the views and interests of developing nations in the formulation and implementation of foreign economic policies. Merely "giving the appearance" of listening to developing-country claims has been, and is, used by developed countries as a device for delaying serious consultations with developing nations on possible solutions to international economic problems. This tactic accounts for a good deal of the skepticism with which developing nations greet new proposals from developed-country capitals. There is no substitute for effective consultations and negotiations between developed and developing nations if viable, long-run systems are to emerge from the current international economic situation. Once the major step of agreeing to seek mutually satisfactory solutions to specific problems has been taken by developed countries, the issues themselves will greatly influence the type of decision-making structures appropriate in each substantive area; a variety of possibilities exist, including precise voting arrangements, systems of representation or delegation of authority that could limit the numbers of countries participating in certain bodies, looser consultative procedures within groups of nations interested in specific issues, and ad hoc treatment of emergencies that takes into consideration a variety of interests.

The great weight of industrialized nations in the world economy ensures that other nations will be affected by their decisions and actions. Consequently, an alternative to the key-country approach would be recognition by developed nations that viable systems require the participation in decision making by countries affected by the results of those decisions. This alternative approach would start from the premise that the pace of political-economic events is now so rapid that the successful "management of interdependence" will depend on developing-country participation in the bodies—small or large—that will determine international policies in security, economic, and other areas, as well as in the field of development.

A prime characteristic of the world economy is the rapid economic change that can take place within sectors or within individual countries. The fact that Brazil, Korea, Yugoslavia, and other countries emerged as major exporters of manufactures in a single decade illustrates this potential. If political-economic institutions are not sufficiently flexible to match such rates of change, institutional bottlenecks or rigidities will eventually hinder the ability of all nations to gain from their participation in international economic systems.

Resistance to Change. Another factor making for sharpened insistence by developing countries on the need to change the "rules of the game" has been the hostile reaction in some industrialized nations to those developing countries that have challenged the activities of private corporations through which developed countries have received raw materials. In many cases, the initiatives of developing countries have been accompanied, or preceded, by a shift to the left by their leaders. This political shift added

142

an element of "cold war" confrontation to their policies and served to justify strong resistance to change by some Western policy makers. In the recent past, reaction to developing-country initiatives has included political-military confrontations, covert subversion of governments, and intervention in the political processes of foreign countries. In the wake of the oil price rise and in response to a growing sensitivity in developed countries to their reliance on imported primary products, there even has been some renewed consideration of resorting to gunboat diplomacy.

From the point of view of the developing countries, the discussion in developed countries of the possibilities of military intervention or of the denial of trade opportunities, capital, and technology to developing countries who do not "play the game" merely illustrates the political-economic obstacle course set before them when they are seen to trespass upon the economic interests of more powerful nations. The obstacles that developing countries meet as they try to obtain a larger share of the gains from their own production and trade—trade barriers, restrictive business practices, political pressure to adhere to Western models of development—suggest that nations may not necessarily *progress* through stages of economic growth but may encounter increasing economic barriers. Indeed, developed-country attempts to counter the "producer power" of certain raw-material exporters or to impose settlements of investment disputes may well strengthen what Robert Heilbroner has called "aggression in the 'normal' direction—that is, aggression by the rich nations against the poor."[8]

Nevertheless, power relationships among and within nations in some instances do change in response to economic growth and social development. The emerging global situation has some parallels in the economic history of developed nations. In the United States, for example, power relationships were altered as industrialization and domestic social change brought new economic and political influence to U.S. labor and minorities. The analogy of course does not apply categorically to the current relationships between rich and poor countries; most developing countries do not yet have influence over the developed nations comparable to that which the Populist movement in the 1890s or minority groups in the 1960s drew upon in the United States or comparable to the pressure applied by organized labor in America and the other Western democracies.

In international relations, as in domestic matters, the rich often equate "order" with existing patterns of power. Their consequent tendency to favor the status quo is likely to lead to attempts to maintain it. Current policy debates over international resource control pit the advocates of strong approaches to breaking embargoes or imposing solutions to resource conflicts against those who oppose military responses to apparent

---

[8]Robert Heilbroner, *An Inquiry into the Human Prospect* (New York: W. W. Norton & Co., Inc., 1974), p. 43.

threats to resource access. But contemplation of interventionist policies or the practice of "Realeconomik" by rich and powerful countries are hardly conducive to constructive negotiations between nations of unequal power. Threats to "withhold trade and technological skills sought by the oil exporting countries"[9] are not an effective means to strike a bargain in the long-term interests of developed and developing countries—nor are suggestions that "the possibilities of withdrawing support from the Saudi regime and even of armed intervention must be made credible."[10]

The London *Economist* noted at the time of the Teheran oil agreement of 1971 that:

> Once upon a time, had a group of backward countries, with highly unstable governments and a reputation for persistent commercial bad faith, tried to hold the Western economies to ransom as the oil-producing governments of the Middle East are now doing, they would have seen the gunboats steaming up the Gulf in double-quick time. Gunboat diplomacy is now a thing of the past. But there are times when big nations feel acutely the loss of a substitute for it.[11]

Perhaps Secretary Kissinger felt just such a loss when he made his guarded but highly publicized remarks about "military action on oil prices" in the event of "some actual strangulation of the industrialized world."[12] Yet if economic disputes are not to escalate into political-military confrontations, negotiation and compromise are the only viable substitutes for gunboat diplomacy.

Cohesion and Pluralism

Although the long-run effect of the events of 1973–1975 on the relative power of developed and developing nations should not be exaggerated, the attitudes and actions of developing countries nevertheless have changed the framework in which the economic policies of developed countries take place. Most trade, monetary, and financial policies appropriate for developed countries therefore must take into account the persistent *cohesion* of the nonaligned countries at a time marked by détente and *pluralism* among the developed nations. The present pluralism within the Western bloc is due in part to the heavily armed truce that prevails between East

---

[9]Editorial, *The New York Times*, June 20, 1974.
[10]Steven D. Krasner, "Chips in the Oil Game," *The New York Times*, May 20, 1974.
[11]*Economist*, January 30, 1971.
[12]Interview of Secretary of State Henry Kissinger with *Business Week*, Department of State Press Release, No. 2, January 2, 1975, p. 6.

and West leaving both "secure" in political-military terms and allowing more freedom of action to the countries within each superpower's camp.

The uniqueness of oil in world trade and of the circumstances leading to the increased power of oil exporters has led some to conclude that comparable problems will not arise between industrialized countries and the developing world. However, the OPEC action and the supportive response it engendered in most other developing countries were not due solely to the peculiarities of the oil industry in the early 1970s. The developing countries' shared sense of long-standing grievances against the industrialized countries will encourage their unity whatever the outcome of the dispute over oil prices.

The fact that the developing countries perceive the industrialized countries as a common adversary or economic threat may be one factor behind the tendency of many in the United States to treat the Third World as a menace to the established order. However, in many areas the Third World does not pose a plausible short-run menace to industrialized-country interests. In fact, unity among developing countries is frequently sustained only by incorporating many diverse objectives in omnibus resolutions that are too general for implementation or too far-reaching in the present political circumstances. Where their perceptions of national interest outweigh expected gains from a concerted approach toward the rich countries—as, for example, in some aspects of the negotiations on the Law of the Sea—the solidarity of the developing nations may be difficult to maintain. There are, moreover, substantial divergences within the developing-country bloc due to differences in level of development, size, and political system. Nevertheless, in the many cases where unity vis-a-vis the industrialized countries serves their domestic and international interests, developing countries will make collective attempts to increase their self-reliance and overcome their poverty. Cohesiveness among developing countries will also serve as a backdrop to efforts by individual or groups of nations to elicit specific gains from developed nations.

Public opinion in developed countries is likely to counter the portrayal of relatively poor African, Asian, and Latin American nations as "the enemy"—although during the 1974-75 recession and in the aftermath of the oil price rises and the Arab oil embargo confrontational tactics by developing countries did engender a "backlash" that was directed in an oversimplified manner toward *all* developing countries. The relatively great dependence of the European countries and of Japan on the resources of the South reduces the likelihood of their unyielding resistance to all Third World demands for international economic change. And consensus already is lacking among the developed countries on approaches to the Third World in the field of raw materials. As resource-dependent countries scramble to meet their own requirements in response to perceived or actual shortages and as raw-material exporters assume tougher bargaining stances, divergence within the Western alliance will increase. The leadership position of the United States already has been eroded by the impact of such developments as well as by the reaction of both rich and poor nations to the United States' past assumption of the role of pre-eminent "cold warrior" and its willingness to intervene covertly or openly in developing nations. For example, the European countries and Japan did not follow the U.S. lead in the Indochina confrontation and have been able to establish contacts in resource-rich developing nations that now hinder a concerted approach with the United States on trade and raw-material issues.

Adjusting to Interdependence

From the perspective of developing nations, the managers of international economic institutions and of the private and official networks that make up global economic systems usually have aimed at achieving the objectives of their own countries or corporations, not at including other parties in *jointly* managed trade, monetary, and investment systems. It is therefore not surprising that the developing countries have set their own priorities for a new international economic order instead of accepting the industrialized world's perception of its own particular interdependence with raw-material suppliers.

Developing countries have of course proposed new policies for their development and their economic relations with developed countries for many years. The record of the first U.N. Conference on Trade and Development (UNCTAD) in 1964 provides examples of their early proposals.[13] Today, however, important new dimensions have been added to statements of developing-country aspirations by the frustrations resulting from more than a decade of largely fruitless efforts to obtain international consideration and implementation of their proposals; by the present determination of developing-country leaders to manifest their dissatisfaction with the responses of developed countries; and by the efforts of OPEC members and some other raw-material exporters.[14]

Like the objectives of the anti-colonial movements, the changes that developing countries now advocate in world political-economic relationships necessarily imply difficult adjustments in the relations between developed and developing nations. At stake in this confrontation is influence over the basic rules governing trade and economic activity.

What are the implications for industrialized countries of the Third World's pressures for change? Those in the developed nations who view increased participation by the developing nations in the world economy as a threat to their own economic interests and continued prosperity are likely

---

[13]See *Proceedings of the United Nations Conference on Trade and Development: Final Act and Report*, Vol. I, U.N. Pub. Sales No. 64.II.B.11 (New York: United Nations, 1964).
[14]See Annexes B-1 and B-3, pp. 185 and 213.

to strengthen their opposition to further geographical shifts of industrial production, increased imports of processed and manufactured goods from developing countries, and greater participation by host countries in activities previously controlled by foreign investors.

An alternative to such resistance might start from the premise suggested by Prime Minister Wilson that " . . . the relationship, the balance, between the rich and poor countries is wrong and must be remedied."[15] Such an approach would include policies designed to optimize all nations' gains from growth in world trade and production. In mid-1975, the members of the Organisation for Economic Co-operation and Development (OECD) took a first step in that direction in declaring their intent " . . . to make real progress toward a more balanced and equitable structure of international economic relations."[16] To realize that objective, developed countries would need to facilitate internal adjustments made necessary by the economic diversification and new trade of developing countries. They also would have to accept political diversity in the Third World and an increasing nonconformity with Western models as social and economic changes bring new forms of government to specific countries.

In the case of the United States, such a new policy approach would need to include substantial governmental support for changes in domestic industrial employment patterns, new trade and development assistance policies, and a new direction for U.S. involvement in the United Nations and other international organizations. Some of these measures would entail substantial costs in the form of U.S. government assistance to specific sectors of the U.S. economy. Others would require adjustments by the private sector. Such costs and their domestic-political implications should not be underestimated; they need to be assessed in relation to the consequences of a failure to meet the required changes in the international economy.

The Dangers of Continued Confrontation. The developing nations were largely taken for granted in the postwar economic systems that were designed primarily to meet the priorities of industrialized countries. Their participation in decisions concerning trade, monetary, and financial affairs has been limited, and the benefits they have gleaned from such "internationally" agreed procedures and guidelines have been imperfect at best. This secondary status of the developing countries in world economic systems also has resulted in the downgrading by developed countries of those international organizations—principally the United Nations and related bodies—in which the developing nations have voiced their grievances and demands.

---

[15]Speech by Prime Minister Harold Wilson at the Commonwealth Heads of Government Meeting, Kingston, Jamaica, May 1, 1975, in *World Economic Interdependence and Trade in Commodities*, Cmnd. 6061 (London: Her Majesty's Stationery Office, 1975), p. 1.

[16]Organisation for Economic Co-operation and Development, *Declaration on Relations with Developing Countries* (Paris), May 28, 1975.

Both developed and developing countries stand to lose by allowing fruitless confrontations and resolutions to continue within the United Nations and other international bodies instead of making more constructive use of these organizations. At the very least, the role of the United Nations as a talking shop provides an opportunity to all parties to air their grievances. The system should also encourage a transition from confrontation to collective bargaining. Without a reversal of the deterioration of the capacity of the U.N. system, that system itself and other related bodies, such as the GATT (which has not yet completed its transition from an organization primarily responsive to rich countries' trading needs to a *global* agency) cannot be expected to serve effectively any group of countries—much less all countries.

Developed nations of course derive most of their international economic strength from their trade and investment relations with one another. It thus would be possible for them to turn inward and rebuff developing-country initiatives without an immediate high cost to their populations' living standards, but the cumulative impact of a failure to find mutually satisfactory bargains would imply economic losses for both rich and poor nations. For the *industrialized nations*, the costs of continued confrontation would include:

(a) Higher prices for imported raw materials—if developing-country policies discouraged new investment in the exploration and development of new resources;

(b) Proliferation and intensification of investment disputes—which, in turn, would affect the overseas operations of numerous corporations, possibly reducing their remittance of royalties and investment income to their home countries;

(c) Possible strengthening of protective trade barriers by developed nations, which would reduce consumer access to inexpensive imports of the manufactured goods now produced efficiently in many developing nations;

(d) Declining foreign markets for developed-country exports as slower growth in developing nations affected the latter's purchasing power; and

(e) Additional difficulties in managing an increasingly complex international economy that—although it is dominated by developed nations—has already shown its vulnerability to actions by raw-materials producers.

Issues such as the settlement of trade disputes over export restraints or subsidies and of conflicts over foreign investment policies will require the cooperation of countries now outside the OECD—the organization that until recently has been the forum in which such matters were discussed most seriously by the United States and other developed nations. Without the involvement of newly powerful and other developing nations in the management of international systems, it would be difficult at this stage for groupings of developed countries to formulate rules, goals, and procedures for their own economic relations that later could be adapted to include participation by new members. Limited agreements on the management of specific sectors of the world economy might well result in enclaves trying to withstand demands for change from outside countries instead of constituting the forefront of international economic reform.

For the *developing countries*, the costs of intensification of their confrontation with the developed world could include:

(a) Defensive commodity stockpiling by individual industrialized countries or groups of these countries;

(b) A drawing inward and a further withdrawal from the family of United Nations institutions by developed countries;

(c) A hardening of the rich-country approach toward trade negotiations with developing nations, both in the multilateral negotiations in Geneva and with regard to primary commodities;

(d) Greater support for protectionist policies in developed countries, and, consequently, more frequent use of such mechanisms as countervailing duties (applied against subsidized foreign exports) and requests for "voluntary" restrictions on developing-country exports of certain "sensitive" products; and

(e) A decline in bilateral development assistance programs and a cutback in support for the lending programs of international financial institutions.

In short, if negotiations do not follow the present confrontation, the economic growth and development of both groups of countries will be impeded. The avoidance of the above costs is probably of greater significance in economic terms to the developing countries, due to the greater adaptability of the economies of the industrialized world. Nevertheless, it is probable that, under circumstances of economic conflict and nuclear proliferation, developed countries also will experience harmful economic and political consequences as a result of unyielding confrontation. The international consideration now being given to problems relating to food, energy, population, environment, and the law of the seas offers many areas in which constructive—and mutually beneficial—solutions can be sought by both rich and poor nations. From the point of view of developing nations, however, such increased gains must include more than a return to satisfactory rates of economic growth by industrial economies. Changes in governmental and corporate policies are called for if new international negotiations are to bring tangible results to developing nations as well as to the industrialized countries.

The Interplay of Domestic and Foreign Policies in the Rich Countries. In the developed countries, policies intended to benefit the development of the poor countries often must face opposition from those interests which feel most threatened by adaptation to international events. For example, the transfer of productive activities to developing nations is opposed by a large segment of organized labor and certain industrial interests. The position of these groups is strengthened by the fact that in many cases elite groups in developing countries are the main beneficiaries of the economic gains obtained through the activities of foreign-based corporations, new trade flows, and foreign assistance. This has made it relatively easy for some to argue that developed countries should not make sacrifices for the benefit of a handful of already rich inhabitants of poor countries. This position has not, however, always been used as an argument against foreign aid of any kind; it was in part responsible, for example, for the new emphasis of U.S. bilateral assistance programs on the poorest people within recipient countries.

Another area in which domestic views have impinged strongly on foreign policy is the consideration of proposals for food aid and for international food reserves. Farm interests became quite outspoken in 1975 over what they regarded as the insufficient attention paid to their concerns in the formulation of U.S. approaches to these two issues. Political uses of food aid and the danger that food reserves would be used to drive down prices received by farmers gave rise to strong expressions of dissatisfaction in the American Midwest. In these two cases, both industrial and farm interests had to be taken explicitly into account in the determination of foreign economic policies toward developing areas.

Yet another major issue that affects the entire range of policies toward developing nations relates to perceptions in rich countries of the state of their own economies and the degree to which living standards are improving for all sectors of their populations. In the midst of a recession and with the possibility of continued low rates of growth in developed nations, the need to reduce inequities and improve domestic employment prospects can lead to opposition to policies toward developing nations that appear to run counter to domestic interests. In circumstances where high rates of economic growth cannot be depended upon to bring gradually improving living standards to the poorer members of the population, rich-nation interest groups affected by events in developing countries are even more reluctant than usually to see a shift in productive resources and economic activity away from industrial economies. Certainly both the transfer of industries from developed to developing countries and the introduction of programs designed to facilitate domestic adjustment in developed countries take place more easily when the economies of industrialized countries are performing well. Without the impetus to new technological development that generally accompanies rapid economic growth in the rich countries, a shift of technological factors to developing countries is virtually certain to be strongly resisted by labor and declining industries. In the long run, therefore, adequate *domestic* growth, economic adjustment, and better income distribution in developed countries can improve the prospects for constructive negotiations aimed at reducing existing inequities and injustices in *international* economic relations.

Multilateral Approaches

The multilateral framework for economic as distinct from political peacekeeping is under severe strain. International cooperation on trade, monetary reform, investment policies, finance, and debt management may well depend upon a mitigation of the confrontation that marred international deliberations in the mid-1970s. Confrontations marked specialized conferences on food and population in 1974, and on the status of women in mid-1975, and were even more conspicuous at the abortive first meeting held in Paris in early 1975 in preparation for a consumer-producer energy and raw-materials conference.

Even as these events took place, however, two major institutions, the World Bank and the International Monetary Fund, were making constructive adjustments to new realities. Until mid-1975, the decision-making structure of the Bank and the Fund reflected for the most part the economic strength of industrialized nations. In both of these institutions, formal votes rarely take place, but negotiated settlements reflect the power structure inherent in the voting weights. However, in response to the increased power and influence of oil exporters and other changes in the position of developing countries, the Fund doubled the quotas of oil exporters while leaving those of other developing countries as a whole unchanged. The effect of this increase was to raise the total share of quotas of oil exporters and other developing countries to nearly one third. The World Bank also has proposed changes that would raise the combined voting power of oil exporters and other developing countries within the Bank to over 40 per cent of the total votes.

Institutional reforms, including changes in decision-making systems, were also proposed by a group established by the U.N. General Assembly to propose measures to strengthen the contribution of the United Nations to economic and social development.[17] And the GATT has also established a small body (18 member countries) designed to improve the capacity of that institution to respond to critical trade policy issues.

Such changes, however, are only first steps in what certainly will be a long process of international adaptation to changes in developing-country influence in international bodies and in negotiations with multinational corporations and individual developed countries. Despite the

---

[17]See Report of the Group of Experts on the Structure of the United Nations System, *A New United Nations Structure for Global Economic Co-Operation*, U.N. Doc. No. E/AC.62/9 (New York: United Nations, 1975).

coordinated activities of both the "Group of 77" developing countries in the United Nations and the nonaligned developing countries, developed countries and the international institutions which they dominate still hold the balance of world economic power. The confrontations that mark U.N. debates thus partly owe their frequently strident tones to the perception of developing countries that they do not yet have much leverage in the decision-making processes in industrialized countries and international institutions that directly affect their economic interests.

With regard to the operations of large private corporations, however, neither rich nor poor countries have a great deal of leverage. Many of these firms have created a global base for their activities that has made it difficult for national authorities to establish instruments with which to regulate and govern transnational corporations. Multilateral guidelines and international codes which incorporate dispute-settlement procedures have been proposed to ensure equitable and satisfactory corporate practices regarding technology, trade, and capital investment. Thus far, both developed and developing countries apparently have preferred to prepare national, or in a few cases, subregional, policies toward foreign investors and the transfer of technology. Apart from overall codes of conduct for foreign investors or broad statements of national policy objectives such as the Charter of Economic Rights and Duties of States, there are specific areas where governments and corporations interact and where multilateral arrangements might be feasible. For example, use of export restraints by both corporations and governments is common; both sides would gain if there were internationally agreed procedures allowing each party to a trade dispute to present its position on the matter. Involvement of corporations in trade-policy codes on this type of issue and in other areas therefore may be an important element of new forms of international economic management.

The Choices Before Rich and Poor Nations

For some time, the principal options before individual developing countries in their relations with developed countries have been the prospects of becoming *dependent partners* of rich countries, their *docile clients*, or, in a few cases, *disciplined rebels* maintaining themselves aloof from international systems.[18] For a few large nations, continued growth may lead to eventual entry into the group of industrialized countries. The accessibility of these options to individual nations is of course affected by their geographic, economic, and political situations.

To these choices we must also add the possibility of the *collective self-reliance* that is now being emphasized by developing countries.[19] This new

[18]Tibor Mende, *From Aid to Recolonization: Lessons of a Failure* (New York: Pantheon Books, 1973), pp. 218–227.
[19]See Annexes B-3 and A-3, pp. 213 and 178.

collective approach draws upon the experience of OPEC and other raw-material producer groups, but it has antecedents in the developing world's economic cooperation and integration movements. Many developing countries have for some time tried to improve their relative strength by coordinating their approaches to trade policies, foreign investment, and other policy issues. The Central American Common Market, the Andean Group, several African groupings, and the Association of Southeast Asian Nations have all—with mixed results—brought developing countries together to contribute to their internal development and to present a common front to the outside world. But the actions of the few disciplined rebels, the tentative steps toward economic integration by other countries, and the OPEC actions of 1973–74, have not yet—despite their great significance—substantially diminished the major economic and political disparities that underlie relations between the rich and powerful countries and most of the developing world.

The persistence of large disparities has led to a recognition that some forms of dependence tend to persist due to factors such as the size of a developing economy relative to external factors (i.e., commodity price fluctuations or the negotiating power of large corporations), or a country's potential for expanding industrial production. However, developing countries also see that a greater capacity for autonomous action on their part would reduce their external dependence. Through collective action, they are seeking to alter the present imbalance of power without necessarily isolating themselves from the world economy.

Such collective action is of course bringing the developing countries face-to-face with the industrialized nations' interests in a number of areas. The industrialized nations, too, face a variety of policy options—notably *confrontation*, selective *accommodation* to newly powerful nations, or *cooperation* in a multilateral framework. The adaptation of international economic systems depends heavily on how the United States and other industrialized nations react to the choices thrust upon them by the "incursions" of new industrial producers and traders and those of the raw-material exporting countries, as well as on how they react to the manner in which developing nations press their claims. Confrontation with some developing-country interests, accommodation to others, and cooperation will all emerge from the clash of policies in the world economy; the question is which of these approaches will predominate.

The confrontation option is illustrated by the negative reaction in some industrialized countries to disruption of established economic patterns by groups of or individual developing countries. Although some multilateral institutions have accommodated themselves to the new influence of petroleum producers, developed countries have opted for a closing of ranks and the establishment of an organization—the International Energy Agency—that is attempting to counter the oil cartel. Developed countries also are seeking bilateral solutions to their energy and resource needs, thereby endangering their own cooperative efforts as well as the framework for multilateral action in other areas.

A second developed-country option now frequently discussed is that of bringing some of the newly rich nations and the more advanced developing countries into the "club" of rich nations as rapidly as possible—thereby neutralizing the leadership that these countries otherwise might exercise within the Third World. Thus encouragement of investment by oil exporters in developed countries is advocated on the ground that a closer relationship between newly rich and industrialized nations may moderate oil price rises and temper the militancy with which oil exporters approach Third World issues. So far, however, the generally hostile attitude of the advanced countries—and of the United States in particular—toward OPEC has reflected a response of confrontation rather than one of accommodation or cooperation. As a consequence, even though the oil exporters have invested heavily in the industrialized countries, they have continued to use the pressure of oil prices to retain their gains. They have also been trying to strengthen their ties with other countries in Africa, Asia, and Latin America through support for their commodity policy objectives and by making substantial financial resources available to them.

The most difficult of the three choices before developed countries is the possibility of a cooperative multilateral approach to international economic issues, including the development of poor nations. This approach implies acceptance of developing-country participation in the decision-making procedures that until recently have been the almost exclusive province of industrialized nations.

Both developing and developed countries will have to move beyond old concepts if this approach is to succeed. A cooperative approach to international economic management would require some enlargement of the small groups within which developed countries have been accustomed to reach agreement—with a possible sacrifice of "efficiency" to ensure viable agreements. Developing countries, for their part, would have to consider whether the "one nation, one vote" system and large, unwieldy organizations are adequate instruments with which to reorder their relations with developed countries and formulate new "rules" to govern international economic relations. A willingness to allow various systems of representation that limit the number of developing countries that can participate directly in decision-making forums—as already has been done in the Interim Committee of the IMF and in the Joint Bank/Fund Development Committee and has been proposed for developed-developing country decision-making on energy, raw-materials, and development assistance issues—is the corollary of the increased autonomy which developing countries could derive from their collective actions.

A policy of "changing only enough to remain the same" may be tempting to developed countries as a way out of the present problems con-

154

fronting international systems. An important premise of this approach is the view that OPEC and "producer power" are transient phenomena. This premise, however, fails to recognize that the developing countries have long sought greater political and economic autonomy and that the oil price rise was not the sole cause of other actions by raw-material producers or of the cohesiveness of the nonaligned group of nations. It was merely the most striking of many on-going efforts to achieve increased economic power. These efforts received impetus from OPEC, but they will continue regardless of the fate of the cartel. Meeting these efforts with palliative measures therefore cannot be expected to eliminate the potential for economic conflict that exists between developing and developed countries. The developing countries will not want to accept any form of cooperation that merely involves minimal changes and leaves international inequalities unchanged.

Having long relied largely on bilateral approaches to developing nations, U.S. policy makers now find it difficult to accept the pluralism and diffusion of power that have resulted from the economic advancement of the Third World. A multiplicity of small gains by developing countries in investment and trade relations has not led to the creation of a center of power that easily can be incorporated into policy-making decisions. The temptation therefore may be to continue to base foreign economic policies on a key-country approach that leaves most of Africa, Asia, and Latin America out of the international decision-making process when it would be far more appropriate to incorporate representative developing countries from the outset in international negotiations dealing with trade, monetary, and financial systems and with other international economic affairs.

One result of the key-country approach to date has been a tendency to rely on aid as a response to the aspirations of developing nations. Indeed, there still are instances in which bilateral aid flows are used as ad hoc measures to ease political or economic disagreements or as quick solutions to problems affecting relations between a developed country and individual developing nations. Such an approach was never an adequate basis for relations between rich and poor countries and declines in real transfers of resources to developing nations now make it even more unacceptable.

Resource transfers are a necessary part of a long-term relationship between the United States and the developing world. But if international economic systems are to be successfully reformed to meet the needs of all nations, increased official and private resource transfers are only one of the steps that must be taken by developed nations. Neither the necessity to make provision for emergency assistance to certain countries nor the need for long-run concessional transfers of resources for development should be permitted to obscure the fact that an "aid relationship" is not appropriate for all developing countries, particularly those that are relatively better off. Furthermore, future transfers must take place without the paternalism that has often accompanied aid in the past. International measures which would link flows of capital from developed to developing countries to *automatically* available sources of finance could improve the presently unfavorable outlook for increased resource transfers and at the same time reduce opportunities for paternalistic intervention in recipient-country development policies.

Attitudes prevailing in developed countries are still impeding an effective dialogue between rich and poor nations. Thus a clearer understanding of the divergent views in developing and developed countries that have "politicized" economic systems are as important to the development of new international systems as are changes in the United Nations and other international agencies or the alteration of rich-country policies on trade, aid, investment, or technology.

The political challenge from the developing world is not something to be shunned by those who shape economic policy in the developed countries, even though it includes a critique of the value system underlying theoretical and applied economics in Western countries. An effort to comprehend the experience of developing countries that has led them to criticize and challenge the present world order would be far preferable to an insistence on the need to depoliticize international economic debates. Leaders of developing countries will interpret that insistence as an attempt to freeze current political-economic relations and thus halt their move beyond dependency.

This in turn would lead to further polarization and a tendency toward a grave North-South split at the very time when the world has become so interdependent that we require economic systems that take all countries into account. Global economic reform must be comprehensive and shaped with such ingenuity that all nations have an opportunity to gain from the operations of new international systems. The industrialized world and the more advanced developing nations need new ways to cope with their growing interdependence, and the poorest billion people on this globe urgently require more effective means to eliminate their abysmal poverty.

Chapter 10

Negotiating a New Bargain with the Rich Countries

Mahbub ul Haq

If history is to be our guide, the world may well be on the threshold of a historical turning point. On the national level, such a turning point was reached in the United States in the 1930s, when the New Deal elevated the working classes to partners in development and accepted them as an essential part of the consuming society. At the international level, we still have not arrived at that philosophic breakthrough when the development of the poor nations is considered an essential element in the sustained development of the rich nations and when the interests of both rich and poor nations are regarded as complementary and compatible rather than conflicting and irreconcilable. And yet we may be nearing that philosophic bridge.

However, if we are to cross this bridge, the rich nations must place the current demands of the Third World in their proper historical perspective, agree on a strategy of serious negotiations, help crystallize certain negotiating areas and principles, and determine the negotiating forums where mutually beneficial agreements can be thrashed out. It is in this spirit that the following few concrete suggestions are offered.

Perspective

It is important that the current demands of the developing countries for a New International Economic Order be perceived in correct perspective.

NOTE: This paper is based on remarks made by the author at a Conference on New Structures for Economic Interdependence (co-sponsored by the Institute on Man and Science and the Aspen Institute for Humanistic Studies, the Overseas Development Council, and the Charles F. Kettering Foundation) held at the United Nations and at the Institute for Man and Science, Rensselaerville, New York, May 15–18, 1975. For the report of that conference, see New Structures for Economic Interdependence (Rensselaerville, New York: Institute on Man and Science, August 1975).

First, the basic objective of the emerging trade union of the poor nations is to negotiate a new deal with the rich nations through the instrument of collective bargaining. The essence of this new deal lies in the objective of the developing countries to obtain greater equality of opportunity and to secure the right to sit as equals around the bargaining tables of the world. No massive redistribution of past income and wealth is being demanded: in fact, even if all the demands are added up, they do not exceed about 1 per cent of the GNP of the rich nations. What is really required, however, is a redistribution of future growth opportunities.

Second, the demand for a New International Economic Order should be regarded as a movement—as part of a historical process to be achieved over time rather than in any single negotiation. Like the political liberation movement of the 1940s and the 1950s, the movement for a new economic deal is likely to dominate the next few decades and cannot be dismissed casually by the rich nations.

Third, whatever deals are eventually negotiated must balance the interests of both the rich and the poor nations. The rich nations have to carefully weigh the costs of disruption against the costs of accommodation and to consider the fact that any conceivable cost of a new deal would amount to a very small proportion of their future growth in an orderly, cooperative framework. The poor nations have to recognize that, in an interdependent world, they cannot hurt the growth prospects of the rich nations without hurting their own chances of negotiating a better deal.

Strategy

The international community must also move quickly to develop a negotiating strategy with a view to:

(a) Reaching agreement that serious negotiations are acceptable on all elements of a New International Economic Order. The rich nations should declare their willingness to enter into such negotiations within the U.N. framework, and the poor nations should accept the fact, in turn, that the meetings of 1975 have merely begun the process of negotiation;

(b) Narrowing down the areas of negotiation to manageable proportions in the first instance and selecting the priorities fairly carefully so that the dialogue can move from the least divisive issues to the more difficult ones in a step-by-step approach. Conferences can seldom produce decisions unless agreement has been reached quietly in advance. At present, such quiet efforts are needed to reach preliminary understandings and a political consensus on the nature and form of the negotiations between the rich and the poor nations;

(c) Developing and agreeing on certain negotiating principles as an umbrella for future discussions. While detailed negotiations may have to proceed on a case-by-case basis, negotiation of an overall umbrella is absolutely essential in the first instance if the advantage of collective bargaining is to be retained;

(d) Formulating specific proposals for implementation. These proposals should bring out various alternatives and their implications for each side; and

(e) Determining the negotiating forums through which agreements can be reached on these proposals in a specified period of time.

Negotiating Principles

It may be useful to focus on a few critical areas to illustrate how the international community can move toward the formulation of certain negotiating principles.

International Trade. What is really wrong with the present economic order from the point of view of the poor nations? First, the exports of about twelve major primary commodities (excluding oil) account for about 80 per cent of the total export earnings of the developing countries. The final consumers pay over $200 billion for these commodities and their products while the primary producers obtain only about $30 billion—with the middlemen enjoying most of the difference. Second, the export earnings from these commodities fluctuate violently at times. Third, the purchasing power of these primary exports keeps declining in terms of manufactured imports. Fourth, the manufactured exports of the developing countries often face tariffs and quotas in the industrialized countries and constitute only about 7 per cent of world manufactured exports.

In order to improve this situation, at least certain negotiating principles can be articulated in the first instance:

(a) Producing countries must get a higher proportion of the final consumer price for their primary commodities. The present marketing and price structure should be examined to determine whether a better return to producers can be ensured by further processing of primary commodities, reduction of present imperfections in the commodity markets, squeezing of middlemen's profits, and organization by the producing countries of their own credit and distribution services;

(b) A better deal on primary commodities must be obtained *before* efforts are made at price stabilization or indexing—as in the case of oil—since stabilization of present low earnings will not achieve much. Possibilities of establishing an international commodity bank should be considered, both to improve present earnings and then to stabilize them;

(c) The consuming countries must be given long-term assurances of the security of supplies, without any deliberate interruptions or embargoes;

(d) Producers' associations in primary commodities should be accepted as legitimate instruments of collective bargaining to offset the present considerable concentration of economic power at the buying end; and,

(e) Present restrictions in the industrialized countries against the manufactured exports of the developing countries should be relaxed, and intra-developing-country trade in these manufactures expanded with a view to increasing the present share of the developing countries in world manufactured exports.

International Monetary System. Let us survey the situation in yet another key area—the present monetary system—from the point of view of the developing countries.

As Professor Triffin has convincingly argued, international liquidity is largely created by the national decisions of the richest industrialized nations as their national reserve currencies (e.g., dollars, sterling) are in international circulation.[1] During 1970–1974, international decisions on special drawing rights (SDRs) accounted for only 9 per cent of the total international reserve creation: even these decisions are primarily dictated by the needs of the rich nations. Not surprisingly, the developing countries obtained very little benefit from the creation of international liquidity: out of $102 billion of international reserves created during 1970–1974, the developing countries received $3.7 billion, or less than 4 per cent. As in any banking system, the poor get little credit.

As such, negotiating principles in this area will have to include the following:

(a) national reserve currencies should be gradually phased out and replaced by the creation of a truly international currency—like the SDRs—through the deliberate decisions of the International Monetary Fund (IMF);

(b) the volume of this international liquidity should be regulated by the IMF in line with the growth requirements in world trade and production, particularly to facilitate such growth in the developing countries;

(c) the distribution of this international liquidity should be adjusted so as to benefit the poorest countries, especially by establishing a link between the creation of international liquidity (SDRs) and long-term assistance; and

(d) in order to carry out these reforms, the present voting strength in the IMF should be changed to establish a near parity between the developing and the developed countries.

---

[1]See Robert Triffin, "The International Monetary System," in *New Structures for Economic Interdependence* (Rensselaerville, New York: The Institute on Man and Science, August 1975). Proceedings of a conference co-sponsored by the Institute on Man and Science and The Aspen Institute for Humanistic Studies, the Overseas Development Council, and the Charles F. Kettering Foundation.

International Resource Transfers. Another area of constant controversy between the rich and the poor nations—the present "aid order"—can serve as a final example. What is really wrong with it from the point of view of the developing countries? First, the present resource transfers from the rich to the poor nations are totally voluntary, dependent only on the fluctuating political will of the rich nations. Second, although a kind of international "deal" was made by the rich nations in accepting a target of 1 per cent of GNP, with 0.7 per cent in Official Development Assistance (ODA), to be transferred annually to the poor countries, in actual practice, ODA has declined in 1975 to 0.3 per cent for all member countries of the OECD's Development Assistance Committee (DAC) and to 0.2 per cent in the case of the United States. Third, not enough attention has been paid to the terms of international resource transfers, so that the developing countries have accumulated over $120 billion in financial debt whose servicing takes away about one half of new assistance every year.

If a negotiated framework for international resource transfers is to emerge, a fresh start needs to be made on a number of fronts:

(a) An element of automaticity must gradually be built into the international resource transfer system—e.g., through an SDR link with aid, certain sources of international financing such as royalties from seabed mining, and a tax on nonrenewable resources—so that these transfers become less than voluntary over time;

(b) The focus of international concessional assistance must shift to the poorest countries, and, within them, to the poorest segments of the population. As such, this assistance should be mainly in the form of grants, without creating a reverse obligation of mounting debt liability at a low level of poverty;

(c) International assistance should be linked in some measure to national programs aimed at satisfying minimum human needs. Such a target for the removal of poverty can be easily understood in the rich nations; it can be the basis of a shared effort between the national governments and the international community; it provides an allocative formula for concessional assistance; and it establishes a specific time period over which the task should be accomplished;

(d) One possible formula for international burden sharing could be to combine an expanding volume of financial funds at commercial rates from the liquidity-surplus members of the Organization of Petroleum Exporting Countries (OPEC) with subsidy funds made available by the industrialized countries and the richest OPEC countries. Such a formula is likely to provide resources on intermediate terms, with a grant element of about 50 to 60 per cent;

(e) Multilateral channels should be used for directing this assistance in preference to bilateral channels, since this will be consistent with greater automaticity of transfers, allocations based on poverty and need rather than on special relationships, and a more orderly system of burden sharing; and

(f) Arrangements must be made to provide a negotiating forum for an orderly settlement of past debts, possibly by convening a conference of principal creditors and debtors.

Conclusion

It is not the intention of this paper to attempt to prepare a concrete blueprint of a new "planetary bargain" that the poor nations seem to be seeking at present—a task that in any case would be impossible in the time available—but rather merely to illustrate a more positive approach toward reaching such a bargain. The report of the Group of Experts on the Structure of the United Nations System is aimed at providing sensible negotiating forums within the U.N. framework for an orderly dialogue on the elements of a New International Economic Order.[2] Technocratic proposals are easy to formulate. But what is really required for the success of the deliberations between rich and poor nations is political vision of an unprecedented nature that is inspired by the promise of the future, not clouded by the controversies of the past nor mired in the short-run problems of the present.

---

[2]Report of the Group of Experts on the Structure of the United Nations System, *A New United Nations Structure for Global Economic Cooperation*, U.N. Doc. No. E/ AC.62/9 (New York: United Nations, 1975).

Annex A

Nongovernmental
Statements

Annex A-1

The Belmont Statement: Self-Reliance and International Reform[1]

The following statement was drawn up and released by the developing-country participants in a North-South dialogue on world development held at the Belmont Conference Center in Elkridge, Maryland, and in Washington, D.C., March 18-21, 1974. Sponsored by the Overseas Development Council and the Charles F. Kettering Foundation, the four-day dialogue also involved in some of its sessions—as participants from the North—members of the staffs of the sponsoring organizations; representatives of the Rockefeller Foundation, the Brookings Institution, the Overseas Development Institute (London), and the Institute for Developing Economies (Tokyo); members and staff of the Trilateral Commission from Canada, Japan, the Netherlands, and the United States; and a group of U.S. Congressmen belonging to Members of Congress for Peace through Law.

The experts from developing countries whose shared views are reflected in the Belmont Statement (and in some individual cases elaborated in chapters contributed to this volume) are: Mr. Abdoul Barry, Regional Director for West Africa, Canadian University Service Overseas, Ouagadougou, Upper Volta; Dr. Pathé Diagne, African Studies Center, DePauw University and the Institut Fondamentale de l'Afrique Noire, Dakar, Senegal; Dr. El-Sayed Dohaia, International Economic Relations Centre, Institute for National Planning, Cairo, Egypt; His Excellency Neville Kanakaratne, Ambassador of Sri Lanka to the United States; Ms. Maria Teresa Moraes, Brazilian lawyer and journalist specializing in mass communications; Dr. Raimi Ola Ojikutu, Nigerian human biologist and anthropologist and former Woodrow Wilson Fellow; Dr. Samuel L. Parmar, Allahabad University, Allahabad, India; Dr. Félix Peña, Instituto para la Integración de América Latina, Buenos Aires, Argentina; Dr. Krishna Roy, Advisor, Centro de Estudios de Población, Lima, Peru; and Dr. Constantine V. Vaitsos, Advisor to the Board, Acuerdo de Cartagena, Lima, Peru.

Released two months prior to the Sixth Special Session of the U.N. General Assembly that produced the controversial "New International Economic Order" documents (see Annex B-1, p. 185), the Belmont Statement gives evidence of deep-rooted, considered support at the private level in the developing countries of the changes in economic relationships that the leaders of these nations are calling for in international forums.

Recent dramatic changes in the international economy severely affect the industrialized countries and the developing countries of Asia, Latin America, and Africa.

---

[1]Reprinted from Overseas Development Council Communique No. 24, May 1974.

Many developing countries will be hurt seriously by a lack of adequate purchasing power to meet their food, energy, and fertilizer requirements. International measures to assist them in dealing with this emergency situation are needed.

But such measures must now break free from the *ad hoc* approach that has characterized efforts to overcome other short-run crises. Even short-term measures—whether taken by individual nations or internationally—must be part of a coherent new framework of international cooperation. Short-term international assistance to help developing countries overcome balance-of-payments crises, for example, should be viewed not merely as a relief operation, but as an important means of enabling these countries to continue their endeavors to change their domestic institutions and policies—efforts which are clearly impeded, and in many instances halted, by the present food and energy emergencies. A new, fundamentally different approach is required at the international level to complement the efforts of many poor countries to increase the participation of their entire populations in the process of development and to ensure the more equitable distribution of its benefits.

A New Realism

There is a striking difference between the character of discussions of international economic cooperation in the 1960s and today. The optimism of the First United Nations Development Decade has disappeared; in its place, there is a new "crisis realism." For too long it was too readily assumed that the scientific and technological revolution of the world's rich nations promised a potential abundance which could, in the not too distant future, meet the growing aspirations resulting from the social revolution taking place in Africa, Asia, and Latin America. Policies of aid, trade, money, investment, and technology were explained in terms of a seeming complementarity between the needs of the developing countries and the capability of the developed. But experience has discredited these hopes.

Unprecedented world population growth has increased demand for essential resources. In many developing countries already oppressed by poverty and social injustice, overpopulation has become an increasingly unbearable burden. At the same time, rising affluence and per capita use of resources in the developed countries has added a second dimension to the global population crisis, thus contributing to the imbalance between world population and resources that is at the core of today's increasingly frequent global scarcities. The technological revolution—harnessed to the economic goals of the developed world—has also contributed greatly both to unprecedented scarcities of basic resources and to the serious maldistribution in their use, with a steadily larger share being consumed by the developed nations.

The Meaning of Self-Reliance

Given these harsh realities, there is a strong inclination in many developing countries today to be self-reliant—that is, to fashion their economic policies according to the needs, problems, and experience of their own economies. Emphasis on the domestic determination of development priorities is becoming increasingly widespread in these countries. It is important for the future of international cooperation—and for the prospect of a genuine dialogue among nations—that the concept of self-reliance not be misunderstood or misrepresented in the developed world.

Experience with the development process over the last two decades has made developing countries wary of two things: 1) concepts, policies, and patterns of development which are borrowed from developed nations and which do not allow the participation of the poor majority in development and 2) patterns of international

166

economic cooperation which continue to make trade, aid, investment, monetary policy, and technology instruments of domination by the developed nations.

Two decades of experience with international economic cooperation have also convinced many leaders in the developing countries that basic changes in their economies and social systems are more important than quantitative increases in external resource transfers. There is, therefore, a greater desire for social justice—not only to meet the immediate needs of the weaker segments of the population but also as the only way to ensure satisfactory economic growth in the long run. It is now clear that popular participation in the production process and a better distribution of domestic income are preconditions of the kind of broadly based growth that developing countries need.

The grave imbalance between population and resource availability in many of these countries makes it urgent for them to avoid the pitfalls of wasteful resource use that characterize industrial countries and to strive at the same time for social justice and economic progress for their populations as a whole. Simultaneous actions on both of these fronts are indispensable to an effective program of population stability.

The new emphasis on self-reliance implies not a lessening of interest in international cooperation but a striving to make relations between developed and underdeveloped countries reflect genuine interdependence and international economic justice. To the extent that developed nations translate their affirmation of interdependence into more equitable international structures, there should be no fundamental conflict between self-reliant development and increased international economic cooperation.

The Lessons of Scarcity

Prior to the energy crisis of recent months, there was little indication that the developed nations—despite their long-standing reliance on resources located in Africa, Asia, and Latin America and their increasing affirmations of global interdependence—really felt any sense of dependence on the developing countries. International cooperation thus tended to be a polite label for unequal relations between the strong and the weak. However, the current situation of worldwide resource scarcities makes it possible, perhaps for the first time, for both developed and developing countries to think of international economic relations in terms of effective mutual dependence and reciprocity.

Because scarcity is a new experience for the industrial countries, they feel threatened and may be tempted to take unilateral actions that could seriously hamper attempts to build a framework of international relations in which all nations have a mutual interest. Yet an objective assessment of the present situation suggests that it is a unique opportunity to make international cooperation into a real partnership. More than ever before, it is necessary for the world community to take a *global* approach to the world's resources and to the structure and operation of international economic relationships. Solving the problem of scarcity of essential resources such as food, energy, fertilizer, other important commodities, as well as raw-material inputs for manufactured goods requires major changes in the institutions, rules, and power relationships that make up the international economic order. While this imposes responsibilities on all countries, those of the developed are necessarily special—both because they control and use a larger part of these resources and because they have much greater influence on the operation of world economic systems.

Toward New "Rules of the Game"

Human needs have to be seen in a global framework. International cooperation has to be geared to these needs not only to overcome short-term problems of scarcity but to begin to come to grips with the long-term problem of a more equitable distribution and use of resources.

The countries of Africa, Asia, and Latin America cannot accept any attempt by the industrial nations to freeze the present structure of international power. Developing countries need to establish control over the development of their own resources. Major changes are necessary in the present "rules of the game" governing trade and access to all resources—raw materials, manufactured products, capital, and technology. These reforms could make development cooperation a reality rather than a dominance-dependence relationship. For example, there must be real participation by the developing countries in international decisions affecting trade, investment, and monetary affairs.

The current scarcity of essential resources has led to the emergence of strong sellers' markets for many raw materials and commodities. This trend will prove advantageous to a number of developing countries and provide them with economic power which could be used to promote much-needed structural changes in their economies. Resource-rich developed countries, notably the United States and Canada, also stand to gain in the balance. But in many poor countries, development efforts and survival itself will be greatly jeopardized by the lack of adequate purchasing power to meet even their basic requirements of these essential resources—not only in 1974, but for the remainder of the decade. These countries therefore will need major additional outside assistance. It is important, however, that this assistance be provided in ways that begin to change the international economic order *now*, and that are designed to lessen the vulnerability of these countries to global scarcities as well as other external political-economic events in the *future*.

To increase their participation in international systems, developing countries will also require greater knowledge of the economic and political factors which shape foreign official and private decisions. Hence the improvement of knowledge through research and development, better information systems, and training will be a significant component of any strengthening of their bargaining capacity.

If international development cooperation continues to concentrate solely on the transfer of financial resources and is not buttressed by institutional changes which seek social justice—both within nations and at the international level—it will fall far short of its maximum contribution to the process of development in the poor countries. Indeed, in the absence of major changes in the conduct of international economic relations, the effectiveness of resource transfers will continue to be restricted by the inadequacy of the institutions that channel and absorb them.

Some Fundamental Questions

If there is to be an effective new framework of international development cooperation, major questions such as the following must be considered jointly by the developed and developing nations:

1. What are the main constraints to partnership in international relations? Why have both developed and developing countries been lacking in political will—and the political power—to translate their expressed good intentions into policies?

2. What kinds of changes are necessary to adapt the institutional framework of international economic relations to the new realities of power and the demands of equitable development? What changes are needed in the structure of international agencies—in the United Nations, the International Monetary Fund, the World Bank, the GATT, and others? Are new institutions or mechanisms needed?

3. How can international economic cooperation help reduce present and po-

tential conflicts of interest among developing nations—particularly those between the large and the relatively less powerful developing nations?

4. What steps should be taken to shape a comprehensive approach to international economic cooperation—one which sees aid, trade, monetary affairs, investment, and technology as interrelated rather than isolated systems and which ensures fair prices and fair access to global resources for all parties?

5. What changes are necessary to promote policies of disarmament and the reduction of waste by consumers to check the existing misdirection of resources?

A Challenge and an Opportunity

The inadequacies of international cooperation over the past twenty years point to a need for a new kind of complementarity: between social justice within nations and international economic justice. This complementarity should be the cornerstone of a new infrastructure of international economic relations—providing for more equitable sharing of resources and economic power through a system of supportive social and political institutions.

The present crisis can also be an opportunity if all nations and international institutions begin to move in this direction.

Annex A-2

The Cocoyoc Declaration[1]

In the fall of 1974, an international symposium on "Patterns of Resource Use, Environment and Development Strategies" was organized by the U.N. Environment Program (UNEP) and the U.N. Conference on Trade and Development (UNCTAD) in close cooperation with the Mexican Government. Held in Cocoyoc, Mexico (October 8-12), the symposium was chaired by Lady Jackson (Barbara Ward), and its participants included the following social scientists, natural scientists, and U.N. officials: Samir Amin, Mauro O. Cardoso Amorelli, Vladimir Baum, Sujatno Birowo, Neoma Castaneda, W. K. Chagula, Gamani Corea, J. J. Ebong, Johan Galtung, José A. Gallego Gredilla, Enrique V. Iglesias, K. Kassas, Vladimir Kollontai, Paul Kaya, M. Kermanj, Thomas A. Lambo, M. Lemeshev, Wassily Leontief, Marc Nerfin, J. Pajestka, Ashok Parthasarathi, George Picht, Ignacy Sachs, Juan Somavia, Rodolfo Stavenhagen, Jack Stone, Maurice Strong, Mostafa Tolba, Shigeto Tsuru, Mahbub ul Haq, Vicente Sanchez, and Alfonso Santa Cruz. All of the symposium's members participated in their personal capacities.

The Declaration—which endorses the "very preliminary step" taken by the U.N. General Assembly's Sixth Special Session (see Annex B-1, p. 185) and encourages the early adoption of the then still pending Charter of Economic Rights and Duties of States (see Annex B-2, p. 203)—constitutes an important personal statement by recognized experts from both developing and developed countries. It places considerable emphasis on the feasibility of designing and implementing new systems "more capable of meeting the 'inner limits' of basic needs for all the world's people . . . without violating the 'outer limits' of the planet's resources and environment."

Thirty years have passed since the signing of the United Nations Charter launched the effort to establish a new international order. Today, that order has reached a critical turning point. Its hopes of creating a better life for the whole human family have been largely frustrated. It has proved impossible to meet the 'inner limits' of satisfying fundamental human needs. On the contrary, more people are hungry, sick, shelterless and illiterate today than when the United Nations was first set up.

At the same time, new and unforeseen concerns have begun to darken the international prospects. Environmental degradation and the rising pressure on resources raise the question whether the 'outer limits' of the planet's physical integrity may not be at risk.

And to these preoccupations must be added the realization that the next thirty years will bring a doubling of world population. Another world on top of this, equal in numbers, demands and hopes.

---

[1]Reprinted from *Development Dialogue*, No. 2 (1974), pp. 88–96. (Published by the Dag Hammarskjold Foundation, Uppsala, Sweden.)

But these critical pressures give no reason to despair of the human enterprise, provided we undertake the necessary changes. The first point to be underlined is that the failure of world society to provide 'a safe and happy life' for all is not caused by any present lack of physical resources. The problem today is not one of absolute physical shortages but of economic and social maldistribution and misuse; mankind's predicament is rooted primarily in economic and social structures and behaviour within and between countries.

Much of the world has not yet emerged from the historical consequences of almost five centuries of colonial control which concentrated economic power so overwhelmingly in the hands of a small group of nations. To this day, at least three quarters of the world's income, investment, services and almost all of the world's research are in the hands of one quarter of its people.

The solution of these problems cannot be left to the automatic operation of market mechanisms. The traditional market makes resources available to those who can buy them rather than those who need them, it stimulates artificial demands and builds waste into the production process, and even underutilizes resources. In the international system the powerful nations have secured the poor countries' raw materials at low prices (for example, the price of petroleum fell decisively between 1950 and 1970), they have engrossed all the value added from processing the materials and they have sold the manufactures back, often at monopoly prices.

At the same time, the very cheapness of the materials was one element in encouraging the industrialized nations to indulge in careless and extravagant use of the imported materials. Once again, energy is the best example. Oil at just over a dollar a barrel stimulated a growth in energy use of between six and eleven per cent a year. In Europe, the annual increase in car registrations reached twenty per cent.

Indeed pre-emption by the rich of a disproportionate share of key resources conflicts directly with the longer term interests of the poor by impairing their ultimate access to resources necessary to their development and by increasing their cost. All the more reason for creating a new system of evaluating resources which takes into account the benefits and the burdens for the developing countries.

The overall effect of such biased economic relationships can best be seen in the contrast in consumption. A North American or a European child, on average, consumes outrageously more than his Indian or African counterpart—a fact which makes it specious to attribute pressure on world resources entirely to the growth of Third World population.

Population growth is, of course, one element in the growing pressures on world supplies. The planet is finite and an indefinite multiplication of both numbers and claims cannot be endlessly sustained. Moreover, shortages can occur locally long before there is any prospect of a general exhaustion of particular resources. A policy for sane resource conservation and for some forms of management of ultimately scarce resources within the framework of new economic order must soon replace today's careless rapacity. But the point in the existing world situation is that the huge contrasts in per capita consumption between the rich minority and the poor majority have far more effect than their relative numbers on resource use and depletion. We can go further. Since a lack of resources for full human development is, as the Bucharest Conference on Population clearly recognized, one of the continuing causes of explosive population growth, to deprive nations of the means of development directly exacerbates their demographic problems.

These unequal economic relationships contribute directly to environmental pressures. The cheapness of materials has been one factor in increasing pollution and encouraging waste and the throwaway economy among the rich. And continued poverty in many developing countries has often compelled the people to cultivate marginal lands at great risk of soil erosion or to migrate to the physically degraded and overcrowded cities.

Nor are the evils which flow from excessive reliance on the market system confined to international relationships. The experience of the last thirty years is that the exclusive pursuit of economic growth, guided by the market and undertaken by and for the powerful cities, has the same destructive effects inside developing countries. The richest 5 per cent engross all the gain while the poorest 20 per cent can actually grow poorer still. And at the local as at the international level the evils of material poverty are compounded by the people's lack of participation and human dignity, by their lack of any power to determine their own fate.

Nothing more clearly illustrates both the need to reform the present economic order and the possibility of doing so than the crisis that has arisen in world markets during the last two years. The trebling of the price of food, fertilizers and manufactures in the wake of world inflation has most severely hit the world's poorest peoples. Indeed, this winter the risk of a complete shortfall in supplies threatens the lives of millions in the Third World. But it cannot be called absolute shortage. The grain exists, but it is being eaten elsewhere by very well-fed people. Grain consumption in North America has grown per capita by 350 pounds, largely in meat products, since 1965—to reach 1900 pounds today. Yet this extra 350 pounds is almost equal to an Indian's total annual consumption. North Americans were hardly starving in 1965. The increase since then has contributed to super-consumption which even threatens health. Thus, in physical terms, there need be no shortage this winter. It requires only a small release from the 'surplus' of the rich to meet the entire Asian shortfall. There could hardly be a more vivid example of the over-consumption of the wealthy nations contributing directly to the underconsumption of the world's poor.

The quadrupling of oil prices through the combined action of the oil producers sharply alters the balance of power in world markets and redistributes resources massively to some Third World countries. Its effect has been to reverse decisively the balance of advantage in the oil trade and to place close to 100 [billion dollars] a year at the disposal of some Third World nations. Moreover, in an area critical to the economies of industrialized states, a profound reversal of power exposes them to the condition long familiar in the Third World—lack of control over vital economic decisions.

Nothing could illustrate more clearly the degree to which the world market system which has continuously operated to increase the power and wealth of the rich and maintain the relative deprivation of the poor is rooted not in unchangeable physical circumstance but in political relationships which can, of their very nature, undergo profound reversals and transformations. In a sense, a new economic order is already struggling to be born. The crisis of the old system can also be the opportunity of the new.

It is true that, at present, the outlook seems to hold little but confrontation, misunderstanding, threats and angry dispute. But again, we repeat, there is no reason to despair. The crisis can also be a moment of truth from which the nations learn to acknowledge the bankruptcy of the old system and to seek the framework of a new economic order.

The task of statemanship is thus to attempt to guide the nations, with all their differences in interest, power and fortune, towards a new system more capable of meeting the 'inner limits' of basic human needs for all the world's people and of doing so without violating the 'outer limits' of the planet's resources and environment. It is because we believe this enterprise to be both vital and possible that we set down a number of changes, in the conduct of economic policy, in the direction of

172

development and in planetary conservation, which appear to us to be essential components of the new system.

The Purpose of Development

Our first concern is to redefine the whole purpose of development. This should not be to develop things but to develop man. Human beings have basic needs: food, shelter, clothing, health, education. Any process of growth that does not lead to their fulfillment—or, even worse, disrupts them—is a travesty of the idea of development. We are still in a stage where the most important concern of development is the level of satisfaction of basic needs for the poorest sections of the population in society. The primary purpose of economic growth should be to ensure the improvement of conditions for these groups. A growth process that benefits only the wealthiest minority and maintains or even increases the disparities between and within countries is not development. It is exploitation. And the time for starting the type of economic growth that leads to better distribution and to the satisfaction of the basic needs for all is today. We believe that thirty years of experience with the hope that rapid economic growth benefiting the few will 'trickle down' to the mass of the people has proved to be illusory. We therefore reject the idea of 'growth first, justice in the distribution of benefits later'.

Development should not be limited to the satisfaction of basic needs. There are other needs, other goals, and other values. Development includes freedom of expression and impression, the right to give and to receive ideas and stimulus. There is a deep social need to participate in shaping the basis of one's own existence, and to make some contribution to the fashioning of the world's future. Above all, development includes the right to work, by which we mean not simply having a job but finding self-realization in work, the right not to be alienated through production processes that use human beings simply as tools.

The Diversity of Development

Many of these more than material needs, goals and values, depend on the satisfaction of the basic needs which are our primary concern. There is no consensus today what strategies to pursue in order to arrive at the satisfaction of basic needs. But there are some good examples even among poor countries. They make clear that the point of departure for the development process varies considerably from one country to another, for historical, cultural and other reasons. Consequently, we emphasize the need for pursuing many different roads of development. We reject the unilinear view which sees development essentially and inevitably as the effort to imitate the historical model of the countries that for various reasons happen to be rich today. For this reason, we reject the concept of 'gaps' in development. The goal is not to 'catch up', but to ensure the quality of life for all with a productive base compatible with the needs of future generations.

We have spoken of the minimum satisfaction of basic needs. But there is also a maximum level, there are ceilings as well as floors. Man must eat to live. But he can also over-eat. It does not help us much to produce and consume more and more if the result is an ever increasing need for tranquilizers and mental hospitals. And just as man has a limited capacity to absorb material goods, we know that the biosphere has a finite carrying capacity. Some countries tax it in a way that is far out of proportion with their share in world population. Thus they create environment problems for others as well as for themselves.

Consequently, the world is today not only faced with the anomaly of underdevelopment. We may also talk about overconsumptive types of development that violate the 'inner limits' of man and the 'outer limits' of nature. Seen in this perspective, we are all in need of a redefinition of our goals, of new development strategies, of new life styles, including more modest patterns of consumption among the rich. Even though the first priority goes to securing the minima we shall be looking for those development strategies that also may help the affluent countries, in their enlightened self-interest, in finding more human patterns of life, less exploitative of nature, of others, of oneself.

Self-Reliance

We believe that one basic strategy of development will have to be increased national self-reliance. It does not mean autarchy. It implies mutual benefits from trade and cooperation and a fairer redistribution of resources satisfying the basic needs. It does mean self-confidence, reliance primarily on one's own resources, human and natural, and the capacity for autonomous goal-setting and decision-making. It excludes dependence on outside influences and powers that can be converted into political pressure. It excludes exploitative trade patterns depriving countries of their natural resources for their own development. There is obviously a scope for transfer of technology, but the thrust should be on adaptation and the generation of local technology. It implies decentralization of the world economy, and sometimes also of the national economy to enhance the sense of personal participation. But it also implies increased international cooperation for collective self-reliance. Above all, it means trust in people and nations, reliance on the capacity of people themselves to invent and generate new resources and techniques, to increase their capacity to absorb them, to put them to socially beneficial use, to take a measure of command over the economy, and to generate their own way of life.

In this process education for full social awareness and participation will play a fundamental role and the extent to which this is compatible with present patterns of schooling will have to be explored.

To arrive at this condition of self-reliance, fundamental economic, social and political changes in the structure of society will often be necessary. Equally necessary is the development of an international system compatible with and capable of supporting moves towards self-reliance.

Self-reliance at national levels may also imply a temporary detachment from the present economic system; it is impossible to develop self-reliance through full participation in a system that perpetuates economic dependence. Large parts of the world of today consist of a center exploiting a vast periphery and also our common heritage, the biosphere. The ideal we need is a harmonized cooperative world in which each part is a center, living at the expense of nobody else, in partnership with nature and in solidarity with future generations.

There is an international power structure that will resist moves in this direction. Its methods are well known: the purposive maintenance of the built-in bias of the existing international market mechanisms, other forms of economic manipulation, withdrawing or withholding credits, embargoes, economic sanctions, subversive use of intelligence agencies, repression including torture, counter-insurgency operations, even full-scale intervention. To those contemplating the use of such methods we say: 'Hands-off. Leave countries to find their own road to a fuller life for their citizens.' To those who are the—sometimes unwilling—tools of such designs—scholars, businessmen, police, soldiers and many others—we would say: 'Refuse to be used for purposes of denying another nation the right to develop itself.' To the natural and social scientists, who help design the instruments of oppression, we would say: 'The world needs your talents for constructive purposes, to develop new technologies that benefit man and do not harm the environment.'

174

Suggestions for Action

We call on political leaders, governments, international organizations and the scientific community to use their imagination and resources to elaborate and start implementing, as soon as possible, programs aimed at satisfying the basic needs of the poorest peoples all over the world, including, wherever appropriate, the distribution of goods in kind. These programs should be designed in such a way as to ensure adequate conservation of resources and protection of the environment.

We consider that the above task could be made easier by instituting a new more cooperative and equitable international economic order.

We are aware that the world system and the national policies cannot be changed overnight. The major changes which are required to answer the critical challenges facing mankind at this turning point of history need some time to mature. But they have to be started immediately, and acquire a growing impetus. The Special Session of the General Assembly of the United Nations on a New Economic Order has given the process a right start and we fully endorse it. This, however, is a very preliminary step which should develop into a great tide of international activities.

The Charter of Economic Rights and Duties of States, proposed by the President of Mexico, Lic. Luis Echeverría, and now under discussion at the United Nations, would be a further important step in the right direction. We urge that it be adopted as early as possible.

In a framework of national sovereignty over natural resources, governments and international institutions should further the management of resources and environment on a global scale. The first aim would be to benefit those who need these resources most and to do so in accordance with the principle of solidarity with future generations.

We support the setting up of strong international regimes for the exploitation of common property resources that do not fall under any national jurisdiction. We especially emphasize the importance of the ocean floor and its subsoil, possibly also the water column above it. An oceans regime has to be established with all countries of the world represented, favoring none and discriminating against none, with jurisdiction over a maximum area of the oceans. Such a regime would gradually develop the type of resource-conserving and environmentally sound technology required to explore, develop, process and distribute ocean resources for the benefit of those who need them most.

The uses of international commons should be taxed for the benefit of the poorest strata of the poor countries. For instance, tolls could be levied from vessels crossing the high seas. This could be a first step towards the establishment of an international taxation system aimed at providing automatic transfers of resources to development assistance. Together with the release of funds through disarmament, international taxation should eventually replace traditional assistance programmes. Pending the establishment of these new mechanisms, we strongly recommend that the flow in international resources to Third World countries should be greatly increased and rigorously dedicated to basic needs of the poorest strata of society.

Science and technology must be responsive to the goals we are pursuing. Present research and development patterns do not effectively contribute to them. We call on universities, other institutions of higher learning, research organizations, scientific associations all over the world to reconsider their priorities. Mindful of the benefits deriving from free and basic research, we underline the fact that there is a reservoir of underutilized creative energy in the whole scientific community of the world, and that it should be more focussed on research for the satis-

175

faction of fundamental needs. This research should be done as far as possible in the poor countries and thus help to reverse the brain-drain.

A rejuvenated United Nations System should be used to strengthen the local capabilities for research and technology assessment in the developing countries, to promote cooperation between them in these areas and to support research in a better and more imaginative utilization of potentially abundant resources for the satisfaction of the fundamental needs of mankind.

At the same time, new approaches to development styles ought to be introduced at the national level. They call for imaginative research into alternative consumption patterns, technological styles, land use strategies as well as the institutional framework and the educational requirements to sustain them. Resource-absorbing and waste-creating overconsumption should be restrained while production of essentials for the poorest sections of the population is stepped up. Low waste and clean technologies should replace the environmentally disruptive ones. More harmonious networks of human settlements could be evolved to avoid further congestion of metropolitan areas and marginalization of the countryside.

In many developing countries the new development styles would imply a much more rational use of the available labour-force to implement programmes aimed at the conservation of natural resources, enhancement of environment, creation of the necessary infrastructure and services to grow more food as well as the strengthening of domestic industrial capacity to turn out commodities satisfying basic needs.

On the assumption of a more equitable international economic order, some of the problems of resource maldistribution and space use could be taken care of by changing the industrial geography of the world. Energy, resource and environmental considerations add new strength to the legitimate aspirations of the poor countries to see their share in world industrial production considerably increased.

Concrete experiments in the field are also necessary. We consider that the present efforts of the United Nations Environment Programme to design strategies and assist projects for ecologically sound socio-economic development (eco-development) at the local and regional level constitute an important contribution to this task. Conditions should be created for people to learn by themselves through practice how to make the best possible use of the specific resources of the ecosystem in which they live, how to design appropriate technologies, how to organize and educate themselves to this end.

We call on leaders of public opinion, on educators, on all interested bodies to contribute to an increased public awareness of both the origins and the severity of the critical situation facing mankind today. Everybody has the right to understand fully the nature of the system of which he is a part, as a producer, as a consumer, as one among the billions populating the earth. He has a right to know who benefits from the fruits of his work, who benefits from what he buys and sells, and the degree to which he enhances or degrades his planetary inheritance.

We call on governments to prepare themselves for action at the 1975 Special Session of the United Nations General Assembly so that the dimension and concepts of development are expanded, that the goals of development are given their rightful place in the United Nations System and the necessary structural changes initiated. We affirm our belief that since the issues of development, environment and resource use are essentially global and concern the well-being of all mankind, governments should fully use the mechanisms of the United Nations for their resolution and that the United Nations system should be renewed and strengthen[ed] to be capable of its new responsibilities.

Epilogue

We recognize the threats to both the 'inner limits' of basic human needs and the 'outer limits' of the planet's physical resources. But we also believe that a new sense of respect for fundamental human rights and for the preservation of our planet is growing up behind the angry divisions and confrontations of our day.

We have faith in the future of mankind on this planet. We believe that ways of life and social systems can be evolved that are more just, less arrogant in their material demands, more respectful of the whole planetary environment. The road forward does not lie through the despair of doom-watching nor through the easy optimism of successive technological fixes. It lies through a careful and dispassionate assessment of the 'outer limits', through the cooperative search for ways to achieve the 'inner limits' of fundamental human rights, through the building of social structures to express those rights, and through all the patient work of devising techniques and styles of development which enhance and preserve our planetary inheritance.

Annex A-3

Communique of the
Third World Forum Conference
in Karachi¹

The Third World Forum is a worldwide association of leading social scientists and intellectuals from the developing countries of Asia, Africa, and Latin America who have a strong personal commitment to the development of their own countries and to the United Nations Charter of Basic Human Rights.

The Third World Forum reflects the aspirations and needs of the Third World countries in the middle 1970s. Its aim is to facilitate the creation of a more just and equitable world, a world in which the basic needs of every human being in terms of clothing, housing, education, medical care and employment are adequately covered.

The Third World Forum is a completely independent organization with no governmental or institutional affiliations. The Forum offers its support to all liberal elements all over the world in working towards the establishment of a more equitable world order.

1. An inaugural meeting of the Third World Forum was held in Karachi from 5 to 10 January 1975 to discuss critical elements in the national and international economic order as well as to discuss means of action to meet the continuing crisis in the relationship between the industrialized and the developing countries.

2. The participants to the Forum supported the objectives stated in the Santiago Declaration and agreed on the need for a continued intellectual revolution to overcome the dependence of the Third World and for profound changes in the internal and external order that the developing countries face today. They felt that they could best make a contribution to the promotion of these aims by organizing a a Third World Forum on a permanent basis. The delegates accordingly considered and adopted a constitution to found such a Forum.

Functions and Organization of the Forum

3. It was agreed that, in line with the Santiago Declaration, the principal functions of the Forum would be to:

   (a) provide an intellectual platform for an exchange of views on alternative development strategies and their policy implications;

---

¹Both the descriptive opening statement and the text of the Communique are reprinted from a mimeographed version issued by the Forum and obtainable from its individual members.

(b) provide intellectual support to the Third World countries in devising their policy options and negotiating alternatives on all relevant development issues;

(c) stimulate and organize relevant socio-economic research, particularly through the regional and national research institutes, in the Third World;

(d) foster the interchange of relevant ideas and research, identify the areas of Third World interdependence and, to this end, seek to influence appropriate international, regional and national decision-making bodies to recognize and protect the legitimate rights and interests of the people of the Third World;

(e) provide support to programmes of action on all types of cooperation among developing countries by:

> (i) suggesting ideas, methods, and types of action that would be most effective for mutual cooperation;
>
> (ii) defining areas in which the Third World countries could offer assistance or could benefit from assistance provided by other Third World countries;
>
> (iii) examining and analyzing mutual cooperation in all fields, including science and technology, with the purpose of facilitating the exchange of ideas, information and an efficient transfer of these between Third World countries;

(f) express views on international issues affecting the Third World and its relations with the developed world.

4. It was agreed that the membership to the Forum will be open to leading social scientists, eminent experts and other intellectuals—both men and women from the Third World acting in their personal capacities.

5. The following were elected to form the first Executive Committee of the Forum for a period of two years. It was decided to enlarge the membership of the Executive Committee to 16 at a later stage as the total membership of the Forum expands.

Enrique V. Iglesias
Enrique Oteiza
Oscar Pino-Santos
Samir Amin
Justinian Rweyemamu
Ikenna Nzimiro
Mohamed Said al Attar
Mahbub ul Haq
Gamani Corea

6. The Executive Committee was authorized to prepare concrete plans for the permanent location of the secretariat of the Forum in a Third World country and for the financing of its activities.

National Development Strategies

7. The participants considered the need for the new development strategies, more responsive to the aspirations of their masses. They agreed that, while there could be many separate roads to development, the new strategies must be based on at least the following principles:

[a] the real focus should be on the satisfaction of basic human needs and on a meaningful participation of the masses in the shaping of economic and social change;

[b] the policies of self-reliance should be encouraged, with emphasis on a self-confident and creative use of local resources, manpower, technology and knowledge, and with growing stress on collective self-reliance between the societies of the Third World;

[c] the concepts of development should embrace the political needs and cultural patterns of their societies, so that life styles in the Third World do not become a pale imitation of somebody else's experience but a proud extension of their own value systems.

8. The participants also reviewed the national development strategies of a few selected countries which had adopted a distinctive style of their own. They agreed that there should be a greater exchange of experience in economic development between the developing countries themselves, with more organized publications and visits to one another than the traditional visits to the centers of the developed countries.

9. In order to promote these concerns, the Forum agreed to:

(a) sponsor specific studies on national development strategies;
(b) discuss and disseminate the results of such studies; and
(c) organize seminars and visits for a more orderly exchange of development experience. The participants authorized the Executive Committee to develop a concrete programme of action to implement these concerns.

New International Economic Order

10. The participants reviewed the nature of the current inequitable world order and discussed specific proposals for the establishment of a more just international economic order.

11. The participants agreed that the present crisis in the world system was neither a "normal" economic recession nor the result of the oil problem. It, in fact, marked the gradual crumbling of an old order in which a group of rich nations constituting the developed center continuously expanded by the use of energy and raw materials provided by the poor nations at the periphery at cheap prices. The increase in the price of oil by the OPEC could, therefore, be seen as a part of the struggle of the Third World to obtain a better deal from the world order. But this struggle would neither be complete nor meaningful until other poor nations at the periphery also obtained a fairer deal and unless the present polarization between the countries at the center and those at the periphery was changed by different patterns of collective self-reliance among the Third World countries.

12. The participants discussed a number of specific proposals to improve the prospects of the Third World in the present world order. These proposals included:

[a] the establishment of a Commodity Bank to strengthen commodities in a weak bargaining position;

[b] the promotion of producers' associations for suitable commodities for ensuring better supply management and for creating countervailing power against the existing concentration of control at the buying end;

[c] more control over the creation and distribution of international credit by the Third World;

[d] bold policy and institutional measures to promote trade among the countries of the Third World including the establishment of payment unions within the Third World;

180

[e] a new alliance of interdependence including the flow of investments towards agriculture production to various Third World countries;

[f] a conference of principal creditors and debtors to reach an agreement on the basic principles of a long term settlement of the past debt that the developing countries have accumulated;

[g] the termination of all unfavorable contracts, leases and concessions given to the multinational corporations by the developing countries for the exploitation of their natural resources and their renegotiation;

[h] establishment of a Third World Development Bank financed by OPEC and other Third World countries;

[i] a new and more automatic basis for international transfer of resources to the poor nations from traditional sources which could be financed from a development cess on non-renewable resources exported from the Third World to the industrialized countries, royalties from ocean bed mining and link between SDRs and aid;

[j] democratization of control over international financial institutions by obtaining at least 50 per cent of the voting power for the Third World;

[k] setting up of institutions of intellectual self-reliance within the Third World financed by a trust fund of the order of $1 billion.

13. In connection with these initiatives the participants considered that close cooperation between OPEC and other parts of the Third World was vital in the next stage of this continuing struggle if the Third World was to succeed in its efforts to obtain more justice from the world order and if oil exporting countries were to expect to consolidate and maintain their gains.

14. It was agreed that, in order to prepare a concrete program of action—

(a) various proposals should be placed in a clear time perspective;

(b) they should be backed up by concrete studies so as to carry both conviction and weight; and

(c) there should be an identification of the specific fora and implementation machinery through which they ought to be pursued.

Besides the need for concrete elaboration of the above proposals, the following studies were identified to examine the legitimacy of existing international economic relations:

[a] the present margins between producers return and consumers price for important commodity exports of the Third World;

[b] the waste and inefficiencies in the consumption as well as the production patterns;

[c] the magnitude of the existing debt as compared with the surpluses which were extracted from the developing world during the colonial era and the surpluses now being extracted through unjust trade and investment patterns;

[d] the systematic intellectual biases which have been diffused in much of the literature produced in the developed world on such questions as economic development, international trade, welfare economics and project criteria;

[e] the means by which the media in the developing world could develop its own networks aimed at informing the peoples of the Third World of each other's needs, aspirations and achievements.

15. The participants authorized the Executive Committee to prepare a concrete plan of studies, including the identification of individuals and institutions for preparing these studies within specified time periods and the selection of fora and instruments through which implementation of concrete proposals should be pressed.

16. The Forum appealed to all intellectuals of the Third World to get organized behind these concerns of vital importance to their societies and to initiate action at all levels to create a climate for more equitable national and international orders.

The Forum concluded by extending its warm thanks to the Government of Pakistan for its generous invitation to hold the plenary session in Karachi and to the National Bank of Pakistan for the excellent arrangements for the conduct of the conference, to the news media of Pakistan for their extensive coverage and support for the activities of the Forum and to the people of Pakistan who are in an essential part of the struggle which the entire Third World is waging and for which the Third World Forum was established on a permanent basis during its historic meeting in Karachi. The Forum expressed its deep appreciation to the Governments of Sweden and Canada for providing funds for the meeting.

Annex B

Official Declarations

Annex B-1

Declaration and Action Programme on the Establishment of a New International Economic Order[1]

The Sixth Special Session of the U.N. General Assembly was convened—on remarkably short notice and largely at the behest of the developing countries, which gave their support to Algeria's initial suggestion for such a meeting—to consider the related problems of raw materials and development.

Many of the provisions of the Declaration and Action Programme produced by that session and reprinted here are entirely consistent with international development objectives and policies subscribed to in principle by the 1960s and early 1970s—and actually made part of the International Strategy for the Second U.N. Development Decade adopted by the General Assembly in 1969. But in the rapidly changing economic and political circumstances of 1974, the very concept of a "New International Economic Order" acquired special political implications and an aura of immediacy, and several of the document's provisions were identified in debate as unacceptable to the United States and several other developed countries.

Under the Assembly's relatively new procedure applicable to situations in which no group of countries chooses formally to record its opposition, the document was "adopted without a vote." But the substance of some of its provisions— particularly the principles enunciated under the Declaration's points 4e, f, g, i, j, and t, and expanded upon throughout the Action Programme's recommendations— continue to make the document a subject of North-South contention.

A seminal provision of the document is Section VII on "collective self-reliance" among developing nations—a concept that has been further elaborated in the Dakar Declaration and Action Programme (see Annex B-3, p. 213) and the Third World Forum Communique (see Annex A-3, p. 178) and that continues to receive much attention in the developing countries on account of both its economic and its political potential.

Declaration on the Establishment of a New International Economic Order

We, the Members of the United Nations,

Having convened a special session of the General Assembly to study for the first time the problems of raw materials and development, devoted to the consideration of the most important economic problems facing the world community,

---

[1]U.N. General Assembly Resolutions 3201 (S-VI) and 3202 (S-VI), May 1, 1974.

Bearing in mind the spirit, purposes and principles of the Charter of the United Nations to promote the economic advancement and social progress of all peoples,

Solemnly proclaim our united determination to work urgently for the establishment of a new international economic order based on equity, sovereign equality, interdependence, common interest and co-operation among all States, irrespective of their economic and social systems which shall correct inequalities and redress existing injustices, make it possible to eliminate the widening gap between the developed and the developing countries and ensure steadily accelerating economic and social development and peace and justice for present and future generations, and, to that end, declare:

1. The greatest and most significant achievement during the last decades has been the independence from colonial and alien domination of a large number of peoples and nations which has enabled them to become members of the community of free peoples. Technological progress has also been made in all spheres of economic activities in the last three decades, thus providing a solid potential for improving the well-being of all peoples. However, the remaining vestiges of alien and colonial domination, foreign occupation, racial discrimination, *apartheid* and neo-colonialism in all its forms continue to be among the greatest obstacles to the full emancipation and progress of the developing countries and all the peoples involved. The benefits of technological progress are not shared equitably by all members of the international community. The developing countries, which constitute 70 per cent of the world's population, account for only 30 per cent of the world's income. It has proved impossible to achieve an even and balanced development of the international community under the existing international economic order. The gap between the developed and the developing countries continues to widen in a system which was established at a time when most of the developing countries did not even exist as independent States and which perpetuates inequality.

2. The present international economic order is in direct conflict with current developments in international political and economic relations. Since 1970, the world economy has experienced a series of grave crises which have had severe repercussions, especially on the developing countries because of their generally greater vulnerability to external economic impulses. The developing world has become a powerful factor that makes its influence felt in all fields of international activity. These irreversible changes in the relationship of forces in the world necessitate the active, full and equal participation of the developing countries in the formulation and application of all decisions that concern the international community.

3. All these changes have thrust into prominence the reality of interdependence of all the members of the world community. Current events have brought into sharp focus the realization that the interests of the developed countries and those of the developing countries can no longer be isolated from each other, that there is close interrelationship between the prosperity of the developed countries and the growth and development of the developing countries, and that the prosperity of the international community as a whole depends upon the prosperity of its constituent parts. International co-operation for development is the shared goal and common duty of all countries. Thus the political, economic and social well-being of present and future generations depends more than ever on co-operation between all members of the international community on the basis of sovereign equality and the removal of the disequilibrium that exists between them.

4. The new international economic order should be founded on full respect for the following principles:

(a) Sovereign equality of States, self-determination of all peoples, inadmissibility of the acquisition of territories by force, territorial integrity and non-interference in the internal affairs of other States;

(b) The broadest co-operation of all the States members of the international community, based on equity, whereby the prevailing disparities in the world may be banished and prosperity secured for all;

(c) Full and effective participation on the basis of equality of all countries in the solving of world economic problems in the common interest of all countries, bearing in mind the necessity to ensure the accelerated development of all the developing countries, while devoting particular attention to the adoption of special measures in favour of the least developed, land-locked and island developing countries as well as those developing countries most seriously affected by economic crises and natural calamities, without losing sight of the interests of other developing countries;

(d) The right [of] every country to adopt the economic and social system that it deems to be the most appropriate for its own development and not to be subjected to discrimination of any kind as a result;

(e) Full permanent sovereignty of every State over its natural resources and all economic activities. In order to safeguard these resources, each State is entitled to exercise effective control over them and their exploitation with means suitable to its own situation, including the right to nationalization or transfer of ownership to its nationals, this right being an expression of the full permanent sovereignty of the State. No State may be subjected to economic, political or any other type of coercion to prevent the free and full exercise of this inalienable right;

(f) The right of all States, territories and peoples under foreign occupation, alien and colonial domination or *apartheid* to restitution and full compensation for the exploitation and depletion of, and damages to, the natural resources and all other resources of those States, territories and peoples;

(g) Regulation and supervision of the activities of transnational corporations by taking measures in the interest of the national economies of the countries where such transnational corporations operate on the basis of the full sovereignty of those countries;

(h) The right of the developing countries and the peoples of territories under colonial and racial domination and foreign occupation to achieve their liberation and to regain effective control over their natural resources and economic activities;

(i) The extending of assistance to developing countries, peoples and territories which are under colonial and alien domination, foreign occupation, racial discrimination or *apartheid* or are subjected to economic, political or any other type of coercive measures to obtain from them the subordination of the exercise of their sovereign rights and to secure from them advantages of any kind, and to neo-colonialism in all its forms, and which have established or are endeavouring to establish effective control over their natural resources and economic activities that have been or are still under foreign control;

(j) Just and equitable relationship between the prices of raw materials, primary products, manufactured and semi-manufactured goods exported by developing countries and the prices of raw materials, primary commodities, manufactures, capital goods and equipment imported by them with the aim of bringing about sustained improvement in their unsatisfactory terms of trade and the expansion of the world economy;

(k) Extension of active assistance to developing countries by the whole international community, free of any political or military conditions;

(l) Ensuring that one of the main aims of the reformed international monetary system shall be the promotion of the development of the developing countries and the adequate flow of real resources to them;

(m) Improving the competitiveness of natural materials facing competition from synthetic substitutes;

(n) Preferential and non-reciprocal treatment for developing countries, wherever feasible, in all fields of international economic co-operation whenever possible;

(o) Securing favourable conditions for the transfer of financial resources to developing countries;

(p) Giving to the developing countries access to the achievements of modern science and technology, and promoting the transfer of technology and the creation of indigenous technology for the benefit of the developing countries in forms and in accordance with procedures which are suited to their economies;

(q) The need for all States to put an end to the waste of natural resources, including food products;

(r) The need for developing countries to concentrate all their resources for the cause of development;

(s) The strengthening, through individual and collective actions, of mutual economic, trade, financial and technical co-operation among the developing countries, mainly on a preferential basis;

(t) Facilitating the role which producers' associations may play within the framework of international co-operation and, in pursuance of their aims, *inter alia* assisting in the promotion of sustained growth of world economy and accelerating the development of developing countries.

5. The unanimous adoption of the International Development Strategy for the Second United Nations Development Decade [General Assembly Resolution 2626 (XXV)] was an important step in the promotion of international economic co-operation on a just and equitable basis. The accelerated implementation of obligations and commitments assumed by the international community within the framework of the Strategy, particularly those concerning imperative development needs of developing countries, would contribute significantly to the fulfilment of the aims and objectives of the present Declaration.

6. The United Nations as a universal organization should be capable of dealing with problems of international economic co-operation in a comprehensive manner and ensuring equally the interests of all countries. It must have an even greater role in the establishment of a new international economic order. The Charter of Economic Rights and Duties of States, for the preparation of which the present Declaration will provide an additional source of inspiration, will constitute a significant contribution in this respect. All the States Members of the United Nations are therefore called upon to exert maximum efforts with a view to securing the implementation of the present Declaration, which is one of the principal guarantees for the creation of better conditions for all peoples to reach a life worthy of human dignity.

7. The present Declaration on the Establishment of a New International Economic Order shall be one of the most important bases of economic relations between all peoples and all nations.

Programme of Action on the Establishment of a New International Economic Order

Introduction

1. In view of the continuing severe economic imbalance in the relations between developed and developing countries, and in the context of the constant and continuing aggravation of the imbalance of the economies of the developing countries and the consequent need for the mitigation of their current economic difficulties, urgent and effective measures need to be taken by the international community to assist the developing countries, while devoting particular attention to the least developed, land-locked and island developing countries and those developing countries most seriously affected by economic crises and natural calamities leading to serious retardation of development processes.

2. With a view to ensuring the application of the Declaration on the Establishment of a New International Economic Order [U.N. General Assembly Resolution 3201(S-VI)] it will be necessary to adopt and implement within a specified period a programme of action of unprecedented scope and to bring about maximum economic co-operation and understanding among all States, particularly between developed and developing countries, based on the principles of dignity and sovereign equality.

I. Fundamental Problems of Raw Materials and Primary Commodities as Related to Trade and Development

1. Raw materials

All efforts should be made:

(a) To put an end to all forms of foreign occupation, racial discrimination, *apartheid*, colonial, neo-colonial and alien domination and exploitation through the exercise of permanent sovereignty over natural resources;

(b) To take measures for the recovery, exploitation, development, marketing and distribution of natural resources, particularly of developing countries, to serve their national interests, to promote collective self-reliance among them and to strengthen mutually beneficial international economic co-operation with a view to bringing about the accelerated development of developing countries;

(c) To facilitate the functioning and to further the aims of producers' associations, including their joint marketing arrangements, orderly commodity trading, improvement in export income of producing developing countries and in their terms of trade, and sustained growth of the world economy for the benefit of all;

(d) To evolve a just and equitable relationship between the prices of raw materials, primary commodities, manufactured and semi-manufactured goods exported by developing countries and the prices of raw materials, primary commodities, food, manufactured and semi-manufactured goods and capital equipment imported by them, and to work for a link between the prices of exports of developing countries and the prices of their imports from developed countries;

(e) To take measures to reverse the continued trend of stagnation or decline in the real price of several commodities exported by developing countries, despite a general rise in commodity prices, resulting in a decline in the export earnings of these developing countries;

(f) To take measures to expand the markets for natural products in relation to synthetics, taking into account the interests of the developing countries, and to utilize fully the ecological advantages of these products;

(g) To take measures to promote the processing of raw materials in the producer developing countries.

2. *Food*

All efforts should be made:

(a) To take full account of specific problems of developing countries, particularly in times of food shortages, in the international efforts connected with the food problem;

(b) To take into account that, owing to lack of means, some developing countries have vast potentialities of unexploited or underexploited land which, if reclaimed and put into practical use, would contribute considerably to the solution of the food crisis;

(c) By the international community to undertake concrete and speedy measures with a view to arresting desertification, salination and damage by locusts or any other similar phenomenon involving several developing countries, particularly in Africa, and gravely affecting the agricultural production capacity of these countries, and also to assist the developing countries affected by this phenomenon to develop the affected zones with a view to contributing to the solution of their food problems;

(d) To refrain from damaging or deteriorating natural resources and food resources, especially those derived from the sea, by preventing pollution and taking appropriate steps to protect and reconstitute those resources;

(e) By developed countries, in evolving their policies relating to production, stocks, imports and exports of food, to take full account of the interests of:
   (i) Developing importing countries which cannot afford high prices for their imports;
   (ii) Developing exporting countries which need increased market opportunities for their exports;

(f) To ensure that developing countries can import the necessary quantity of food without undue strain on their foreign exchange resources and without unpredictable deterioration in their balance of payments, and, in this context, that special measures are taken in respect of the least developed, the land-locked and island developing countries as well as those developing countries most seriously affected by economic crises and natural calamities;

(g) To ensure that concrete measures to increase food production and storage facilities in developing countries are introduced, *inter alia*, by ensuring an increase in all available essential inputs, including fertilizers, from developed countries on favourable terms;

(h) To promote exports of food products of developing countries through just and equitable arrangements, *inter alia*, by the progressive elimination of such protective and other measures as constitute unfair competition.

3. *General trade*

All efforts should be made:

(a) To take the following measures for the amelioration of terms of trade of developing countries and concrete steps to eliminate chronic trade deficits of developing countries:
   (i) Fulfillment of relevant commitments already undertaken in the United

Nations Conference on Trade and Development and in the International Development Strategy for the Second United Nations Development Decade [General Assembly Resolution 2626(XXV)];

(ii) Improved access to markets in developed countries through the progressive removal of tariff and non-tariff barriers and of restrictive business practices;

(iii) Expeditious formulation of commodity agreements where appropriate, in order to regulate as necessary and to stabilize the world markets for raw materials and primary commodities;

(iv) Preparation of an over-all integrated programme, setting out guidelines and taking into account the current work in this field, for a comprehensive range of commodities of export interest to developing countries;

(v) Where products of developing countries compete with the domestic production in developed countries, each developed country should facilitate the expansion of imports from developing countries and provide a fair and reasonable opportunity to the developing countries to share in the growth of the market;

(vi) When the importing developed countries derive receipts from customs duties, taxes and other protective measures applied to imports of these products, consideration should be given to the claim of the developing countries that these receipts should be reimbursed in full to the exporting developing countries or devoted to providing additional resources to meet their development needs;

(vii) Developed countries should make appropriate adjustments in their economies so as to facilitate the expansion and diversification of imports from developing countries and thereby permit a rational, just and equitable international division of labour;

(viii) Setting up general principles for pricing policy for exports of commodities of developing countries, with a view to rectifying and achieving satisfactory terms of trade for them;

(ix) Until satisfactory terms of trade are achieved for all developing countries, consideration should be given to alternative means, including improved compensatory financing schemes for meeting the development needs of the developing countries concerned;

(x) Implementation, improvement and enlargement of the generalized system of preferences for exports of agricultural primary commodities, manufactures and semi-manufactures from developing to developed countries and consideration of its extension to commodities, including those which are processed or semi-processed; developing countries which are or will be sharing their existing tariff advantages in some developed countries as the result of the introduction and eventual enlargement of the generalized system of preferences should, as a matter of urgency, be granted new openings in the markets of other developed countries which should offer them export opportunities that at least compensate for the sharing of those advantages;

(xi) The setting up of buffer stocks within the framework of commodity arrangements and their financing by international financial institutions, wherever necessary, by the developed countries and, when they are able to do so, by the developing countries, with the aim of favouring the producer developing and consumer developing countries and of contributing to the expansion of world trade as a whole;

(xii) In cases where natural materials can satisfy the requirements of the market, new investment for the expansion of the capacity to produce synthetic materials and substitutes should not be made.

(b) To be guided by the principles of non-reciprocity and preferential treatment of developing countries in multilateral trade negotiations between developed and developing countries, and to seek sustained and additional benefits for the international trade of developing countries, so as to achieve a substantial increase in their foreign exchange earnings, diversification of their exports and acceleration of the rate of their economic growth.

4. *Transportation and insurance*

All efforts should be made:

(a) To promote an increasing and equitable participation of developing countries in the world shipping tonnage;

(b) To arrest and reduce the ever-increasing freight rates in order to reduce the cost of imports to, and exports from, the developing countries;

(c) To minimize the cost of insurance and reinsurance for developing countries and to assist the growth of domestic insurance and reinsurance markets in developing countries and the establishment to this end, where appropriate, of institutions in these countries or at the regional level;

(d) To ensure the early implementation of the code of conduct for liner conferences;

(e) To take urgent measures to increase the import and export capability of the least developed countries and to offset the disadvantages of the adverse geographic situation of land-locked countries, particularly with regard to their transportation and transit costs, as well as developing island countries in order to increase their trading ability;

(f) By the developed countries to refrain from imposing measures or implementing policies designed to prevent the importation, at equitable prices, of commodities from the developing countries or from frustrating the implementation of legitimate measures and policies adopted by the developing countries in order to improve prices and encourage the export of such commodities.

II. *International Monetary System and Financing of the Development of Developing Countries*

1. *Objectives*

All efforts should be made to reform the international monetary system with, *inter alia*, the following objectives:

(a) Measures to check the inflation already experienced by the developed countries, to prevent it from being transferred to developing countries and to study and devise possible arrangements within the International Monetary Fund to mitigate the effects of inflation in developed countries on the economies of developing countries;

(b) Measures to eliminate the instability of the international monetary system, in particular the uncertainty of the exchange rates, especially as it affects adversely the trade in commodities;

(c) Maintenance of the real value of the currency reserves of the developing countries by preventing their erosion from inflation and exchange rate depreciation of reserve currencies;

(d) Full and effective participation of developing countries in all phases of decision-making for the formulation of an equitable and durable monetary system and adequate participation of developing countries in all bodies entrusted with this reform and, particularly, in the Board of Governors of the International Monetary Fund;

(e) Adequate and orderly creation of additional liquidity with particular regard to the needs of the developing countries through the additional allocation of special drawing rights based on the concept of world liquidity needs to be appropriately revised in the light of the new international environment; any creation of international liquidity should be made through international multilateral mechanisms;

(f) Early establishment of a link between special drawing rights and additional development financing in the interest of developing countries, consistent with the monetary characteristics of special drawing rights;

(g) Review by the International Monetary Fund of the relevant provisions in order to ensure effective participation by developing countries in the decision-making process;

(h) Arrangements to promote an increasing net transfer of real resources from the developed to the developing countries;

(i) Review of the methods of operation of the International Monetary Fund, in particular the terms for both credit repayments and "stand-by" arrangements, the system of compensatory financing, and the terms of the financing of commodity buffer stocks, so as to enable the developing countries to make more effective use of them.

2. *Measures*

All efforts should be made to take the following urgent measures to finance the development of developing countries and to meet the balance-of-payment crises in the developing world:

(a) Implementation at an accelerated pace by the developed countries of the time-bound programme, as already laid down in the International Development Strategy for the Second United Nations Development Decade, for the net amount of financial resource transfers to developing countries; increase in the official component of the net amount of financial resource transfers to developing countries so as to meet and even to exceed the target of the Strategy;

(b) International financing institutions should effectively play their role as development financing banks without discrimination on account of the political or economic system of any member country, assistance being untied;

(c) More effective participation by developing countries, whether recipients or contributors, in the decision-making process in the competent organs of the International Bank for Reconstruction and Development and the International Development Association, through the establishment of a more equitable pattern of voting rights;

(d) Exemption, wherever possible, of the developing countries from all import and capital outflow controls imposed by the developed countries;

(e) Promotion of foreign investment, both public and private, from developed to developing countries in accordance with the needs and requirements in sectors of their economies as determined by the recipient countries;

(f) Appropriate urgent measures, including international action, should be taken to mitigate adverse consequences for the current and future development of developing countries arising from the burden of external debt contracted on hard terms;

(g) Debt renegotiation on a case-by-case basis with a view to concluding agreements on debt cancellation, moratorium, rescheduling or interest subsidization;

(h) International financial institutions should take into account the special situation of each developing country in reorienting their lending policies to suit these urgent needs; there is also need for improvement in practices of international financial institutions in regard to, *inter alia*, development financing and international monetary problems;

(i) Appropriate steps should be taken to give priority to the least developed, land-locked and island developing countries and to the countries most seriously affected by economic crises and natural calamities, in the availability of loans for development purposes which should include more favourable terms and conditions.

III. *Industrialization*

All efforts should be made by the international community to take measures to encourage the industrialization of the developing countries, and, to this end:

(a) The developed countries should respond favourably, within the framework of their official aid as well as international financial institutions, to the requests of developing countries for the financing of industrial projects;

(b) The developed countries should encourage investors to finance industrial production projects, particularly export-oriented production, in developing countries, in agreement with the latter and within the context of their laws and regulations;

(c) With a view to bringing about a new international economic structure which should increase the share of the developing countries in world industrial production, the developed countries and the agencies of the United Nations system, in co-operation with the developing countries, should contribute to setting up new industrial capacities including raw materials and commodity-transforming facilities as a matter of priority in the developing countries that produce those raw materials and commodities;

(d) The international community should continue and expand, with the aid of the developed countries and the international institutions, the operational and instruction-oriented technical assistance programmes, including vocational training and management development of national personnel of the developing countries, in the light of their special development requirements.

IV. *Transfer of Technology*

All efforts should be made:

(a) To formulate an international code of conduct for the transfer of technology corresponding to needs and conditions prevalent in developing countries;

(b) To give access on improved terms to modern technology and to adapt that technology, as appropriate, to specific economic, social and ecological conditions and varying stages of development in developing countries;

(c) To expand significantly the assistance from developed to developing countries in research and development programmes and in the creation of suitable indigenous technology;

(d) To adapt commercial practices governing transfer of technology to the requirements of the developing countries and to prevent abuse of the rights of sellers;

(e) To promote international co-operation in research and development in exploration and exploitation, conservation and the legitimate utilization of natural resources and all sources of energy.

In taking the above measures, the special needs of the least developed and land-locked countries should be borne in mind.

V. *Regulation and Control Over the Activities of Transnational Corporations*

All efforts should be made to formulate, adopt and implement an international code of conduct for transnational corporations:

(a) To prevent interference in the internal affairs of the countries where they operate and their collaboration with racist régimes and colonial administrations;

(b) To regulate their activities in host countries, to eliminate restrictive business practices and to conform to the national development plans and objectives of developing countries, and in this context facilitate, as necessary, the review and revision of previously concluded arrangements;

(c) To bring about assistance, transfer of technology and management skills to developing countries on equitable and favourable terms;

(d) To regulate the repatriation of the profits accruing from their operations, taking into account the legitimate interests of all parties concerned;

(e) To promote reinvestment of their profits in developing countries.

VI. *Charter of Economic Rights and Duties of States*

The Charter of Economic Rights and Duties of States, the draft of which is being prepared by a working group of the United Nations and which the General Assembly has already expressed the intention of adopting at its twenty-ninth regular session, shall constitute an effective instrument towards the establishment of a new system of international economic relations based on equity, sovereign equality, and interdependence of the interests of developed and developing countries. It is therefore of vital importance that the aforementioned Charter be adopted by the General Assembly at its twenty-ninth session.

VII. *Promotion of Co-operation Among Developing Countries*

1. Collective self-reliance and growing co-operation among developing countries will further strengthen their role in the new international economic order. Developing countries, with a view to expanding co-operation at the regional, subregional and interregional levels, should take further steps, *inter alia*:

(a) To support the establishment and/or improvement of an appropriate mechanism to defend the prices of their exportable commodities and to improve access to and stabilize markets for them. In this context the increasingly effective mobilization by the whole group of oil-exporting countries of their natural resources for the benefit of their economic development is to be welcomed. At the same time there is the paramount need for co-operation among the developing countries in evolving urgently and in a spirit of solidarity all possible means to assist developing countries to cope with the immediate problems resulting from this legitimate and perfectly justified action. The measures already taken in this regard are a positive indication of the evolving co-operation between developing countries;

(b) To protect their inalienable right to permanent sovereignty over their natural resources;

(c) To promote, establish or strengthen economic integration at the regional and subregional levels;

(d) To increase considerably their imports from other developing countries;

(e) To ensure that no developing country accords to imports from developed countries more favourable treatment than that accorded to imports from developing countries. Taking into account the existing international agreements, current limitations and possibilities and also their future evolution, preferential treatment should be given to the procurement of import requirements from other developing countries. Wherever possible, preferential treatment should be given to imports from developing countries and the exports of those countries;

(f) To promote close co-operation in the fields of finance, credit relations and monetary issues, including the development of credit relations on a preferential basis and on favourable terms;

(g) To strengthen efforts which are already being made by developing countries to utilize available financial resources for financing development in the developing countries through investment, financing of export-oriented and emergency projects and other long-term assistance;

(h) To promote and establish effective instruments of co-operation in the fields of industry, science and technology, transport, shipping and mass communication media.

2. Developed countries should support initiatives in the regional, subregional and interregional co-operation of developing countries through the extension of financial and technical assistance by more effective and concrete actions, particularly in the field of commercial policy.

VIII. *Assistance in the Exercise of Permanent Sovereignty of States Over Natural Resources*

All efforts should be made:

(a) To defeat attempts to prevent the free and effective exercise of the rights of every State to full and permanent sovereignty over its natural resources;

(b) To ensure that competent agencies of the United Nations system meet requests for assistance from developing countries in connexion with the operation of nationalized means of production.

IX. *Strengthening the Role of the United Nations System in the Field of International Economic Co-operation*

1. In furtherance of the objectives of the International Development Strategy for the Second United Nations Development Decade and in accordance with the aims and objectives of the Declaration on the Establishment of a New International Economic Order, all Member States pledge to make full use of the United Nations system in the implementation of the present Programme of Action, jointly adopted by them, in working for the establishment of a new international economic order and thereby strengthening the role of the United Nations in the field of world-wide co-operation for economic and social development.

2. The General Assembly of the United Nations shall conduct an over-all review of the implementation of the Programme of Action as a priority item. All the activities of the United Nations system to be undertaken under the Programme of Action

as well as those already planned, such as the World Population Conference, 1974, the World Food Conference, the Second General Conference of the United Nations Industrial Development Organization and the mid-term review and appraisal of the International Development Strategy for the Second United Nations Development Decade should be so directed as to enable the special session of the General Assembly on development, called for under Assembly resolution 3172 (XXVIII) of 17 December 1973, to make its full contribution to the establishment of the new international economic order. All Member States are urged, jointly and individually, to direct their efforts and policies towards the success of that special session.

3. The Economic and Social Council shall define the policy framework and co-ordinate the activities of all organizations, institutions and subsidiary bodies within the United Nations system which shall be entrusted with the task of implementing the present Programme of Action. In order to enable the Economic and Social Council to carry out its tasks effectively:

(a) All organizations, institutions and subsidiary bodies concerned within the United Nations system shall submit to the Economic and Social Council progress reports on the implementation of the Programme of Action within their respective fields of competence as often as necessary, but not less than once a year;

(b) The Economic and Social Council shall examine the progress reports as a matter of urgency, to which end it may be convened, as necessary, in special session or, if need be, may function continuously. It shall draw the attention of the General Assembly to the problems and difficulties arising in connexion with the implementation of the Programme of Action.

4. All organizations, institutions, subsidiary bodies and conferences of the United Nations system are entrusted with the implementation of the Programme of Action. The activities of the United Nations Conference on Trade and Development, as set forth in General Assembly resolution 1995 (XIX) of 30 December 1964, should be strengthened for the purpose of following in collaboration with other competent organizations the development of international trade in raw materials throughout the world.

5. Urgent and effective measures should be taken to review the lending policies of international financial institutions, taking into account the special situation of each developing country, to suit urgent needs, to improve the practices of these institutions in regard to, *inter alia*, development financing and international monetary problems, and to ensure more effective participation by developing countries—whether recipients or contributors—in the decision-making process through appropriate revision of the pattern of voting rights.

6. The developed countries and others in a position to do so should contribute substantially to the various organizations, programmes and funds established within the United Nations system for the purpose of accelerating economic and social development in developing countries.

7. The present Programme of Action complements and strengthens the goals and objectives embodied in the International Development Strategy for the Second United Nations Development Decade as well as the new measures formulated by the General Assembly at its twenty-eighth session to offset the short-falls in achieving those goals and objectives.

8. The implementation of the Programme of Action should be taken into account at the time of the mid-term review and appraisal of the International Development

Strategy for the Second United Nations Development Decade. New commitments, changes, additions and adaptations in the Strategy should be made, as appopriate, taking into account the Declaration on the Establishment of a New International Economic Order and the present Programme of Action.

X. *Special Programme*

The General Assembly adopts the following Special Programme, including particularly emergency measures to mitigate the difficulties of the developing countries most seriously affected by economic crisis, bearing in mind the particular problem of the least developed and land-locked countries:

The General Assembly,

Taking into account the following considerations:

(a) The sharp increase in the prices of their essential imports such as food, fertilizers, energy products, capital goods, equipment and services, including transportation and transit costs, has gravely exacerbated the increasingly adverse terms of trade of a number of developing countries, added to the burden of their foreign debt and, cumulatively, created a situation which, if left untended, will make it impossible for them to finance their essential imports and development and result in a further deterioration in the levels and conditions of life in these countries. The present crisis is the outcome of all the problems that have accumulated over the years: in the field of trade, in monetary reform, the world-wide inflationary situation, inadequacy and delay in provision of financial assistance and many other similar problems in the economic and developmental fields. In facing the crisis, this complex situation must be borne in mind so as to ensure that the Special Programme adopted by the international community provides emergency relief and timely assistance to the most seriously affected countries. Simultaneously, steps are being taken to resolve these outstanding problems through a fundamental restructuring of the world economic system, in order to allow these countries while solving the present difficulties to reach an acceptable level of development.

(b) The special measures adopted to assist the most seriously affected countries must encompass not only the relief which they require on an emergency basis to maintain their import requirements, but also, beyond that, steps to consciously promote the capacity of these countries to produce and earn more. Unless such a comprehensive approach is adopted, there is every likelihood that the difficulties of the most seriously affected countries may be perpetuated. Nevertheless, the first and most pressing task of the international community is to enable these countries to meet the short-fall in their balance-of-payments positions. But this must be simultaneously supplemented by additional development assistance to maintain and thereafter accelerate their rate of economic development.

(c) The countries which have been most seriously affected are precisely those which are at the greatest disadvantage in the world economy: the least developed, the land-locked and other low-income developing countries as well as other developing countries whose economies have been seriously dislocated as a result of the present economic crisis, natural calamities, and foreign aggression and occupation. An indication of the countries thus affected, the level of the impact on their economies and the kind of relief and assistance they require can be assessed on the basis, *inter alia*, of the following criteria:

    (i) Low *per capita* income as a reflection of relative poverty, low productivity, low level of technology and development;

(ii) Sharp increase in their import cost of essentials relative to export earnings;

(iii) High ratio of debt servicing to export earnings;

(iv) Insufficiency in export earnings, comparative inelasticity of export income and unavailability of exportable surplus;

(v) Low level of foreign exchange reserves or their inadequacy for requirements;

(vi) Adverse impact of higher transportation and transit costs;

(vii) Relative importance of foreign trade in the development process.

(d) The assessment of the extent and nature of the impact on the economies of the most seriously affected countries must be made flexible, keeping in mind the present uncertainty in the world economy, the adjustment policies that may be adopted by the developed countries and the flow of capital and investment. Estimates of the payments situation and needs of these countries can be assessed and projected reliably only on the basis of their average performance over a number of years. Long-term projections, at this time, cannot but be uncertain.

(e) It is important that, in the special measures to mitigate the difficulties of the most seriously affected countries, all the developed countries as well as the developing countries should contribute according to their level of development and the capacity and strength of their economies. It is notable that some developing countries, despite their own difficulties and development needs, have shown a willingness to play a concrete and helpful role in ameliorating the difficulties faced by the poorer developing countries. The various initiatives and measures taken recently by certain developing countries with adequate resources on a bilateral and multilateral basis to contribute to alleviating the difficulties of other developing countries are a reflection of their commitment to the principle of effective economic cooperation among developing countries.

(f) The response of the developed countries which have by far the greater capacity to assist the affected countries in overcoming their present difficulties must be commensurate with their responsibilities. Their assistance should be in addition to the presently available levels of aid. They should fulfil and if possible exceed the targets of the International Development Strategy for the Second United Nations Development Decade on financial assistance to the developing countries, especially that relating to official development assistance. They should also give serious consideration to the cancellation of the external debts of the most seriously affected countries. This would provide the simplest and quickest relief to the affected countries. Favourable consideration should also be given to debt moratorium and rescheduling. The current situation should not lead the industrialized countries to adopt what will ultimately prove to be a self-defeating policy aggravating the present crisis.

Recalling the constructive proposals made by His Imperial Majesty the Shahanshah of Iran [U.N. Doc. A/9548, annex], and His Excellency Mr. Houari Boumediène, President of the People's Democratic Republic of Algeria [U.N. Doc. A/PV.2208, pp. 2–50];

1. *Decides* to launch a Special Programme to provide emergency relief and development assistance to the developing countries most seriously affected, as a matter of urgency, and for the period of time necessary, at least until the end of the Second United Nations Development Decade, to help them overcome their present difficulties and to achieve self-sustaining economic development;

2. *Decides* as a first step in the Special Programme to request the Secretary-General to launch an emergency operation to provide timely relief to the most seriously

affected developing countries, as defined in subparagraph (c) above, with the aim of maintaining unimpaired essential imports for the duration of the coming 12 months and to invite the industrialized countries and other potential contributors to announce their contributions for emergency assistance, or intimate their intention to do so, by 15 June 1974 to be provided through bilateral or multilateral channels, taking into account the commitments and measures of assistance announced or already taken by some countries, and further requests the Secretary-General to report the progress of the emergency operation to the General Assembly at its twenty-ninth session, through the Economic and Social Council at its fifty-seventh session;

3. *Calls upon* the industrialized countries and other potential contributors to extend to the most seriously affected countries immediate relief and assistance which must be of an order of magnitude that is commensurate with the needs of these countries. Such assistance should be in addition to the existing level of aid and provided at a very early date to the maximum possible extent on a grant basis and, where not possible, on soft terms. The disbursement and relevant operational procedures and terms must reflect this exceptional situation. The assistance could be provided either through bilateral or multilateral channels, including such new institutions and facilities that have been or are to be set up. The special measures may include the following:

(a) Special arrangements on particularly favourable terms and conditions including possible subsidies for and assured supplies of essential commodities and goods;

(b) Deferred payments for all or part of imports of essential commodities and goods;

(c) Commodity assistance, including food aid, on a grant basis or deferred payments in local currencies, bearing in mind that this should not adversely affect the exports of developing countries;

(d) Long-term suppliers' credits on easy terms;

(e) Long-term financial assistance on concessionary terms;

(f) Drawings from special International Monetary Fund facilities on concessional terms;

(g) Establishment of a link between the creation of special drawing rights and development assistance, taking into account the additional financial requirements of the most seriously affected countries;

(h) Subsidies, provided bilaterally or multilaterally, for interest on funds available on commercial terms borrowed by the most seriously affected countries;

(i) Debt renegotiation on a case-by-case basis with a view to concluding agreements on debt cancellation, moratorium or rescheduling;

(j) Provision on more favourable terms of capital goods and technical assistance to accelerate the industrialization of the affected countries;

(k) Investment in industrial and development projects on favourable terms;

(l) Subsidizing the additional transit and transport costs, especially of the land-locked countries;

4. *Appeals* to the developed countries to consider favourably the cancellation, moratorium or rescheduling of the debts of the most seriously affected developing countries, on their request, as an important contribution to mitigating the grave and urgent difficulties of these countries;

5. *Decides* to establish a Special Fund under the auspices of the United Nations, through voluntary contributions from industrialized countries and other potential

contributors, as a part of the Special Programme, to provide emergency relief and development assistance, which will commence its operations at the latest by 1 January 1975;

6. *Establishes* an *Ad Hoc* Committee on the Special Programme, composed of 36 Member States appointed by the President of the General Assembly, after appropriate consultations, bearing in mind the purposes of the Special Fund and its terms of reference:

    (a) To make recommendations, *inter alia*, on the scope, machinery and modes of operation of the Special Fund, taking into account the need for:
        (i) Equitable representation on its governing body;
        (ii) Equitable distribution of its resources;
        (iii) Full utilization of the services and facilities of existing international organizations;
        (iv) The possibility of merging the United Nations Capital Development Fund with the operations of the Special Fund;
        (v) A central monitoring body to oversee the various measures being taken both bilaterally and multilaterally;
and, to this end, bearing in mind the different ideas and proposals submitted at the sixth special session, including those put forward by Iran [U.N. Doc. A/AC.166/L.15] and those made at the 2208th plenary meeting, and the comments thereon, and the possibility of utilizing the Special Fund to provide an alternative channel for normal development assistance after the emergency period;

    (b) To monitor, pending commencement of the operations of the Special Fund, the various measures being taken both bilaterally and multilaterally to assist the most seriously affected countries;

    (c) To prepare, on the basis of information provided by the countries concerned and by appropriate agencies of the United Nations system, a broad assessment of:
        (i) The magnitude of the difficulties facing the most seriously affected countries;
        (ii) The kind and quantities of the commodities and goods essentially required by them;
        (iii) Their need for financial assistance;
        (iv) Their technical assistance requirements, including especially access to technology;

7. *Requests* the Secretary-General of the United Nations, the Secretary-General of the United Nations Conference on Trade and Development, the President of the International Bank for Reconstruction and Development, the Managing Director of the International Monetary Fund, the Administrator of the United Nations Development Programme and the heads of the other competent international organizations to assist the *Ad Hoc* Committee on the Special Programme in performing the functions assigned to it under paragraph 6 above, and to help, as appropriate, in the operations of the Special Fund;

8. *Requests* the International Monetary Fund to expedite decisions on:
    (a) The establishment of an extended special facility with a view to enabling the most seriously affected developing countries to participate in it on favourable terms;
    (b) The creation of special drawing rights and the early establishment of the link between their allocation and development financing;

(c) The establishment and operation of the proposed new special facility to extend credits and subsidize interest charges on commercial funds borrowed by Member States, bearing in mind the interests of the developing countries and especially the additional financial requirements of the most seriously affected countries;

9. *Requests* the World Bank Group and the International Monetary Fund to place their managerial, financial and technical services at the disposal of Governments contributing to emergency financial relief so as to enable them to assist without delay in channelling funds to the recipients, making such institutional and procedural changes as may be required;

10. *Invites* the United Nations Development Programme to take the necessary steps, particularly at the country level, to respond on an emergency basis to requests for additional assistance which it may be called upon to render within the framework of the Special Programme;

11. *Requests* the *Ad Hoc* Committee on the Special Programme to submit its report and recommendations to the Economic and Social Council at its fifty-seventh session and invites the Council, on the basis of its consideration of that report, to submit suitable recommendations to the General Assembly at its twenty-ninth session;

12. *Decides* to consider as a matter of high priority at its twenty-ninth session, within the framework of a new international economic order, the question of special measures for the most seriously affected countries.

Annex B-2

Charter of Economic Rights and Duties of States[1]

Originally proposed by the President of Mexico, Luis Echeverria, the Charter was drafted over a two-year period under the auspices of the U.N. Conference on Trade and Development (UNCTAD) by a working group of representatives of U.N. Member States.

The hope had been that the new Charter, like the 1948 Universal Declaration of Human Rights, would be adopted unanimously and thus constitute a set of standards that would become part of international law. This aim was abandoned, however, when—in the atmosphere of mutual distrust that characterized the North-South debate at the twenty-ninth General Assembly session—an amendment (sponsored by France and eight other developed nations) to postpone action on the Charter until the September 1975 Special Session in the hope of reconciling differences was rejected.

Apparently persuaded that further negotiations would only mean further delay and would not bridge continuing fundamental disagreements, the developing countries determined to press the draft to final decision by a roll-call vote of 120 in favor, 6 opposed (including the United States), and 10 abstentions. The Charter's most controversial provisions—in the General Assembly debate preceding the vote and since—are its Articles 2, 5, 19, and 28.

Preamble

The General Assembly

Reaffirming the fundamental purposes of the United Nations, in particular, the maintenance of international peace and security, the development of friendly relations among nations and the achievement of international co-operation in solving international problems in the economic and social fields,

Affirming the need for strengthening international co-operation in these fields,

Reaffirming further the need for strengthening international co-operation for development,

Declaring that it is a fundamental purpose of this Charter to promote the establishment of the new international economic order, based on equity, sovereign equality, interdependence, common interest and co-operation among all States, irrespective of their economic and social systems,

---

[1]U.N. General Assembly Resolution 3281 (XXIX), December 12, 1974.

Desirous of contributing to the creation of conditions for:

(a) The attainment of wider prosperity among all countries and of higher standards of living for all peoples,

(b) The promotion by the entire international community of economic and social progress of all countries, especially developing countries,

(c) The encouragement of co-operation, on the basis of mutual advantage and equitable benefits for all peace-loving States which are willing to carry out the provisions of this Charter, in the economic, trade, scientific and technical fields, regardless of political, economic or social systems,

(d) The overcoming of main obstacles in the way of the economic development of the developing countries,

(e) The acceleration of the economic growth of developing countries with a view to bridging the economic gap between developing and developed countries,

(f) The protection, preservation and enhancement of the environment,

Mindful of the need to establish and maintain a just and equitable economic and social order through:

(a) The achievement of more rational and equitable international economic relations and the encouragement of structural changes in the world economy,

(b) The creation of conditions which permit the further expansion of trade and intensification of economic co-operation among all nations,

(c) The strengthening of the economic independence of developing countries,

(d) The establishment and promotion of international economic relations, taking into account the agreed differences in development of the developing countries and their specific needs,

Determined to promote collective economic security for development, in particular of the developing countries, with strict respect for the sovereign equality of each State and through the co-operation of the entire international community,

Considering that genuine co-operation among States, based on joint consideration of and concerted action regarding international economic problems, is essential for fulfilling the international community's common desire to achieve a just and rational development of all parts of the world,

Stressing the importance of ensuring appropriate conditions for the conduct of normal economic relations among all States, irrespective of differences in social and economic systems, and for the full respect for the rights of all peoples, as well as the strengthening of instruments of international economic co-operation as means for the consolidation of peace for the benefit of all,

Convinced of the need to develop a system of international economic relations on the basis of sovereign equality, mutual and equitable benefit and the close interrelationship of the interests of all States,

Reiterating that the responsibility for the development of every country rests primarily upon itself but that concomitant and effective international co-operation is an essential factor for the full achievement of its own development goals,

Firmly convinced of the urgent need to evolve a substantially improved system of international economic relations,

Solemnly adopts the present Charter of Economic Rights and Duties of States.

Chapter I. Fundamentals of International Economic Relations

Economic as well as political and other relations among States shall be governed, *inter alia*, by the following principles:

(a) Sovereignty, territorial integrity and political independence of States;
(b) Sovereign equality of all States;
(c) Non-aggression;
(d) Non-intervention;
(e) Mutual and equitable benefit;
(f) Peaceful coexistence;
(g) Equal rights and self-determination of peoples;
(h) Peaceful settlement of disputes;
(i) Remedying of injustices which have been brought about by force and which deprive a nation of the natural means necessary for its normal development;
(j) Fulfillment in good faith of international obligations;
(k) Respect for human rights and fundamental freedoms;
(l) No attempt to seek hegemony and spheres of influence;
(m) Promotion of international social justice;
(n) International co-operation for development;
(o) Free access to and from the sea by land-locked countries within the framework of the above principles.

Chapter II. Economic Rights and Duties of States

Article 1

Every State has the sovereign and inalienable right to choose its economic system as well as its political, social and cultural systems in accordance with the will of its people, without outside interference, coercion or threat in any form whatsoever.

Article 2

1. Every State has and shall freely exercise full permanent sovereignty, including possession, use and disposal, over all its wealth, natural resources and economic activities.

2. Each State has the right:

(a) To regulate and exercise authority over foreign investment within its national jurisdiction in accordance with its laws and regulations and in conformity with its national objectives and priorities. No State shall be compelled to grant preferential treatment to foreign investment;

(b) To regulate and supervise the activities of transnational corporations within its national jurisdiction and take measures to ensure that such activities comply with its laws, rules and regulations and conform with its economic and social policies. Transnational corporations shall not intervene in the internal affairs of a host State. Every State should, with full regard for its sovereign rights, co-operate with other States in the exercise of the right set forth in this subparagraph;

(c) To nationalize, expropriate or transfer ownership of foreign property, in which case appropriate compensation should be paid by the State adopting such measures, taking into account its relevant laws and regulations and all circumstances that the State considers pertinent. In any case where the question of compensation gives rise to a controversy, it shall be settled under the domestic law of the nationalizing State and by its tribunals, unless it is freely and mutually agreed by all States concerned that other peaceful means be sought on the basis of the sovereign equality of States and in accordance with the principle of free choice of means.

Article 3

In the exploitation of natural resources shared by two or more countries, each State must co-operate on the basis of a system of information and prior consultations in order to achieve optimum use of such resources without causing damage to the legitimate interest of others.

Article 4

Every State has the right to engage in international trade and other forms of economic co-operation irrespective of any differences in political, economic and social systems. No State shall be subjected to discrimination of any kind based solely on such differences. In the pursuit of international trade and other forms of economic co-operation, every State is free to choose the forms of organization of its foreign economic relations and to enter into bilateral and multilateral arrangements consistent with its international obligations and with the needs of international economic co-operation.

Article 5

All States have the right to associate in organizations of primary commodity producers in order to develop their national economies to achieve stable financing for their development, and in pursuance of their aims, to assist in the promotion of sustained growth of the world economy, in particular accelerating the development of developing countries. Correspondingly all States have the duty to respect that right by refraining from applying economic and political measures that would limit it.

Article 6

It is the duty of States to contribute to the development of international trade of goods, particularly by means of arrangements and by the conclusion of long-term multilateral commodity agreements, where appropriate, and taking into account the interests of producers and consumers. All States share the responsibility to promote the regular flow and access of all commercial goods traded at stable, remunerative and equitable prices, thus contributing to the equitable development of the world economy, taking into account, in particular, the interests of developing countries.

Article 7

Every State has the primary responsibility to promote the economic, social and cultural development of its people. To this end, each State has the right and the responsibility to choose its means and goals of development, fully to mobilize and use its resources, to implement progressive economic and social reforms and to ensure the full participation of its people in the process and benefits of development. All States have the duty, individually and collectively, to co-operate in order to eliminate obstacles that hinder such mobilization and use.

Article 8

States should co-operate in facilitating more rational and equitable international economic relations and in encouraging structural changes in the context of a balanced world economy in harmony with the needs and interests of all countries, especially developing countries, and should take appropriate measures to this end.

Article 9

All States have the responsibility to co-operate in the economic, social, cultural, scientific and technological fields for the promotion of economic and social progress throughout the world, especially that of the developing countries.

Article 10

All States are juridically equal and, as equal members of the international community, have the right to participate fully and effectively in the international decision-making process in the solution of world economic, financial and monetary problems, *inter alia*, through the appropriate international organizations in accordance with their existing and evolving rules, and to share equitably in the benefits resulting therefrom.

Article 11

All States should co-operate to strengthen and continuously improve the efficiency of international organizations in implementing measures to stimulate the general economic progress of all countries, particularly of developing countries, and therefore should co-operate to adapt them, when appropriate, to the changing needs of international economic co-operation.

Article 12

1. States have the right, in agreement with the parties concerned, to participate in subregional, regional and interregional co-operation in the pursuit of their economic and social development. All States engaged in such co-operation have the duty to ensure that the policies of those groupings to which they belong correspond to the provisions of the Charter and are outward-looking, consistent with their international obligations and with the needs of international economic co-operation and have full regard for the legitimate interests of third countries, especially developing countries.

2. In the case of groupings to which the States concerned have transferred or may transfer certain competences as regards matters that come within the scope of the present Charter, its provisions shall also apply to those groupings, in regard to such matters, consistent with the responsibilities of such States as members of such groupings. Those States shall co-operate in the observance by the groupings of the provisions of this Charter.

Article 13

1. Every State has the right to benefit from the advances and developments in science and technology for the acceleration of its economic and social development.

2. All States should promote international scientific and technological co-operation and the transfer of technology, with proper regard for all legitimate interests including, *inter alia*, the rights and duties of holders, suppliers and recipients of technology. In particular, all States should facilitate the access of developing countries to the achievements of modern science and technology, the transfer of technology and the creation of indigenous technology for the benefit of the developing countries in forms and in accordance with procedures which are suited to their economies and their needs.

3. Accordingly, developed countries should co-operate with the developing countries in the establishment, strengthening and development of their scientific and technological infrastructures and their scientific research and technological activities so as to help to expand and transform the economies of developing countries.

4. All States should co-operate in exploring with a view to evolving further internationally accepted guidelines or regulations for the transfer of technology, taking fully into account the interests of developing countries.

Article 14

Every State has the duty to co-operate in promoting a steady and increasing expansion and liberalization of world trade and an improvement in the welfare and living standards of all peoples, in particular those of developing countries. Accordingly, all States should co-operate, *inter alia*, towards the progressive dismantling of obstacles to trade and the improvement of the international framework for the conduct of world trade and, to these ends, co-ordinated efforts shall be made to solve in an equitable way the trade problems of all countries, taking into account the specific trade problems of the developing countries. In this connexion, States shall take measures aimed at securing additional benefits for the international trade of developing countries so as to achieve a substantial increase in their foreign exchange earnings, the diversification of their exports, the acceleration of the rate of growth of their trade, taking into account their development needs, an improvement in the possibilities for these countries to participate in the expansion of world trade and a balance more favourable to developing countries in the sharing of the advantages resulting from this expansion, through, in the largest possible measure, a substantial improvement in the conditions of access for the products of interest to the developing countries and, wherever appropriate, measures designed to attain stable, equitable and remunerative prices for primary products.

Article 15

All States have the duty to promote the achievement of general and complete disarmament under effective international control and to utilize the resources freed by effective disarmament measures for the economic and social development of countries, allocating a substantial portion of such resources as additional means for the development needs of developing countries.

Article 16

1. It is the right and duty of all States, individually and collectively, to eliminate colonialism, *apartheid*, racial discrimination, neo-colonialism and all forms of foreign aggression, occupation and domination, and the economic and social consequences thereof, as a prerequisite for development. States which practise such coercive policies are economically responsible to the countries, territories and

peoples affected for the restitution and full compensation for the exploitation and depletion of, and damages to, the natural and all other resources of those countries, territories and peoples. It is the duty of all States to extend assistance to them.

2. No State has the right to promote or encourage investments that may constitute an obstacle to the liberation of a territory occupied by force.

Article 17

International co-operation for development is the shared goal and common duty of all States. Every State should co-operate with the efforts of developing countries to accelerate their economic and social development by providing favourable external conditions and by extending active assistance to them, consistent with their development needs and objectives, with strict respect for the sovereign equality of States and free of any conditions derogating from their sovereignty.

Article 18

Developed countries should extend, improve and enlarge the system of generalized non-reciprocal and non-discriminatory tariff preferences to the developing countries consistent with the relevant agreed conclusions and relevant decisions as adopted on this subject, in the framework of the competent international organizations. Developed countries should also give serious consideration to the adoption of other differential measures, in areas where this is feasible and appropriate and in ways which will provide special and more favourable treatment, in order to meet the trade and development needs of the developing countries. In the conduct of international economic relations the developed countries should endeavour to avoid measures having a negative effect on the development of the national economies of the developing countries, as promoted by generalized tariff preferences and other generally agreed differential measures in their favour.

Article 19

With a view to accelerating the economic growth of developing countries and bridging the economic gap between developed and developing countries, developed countries should grant generalized preferential, non-reciprocal and non-discriminatory treatment to developing countries in those fields of international economic co-operation where it may be feasible.

Article 20

Developing countries should, in their efforts to increase their over-all trade, give due attention to the possibility of expanding their trade with socialist countries, by granting to these countries conditions for trade not inferior to those granted normally to the developed market economy countries.

Article 21

Developing countries should endeavour to promote the expansion of their mutual trade and to this end may, in accordance with the existing and evolving provisions and procedures of international agreements where applicable, grant trade preferences to other developing countries without being obliged to extend such preferences to developed countries, provided these arrangements do not constitute an impediment to general trade liberalization and expansion.

Article 22

1. All States should respond to the generally recognized or mutually agreed development needs and objectives of developing countries by promoting increased net flows of real resources to the developing countries from all sources, taking into account any obligations and commitments undertaken by the States concerned, in order to reinforce the efforts of developing countries to accelerate their economic and social development.

2. In this context, consistent with the aims and objectives mentioned above and taking into account any obligations and commitments undertaken in this regard, it should be their endeavour to increase the net amount of financial flows from official sources to developing countries and to improve the terms and conditions thereof.

3. The flow of development assistance resources should include economic and technical assistance.

Article 23

To enhance the effective mobilization of their own resources, the developing countries should strengthen their economic co-operation and expand their mutual trade so as to accelerate their economic and social development. All countries, especially developed countries, individually as well as through the competent international organizations of which they are members, should provide appropriate and effective support and co-operation.

Article 24

All States have the duty to conduct their mutual economic relations in a manner which takes into account the interests of other countries. In particular, all States should avoid prejudicing the interests of developing countries.

Article 25

In furtherance of world economic development, the international community, especially its developed members, shall pay special attention to the particular needs and problems of the least developed among the developing countries, of land-locked developing countries and also island developing countries, with a view to helping them to overcome their particular difficulties and thus contribute to their economic and social development.

Article 26

All States have the duty to coexist in tolerance and live together in peace, irrespective of differences in political, economic, social and cultural systems, and to facilitate trade between States having different economic and social systems. International trade should be conducted without prejudice to generalized non-discriminatory and non-reciprocal preferences in favour of developing countries, on the basis of mutual advantage, equitable benefits and the exchange of most-favoured-nation treatment.

Article 27

1. Every State has the right to enjoy fully the benefits of world invisible trade and to engage in the expansion of such trade.

2. World invisible trade, based on efficiency and mutual and equitable benefit, furthering the expansion of the world economy, is the common goal of all States.

The role of developing countries in world invisible trade should be enhanced and strengthened consistent with the above objectives, particular attention being paid to the special needs of developing countries.

3. All States should co-operate with developing countries in their endeavours to increase their capacity to earn foreign exchange from invisible transactions, in accordance with the potential and needs of each developing country and consistent with the objectives mentioned above.

Article 28

All States have the duty to co-operate in achieving adjustments in the prices of exports of developing countries in relation to prices of their imports so as to promote just and equitable terms of trade for them, in a manner which is remunerative for producers and equitable for producers and consumers.

Chapter III. Common Responsibilities Towards the International Community

Article 29

The sea-bed and ocean floor and the subsoil thereof, beyond the limits of national jurisdiction, as well as the resources of the area, are the common heritage of mankind. On the basis of the principles adopted by the General Assembly in resolution 2749 (XXV) of 17 December 1970, all States shall ensure that the exploration of the area and exploitation of its resources are carried out exclusively for peaceful purposes and that the benefits derived therefrom are shared equitably by all States, taking into account the particular interests and needs of developing countries; an international régime applying to the area and its resources and including appropriate international machinery to give effect to its provisions shall be established by an international treaty of a universal character, generally agreed upon.

Article 30

The protection, preservation and the enhancement of the environment for the present and future generations is the responsibility of all States. All States shall endeavour to establish their own environmental and developmental policies in conformity with such responsibility. The environmental policies of all States should enhance and not adversely affect the present and future development potential of developing countries. All States have the responsibility to ensure that activities within their jurisdiction or control do not cause damage to the environment of other States or of areas beyond the limits of national jurisdiction. All States should co-operate in evolving international norms and regulations in the field of the environment.

Chapter IV. Final Provisions

Article 31

All States have the duty to contribute to the balanced expansion of the world economy, taking duly into account the close interrelationship between the well-being of the developed countries and the growth and development of the developing countries, and the fact that the prosperity of the international community as a whole depends upon the prosperity of its constituent parts.

Article 32

No State may use or encourage the use of economic, political or any other type of measures to coerce another State in order to obtain from it the subordination of the exercise of its sovereign rights.

Article 33

1. Nothing in the present Charter shall be construed as impairing or derogating from the provisions of the Charter of the United Nations or actions taken in pursuance thereof.

2. In their interpretation and application, the provisions of the present Charter are interrelated and each provision should be construed in the context of the other provisions.

Article 34

An item on the Charter of Economic Rights and Duties of States shall be inscribed in the agenda of the General Assembly at its thirtieth session, and thereafter on the agenda of every fifth session. In this way a systematic and comprehensive consideration of the implementation of the Charter, covering both progress achieved and any improvements and additions which might become necessary, would be carried out and appropriate measures recommended. Such consideration should take into account the evolution of all the economic, social, legal and other factors related to the principles upon which the present Charter is based and on its purpose.

Annex B-3

The Dakar Declaration and Action Programme of the Conference of Developing Countries on Raw Materials[1]

Drawn up in Dakar, Senegal, by a major conference attended by representatives of 110 developing nations, the Declaration and Action Programme—although a descendant of earlier developing-country position statements such as the Charter of Algiers and the Declaration of Lima (prepared, respectively, for the 1968 and 1972 sessions of the U.N. Conference on Trade and Development)—contains significant new material on the cooperation possible among the developing countries themselves and the implications of such cooperation for the rest of the world. It represents an important step in the elaboration of the concept of "collective self-reliance" first advanced—in the aftermath of OPEC action—at the Sixth Special Session of the U.N. General Assembly and included in its Action Programme (see Annex B-1, p. 185).

The Dakar Declaration

The developing countries, meeting in Dakar on 4-8 February [1975] on the initiative of the Fourth Summit Conference of Non-Aligned Countries, carried out a detailed analysis of the fundamental problems of raw materials and development in the light of recent trends in international economic relations, and taking into account the decisions of the Sixth Special Session of the United Nations General Assembly on raw materials and development.

They noted the trends in the international economic situation, which was marked by the perpetuation of inequalities in economic relations, imperialist domination, neo-colonialist exploitation and a total lack of solutions to the basic problems of the developing countries.

Determined to pursue together and in unity a joint action to broaden the irreversible process which has been initiated in international economic relations and which has opened the way for the developing countries to put an end to their position of dependence vis-à-vis imperialism;

---

[1]Both the text and the numbering (despite the latter's apparent discontinuities) are reproduced in entirety as issued (in mimeographed form) by the Conference and as circulated by the U.N. Economic and Social Council (U.N. Doc. No. E/AC.62/6, April 15, 1975).

Convinced that the only way for them to achieve full and complete economic emancipation is to recover and control their natural resources and wealth and the means of economic development in order to secure the economic, social and cultural progress of their peoples;

Decide, in accordance with the principles and objectives of the Declarations and Programmes of Action of the Fourth Summit Conference of Non-Aligned Countries and the Sixth Special Session of the United Nations General Assembly, on the basis of a common course of action, to adopt the following declaration:

1. The present structure of international trade, which had its origins in imperialist and colonialist exploitation, and which has continued in force up to the present day, in most cases through various forms of neo-colonialism, needs to be replaced by a new international economic order based on principles of justice and equity, designed to safeguard the common interests of all peoples, to correct present injustices and to prevent the occurrence of further injustices. The profound crisis now affecting the international economic system has once again demonstrated the breakdown of traditional mechanisms, and with it the particular vulnerability of the economies of developing countries. It cannot be denied that the structure and organization of world import and export trade operate for the most part to the advantage of developed countries. A powerful weapon which the developing countries can use to change this state of affairs is to defend their natural resources and to grasp the fact (as they are in fact doing) that it is only by combining their forces to strengthen their negotiating power that they will ever succeed in obtaining their rights to just and equitable treatment, something for which our peoples have lived and fought for centuries. Despite innumerable efforts at [the] international level to tackle the problems which confront developing countries which export primary products, no perceptible progress has in fact been made for several decades in solving any aspect of the primary products problem.

2. According to the views imposed by the industrialized capitalist countries concerning world trade in primary products, the free working of the primary products markets should normally ensure an optimum distribution of the world resources, and the rising trend of demand in the industrialised countries for exports of primary products from developing countries should stimulate the economic growth of this latter group of countries. This would have been the case if favourable conditions had been created, especially with regard to free access to the markets of the developed countries and the marketing of primary products, but the developing countries have, in the performance of this function of suppliers of raw materials to the industrialized countries, run into other obstacles imposed on them.

3. The framework and organization of commodity trade, and especially the marketing and distribution systems for individual commodities prevailing at present, were developed in the nineteenth century by colonial powers and are wholly inadequate today as instruments of economic change and advancement. Under such systems, transnational corporations control the production of and trade in many primary commodities, particularly through the exercise of bargaining power against a large number of weak competing sellers in developing countries. World commodity markets experience a chronic instability which arises through sudden and substantial shifts in the balance of world supply and demand as well as through excessive speculative activities encouraged by the lack of adequate regulation of these markets.

4. The fact that developing countries have been denied adequate participation in the determination of the international prices of their export commodities has led

to a permanent transfer of real resources from developing to developed countries, because the benefits from the improvements in productivity in the production of primary commodities and raw materials are transferred to developed consumer countries rather than translated into higher earnings for commodity producers, in marked contrast with what occurs in developed countries where improvements in productivity result in higher profits for those countries. Furthermore the low level of commodity prices has stimulated an excessive consumption and considerable waste of scarce raw materials in the affluent countries, resulting in the rapid depletion of non-renewable resources.

5. The repeated MFN tariff reductions in the post-war period which resulted from trade negotiations in GATT covered mostly industrial products traded mainly between developed countries. Moreover efforts towards the liberalization of international trade tended to ignore non-tariff barriers, which more particularly affect raw or semi-processed primary commodities of export interest to developing countries, and also left unresolved the problem of tariff escalation, which greatly hampers the trade of developing countries.

6. In addition, developed countries or groupings of developed countries spent on the subsidization of their domestic production of primary commodities competing with those exported by developing countries a much larger amount than that allocated to official development assistance to developing countries. Moreover, they have violated the principles adopted in the framework of the GATT and have failed to meet their obligations under the International Development Strategy with regard to the readjustments of their respective economies. As a result, their self-sufficiency ratios for most of these commodities increased substantially, and in some cases surpluses became available for dumping on third countries' markets, thus reducing the export outlets available to producer developing countries.

7. At the same time considerable research and development efforts were undertaken, in particular by transnational corporations—partly financed out of the excess profits they had made by controlling the exploitation and marketing of the natural resources of the developing countries—and led to the large-scale production of synthetics and substitutes which displaced in well-protected markets the natural products exported by developing countries.

8. The fast growth of developed countries was partly financed through an international monetary system tailored to their needs, allowing inflationary trends to affect not only their domestic economies but also international trade. Developing countries, being the weakest partners in this trade, were those who suffered most from inflation. Moreover, speculative monetary activities by transnational corporations contributed significantly to the destabilization of the international monetary system. The monetary instability and devaluation of the early 1970s affected adversely the currency reserves held by developing countries.

9. The above constraints imposed on the commodity trade of developing countries have resulted in a persistent long-term deterioration in their terms of trade, despite occasional improvements such as those which occurred at the beginning of the fifties or recently in 1973 and at the beginning of 1974. The sudden increase in commodity prices which occurred in 1973 and part of 1974, however, was due to exceptional circumstances and to an increase in demand as a hedge against inflation and exchange-rate changes rather than to any conscious international policy. Furthermore, this rise in commodity prices was uneven among the various commodities, the prices of some important commodities having actually remained stagnant or decreased in real terms.

10. Finally, this increase in commodity prices, including oil prices, followed a long period of deterioration in the terms of trade of the developing countries.

11. The prices of several major commodities have begun to decline significantly, leading to a further deterioration in the terms of trade of developing countries. There is also a real possibility that other commodities may also experience a decline in prices, given the likelihood that developed countries will take measures to reduce their imports of many of these commodities as part of their strategy of dividing the developing countries.

12. Ever rising freight rates and the failure by the Liner Conferences in most cases to grant promotional freight rates in respect of primary commodities of export interest to the developing countries have further impeded export promotion, particularly in countries which are land-locked and geographically handicapped.

13. The high rates of inflation generated within the economies of the industrialized developed countries have been exported to the economies of the developing countries by raising their import bills to unbearable limits. The balance-of-payments difficulties already being experienced by many developing countries have been seriously aggravated by, *inter alia*, the enormous increase in the cost of imports of food, fertilizers, capital equipment and fuel and in the cost of transport, ocean freight, services and insurance, and the implementation of the development plans of developing countries facing such difficulties has been seriously impeded.

In this respect the land-locked developing countries are in a very difficult position, which certainly deserves special attention in view of the special problems with which these countries are confronted.

14. Finally, the potential mineral resources of the seabed, the ocean floor and the sub-soil thereof outside the limits of national jurisdiction, the extraction of which might become a reality towards 1985, threaten seriously to reduce the export earnings of developing countries, particularly given the danger that the exploitation of these resources may be undertaken under a régime which will not fully safeguard the interests of the producer developing countries concerned.

15. The fundamental problem remains the same: developing countries still depend on their commodity exports for 75 to 80 per cent of their foreign exchange earnings. The process of their development is still largely dependent upon external factors, i.e. the demand from the developed countries for their export commodities.

16. There is no price support at just and remunerative levels in the world market for primary commodities, in marked contrast to the systems operating in the domestic markets of the developed countries in favour of their own farmers. Finally, the existing system of organization of the world food trade has been unable to meet the essential requirements of food-deficient developing countries.

17. By the middle of the second United Nations Development Decade, the first measures for the implementation of the International Strategy which were to be taken by developed countries have not yet been applied, or in some cases even agreed upon. The lack of action by developed countries to tackle the commodity problem of the developing countries is particularly apparent in the following areas:

(1) Non-implementation of the provisions of the International Development Strategy for the Second United Nations Development Decade concerning world trade in commodities, and concerning the reduction and elimination of duties

and other barriers to imports of primary products, including those in processed and semi-processed form, of export interest to developing countries;

(2) Failure of the international community to establish comprehensive international arrangements on most individual commodities owing to the intransigence of developed countries;

(3) Non-implementation of resolutions adopted in UNCTAD and other forums with respect to pricing policy and access to markets and the increasing trend towards protectionism in developed countries;

(4) Failure of the recent round of intensive intergovernmental consultations on individual commodities, pursuant to resolution 83 (III) of the United Nations Conference on Trade and Development and resolution 7 (VII) of the UNCTAD Committee on Commodities, to achieve concrete results;

(5) Long delay in the commencement of the multilateral trade negotiations and in the implementation of provisions of the Tokyo Declaration, which referred *inter alia* to (i) the need to secure additional benefits for the international trade of developing countries so as to achieve a substantial increase in their foreign exchange earnings, the diversification of their exports, and the acceleration of the growth of their trade, and (ii) the need to treat tropical products as a special and priority sector.

18. To this must be added the anarchical exploitation by the multinational corporations and the misuse and squandering of non-renewable raw materials by the developed countries, which constitute a threat to the indispensable conservation of the natural resources needed for promoting development and satisfying in the long term the real needs of mankind as a whole. At the same time the food deficit in the developing countries, caused by the economic policies pursued by the developed countries, which aggravate the dependent position and accentuate the external disequilibrium and under-development of the developing countries, makes it essential that the developed countries make an effective contribution to the long-term solution of the world food problem.

The developed countries should undertake action to alleviate the position of the deficit developing countries, making both food supplies and also adequate technical and financial aid available to them, the latter being directed in particular to developing countries enjoying comparative advantages so that they may expand as far as possible their local production of food. This action must however in no way hamper the production and exports of developing countries which are traditional exporters of food.

19. Given this lack of adequate action by the international community owing to the lack of political will on the part of developed countries, there is an urgent need for the developing countries to change their traditional approach to negotiations with the developed countries, hitherto consisting in the presentation of a list of requests to the developed countries and an appeal to their political good will, which in reality was seldom forthcoming. To achieve this change, the developing countries must undertake common action to strengthen their bargaining position in relation to the developed countries. It is more imperative than ever for the developing countries to take practical steps to strengthen economic co-operation among themselves on the lines of the Programme of Action adopted by the Fourth Summit Conference of Non-Aligned Countries in September 1973 and to agree on a common strategy and on specific lines of action in the field of raw materials and other primary commodities, based on the principle of relying first and foremost on themselves and their own resources to obtain the means for their own development and to establish a new international economic order.

20. The causes of the current economic crisis are rooted in the colonial past of many developing countries, characterized by centuries of uninhibited exploitation of their natural resources. Although colonialism is disappearing, economic exploitation of the developing countries by the developed countries continues to be a major obstacle to the even and balanced development of all countries. The developing countries, which have 70 per cent of the world's population, generate only 30 per cent of the world's income, and the gap between the developed and the developing countries continues to widen.

21. Moreover, some peoples, still victims of direct colonialism or racism, are deprived of their fundamental rights to sovereignty and independence and any possibility of development.

On the other hand, many countries are still subject to imperialist domination and neo-colonialist exploitation, which constitute a reality and a serious obstacle to their independence.

22. The inequities and weaknesses of the present economic system are particularly glaring in the conduct of world trade in raw materials. Those who control the levers of the price mechanism have successfully denied to the producers of a number of raw materials their due profit from their labour and from their natural endowment, while they have themselves continued to make excessive profits by charging high prices for the finished products.

23. The prevailing economic order, and the international division of labour on which it depends, have been based essentially on the exploitation and processing by industrialized countries of the raw materials produced by developing countries and on the enjoyment of the value added which determines both the final overall price and the unfair terms of trade resulting therefrom. To these must be added the further profits accruing from the processes of marketing, financing, freight and insurance.

24. Consequently, the only possibility of correcting this economic order and such a division of labour lies essentially in transferring to the developing countries the job of processing the raw materials they produce in their own national territories, so that they may be able to derive maximum benefit from their potential wealth and improve their real terms of trade with developed countries.

25. For this reason, when the developing countries meet at Algiers from the 15th to 18th February 1975 for the Ministerial Conference of the Group of 77, they will have to decide on concerted action and follow the same line if they are to acquire a larger share in world industrial output by processing and upgrading their raw materials within their own frontiers and by this means helping to establish new forms of international industrial co-operation.

26. That is why the Algiers Ministerial Conference marks a decisive step forward for developing countries in the preparation for the Second General Conference of UNIDO which is to be held at Lima from the 12th to the 26th March, and during which a Declaration will be made and a plan of action for industrialization adopted by the international community in line with the principles for the establishment of a new international economic order.

27. Recent events have shown that traditional ideas about international trade conflict with reality, for they are based on an increasingly outmoded conception of international specialization. This conception is simply that trade relations depend

on factors with which the various countries participating in international trade are endowed. Based as it is on a false assumption, it disregards some essential features of present-day economic reality.

28. These events have thrust into prominence the reality of interdependence of all members of the international community and have made it clear that a few developed countries can no longer decide the community's fate. This realization led to the convening of a special session of the General Assembly devoted exclusively to the problems of raw materials and development, and to the adoption of the historic Declaration and Programme of Action on the establishment of a new international economic order, whose provisions must be implemented as a matter of urgency.

The Sixth Special Session of the United Nations General Assembly on raw materials and development has set in motion an irreversible process in international relations and made it possible to reaffirm the intention of developing countries to engage in dialogue, to concert policies and to co-operate in order to establish new economic relations between Members of the international community. This necessary shift in international relations obliges developed countries to take full cognisance of economic and political facts in the world today and to accept precise commitments to assume their responsibilities within the framework of the inevitable alterations which must be made for the establishment of a new international economic order.

29. Considering that there is now a general tendency among developing countries to mobilise and more rationally exploit their natural resources, these countries undertake to advance along the road towards the complete eradication of their economic dependence on imperialism, to develop their economies, their science and their technology, to achieve prosperity in their countries, to systematically improve the lives of their people, to achieve complete economic independence, social justice and political sovereignty and to eliminate inequalities between nations in international relations, and so to establish a new international economic order.

30. The new international economic order must be based on the principles of equality and equity, and conceived in the common interest for the benefit of all the peoples of the world. It entails reversal of the existing trends in world commodity trade. Primary commodities form an area of the world economy in which structural changes are necessary and inevitable. The introduction of the new international economic order, which must provide for the broadest possible co-operation between all States in eliminating the existing disparities and securing prosperity for all, is a prerequisite for the establishment of a new distribution of productive activities throughout the world and a new type of economic relations based on respect of the right of every State to exercise permanent sovereignty over its natural resources and to dispose of them freely.

31. The principles set out in the Charter of the Economic Rights and Obligations of States must be fully implemented. Consequently, it is the right and duty of all states, individually and collectively, to eliminate colonialism, apartheid, racial discrimination, neo-colonialism and all forms of foreign aggression, occupation and domination, and the economic and social consequences thereof, as a prerequisite for development. States which practice such coercive policies are economically responsible to the countries, territories and peoples affected for the restitution and full compensation for the exploitation and depletion of, and damage to, the natural and all other resources of those countries, territories and peoples. It is the duty of all states to extend assistance to them.

Action Programme

1. *Cooperation Between Developing Countries in the Field of Raw Materials and Other Primary Commodities*

It is more imperative than ever to strengthen cooperation between developing countries on the lines of the principles and programmes adopted by the Fourth Summit Conference of Non-Aligned Countries held at Algiers in September 1973 and by the General Assembly of the United Nations at its sixth special session: programmes in which the developing countries have re-affirmed their conviction that the responsibility for the speedy development of their countries is first incumbent on them. In this connection, cooperation among developing countries in the field of raw materials and other primary commodities should aim to achieve the following main objectives:

(a) to strengthen the negotiating position of the developing countries in relation to the developed countries;

(b) to secure for the developing countries control over their natural resources;

(c) to expand the markets for, and increase the returns from the exports of commodities produced by developing countries;

(d) to maintain and strengthen the purchasing power of the developing countries through the establishment of an indexation mechanism for the price of the raw materials and agricultural produce which they export in relation to the price of the principal products and services which they import from the industrialized countries;

(e) to promote the processing by developing countries of their raw materials to the highest degree possible in their national territory;

(f) to promote direct trade in raw and processed commodities between developing countries, i.e. to put an end to the prevailing triangular system of trade under which a developed country serves as an intermediary in importing an unprocessed commodity from a developing country and re-exporting it in a semi-processed or processed form to another developing country;

(g) to improve the competitive position of natural products exported by developing countries *versus* synthetic products;

(h) to promote the diversification of the economic structure in the developing countries by cooperation in their investment and production projects and programmes and intensification of industrial, financial, scientific, technical and all other forms of mutual cooperation;

(i) to support, wherever possible, measures adopted with a view to implementing the Action Programme adopted at Georgetown, enlarged upon at Algiers and further elaborated on at the Belgrade meeting of the Co-ordinators with a view to promoting economic cooperation among all developing countries concerned in the fields of trade, industry and transport; exchange of technology, know-how, and technical assistance, monetary and financial cooperation, and economic cooperation in general, in order to achieve economic progress for the developing countries;

and to this end:

2. (37) Recalling the decisions taken at the Fourth Summit Conference of Non-Aligned Countries held at Algiers in September 1973, and the resolutions adopted by the United Nations Sixth Special Session in April-May 1974 to establish asso-

ciations of producers among developing countries, the Conference invites the Governments of developing countries to implement all possible means of strengthening the action of established producers' associations and of encouraging the establishment of other associations for the main commodities of export interest to developing countries, and for this purpose, invites them to set up a council for consultation and cooperation between the various associations of producers with a view to the coordination and mutual support of their activities.

This council shall have the following aims and objectives:

(a) implementation of measures for the recovery of resources and production and marketing structures;
(b) to organize on a regular basis an exchange of experience and results between the various producer-exporter associations and make their common expertise available to any group of developing producing countries willing to establish a similar association among themselves;
(c) to harmonize the actions of the various associations and mobilize their support for any one of them when required, within the framework of the solidarity among developing countries and the exercise of their sovereignty over their natural resources, and the exploitation, processing and marketing thereof;
(d) defence against all forms of aggression, economic or otherwise;
(e) to promote financial assistance between the various producer-exporter associations in the financing of buffer stocks and other forms of market intervention as appropriate;
(f) to define common measures to be taken by producer-exporter associations in order to control and regulate the activities of transnational corporations with a view to preserving and consolidating the permanent sovereignty of developing countries over their natural resources.

3. (38) The Conference reaffirms the collective active support of all developing countries for any developing country engaged in the process of recovering and consolidating its sovereignty and control over its natural resources and the exploitation, processing and marketing thereof, and full control of all aspects of foreign trade. In this context, producers' associations should make their expertise available and provide all possible assistance to developing countries in establishing control over industries in their territory, particularly those concerned with the processing and marketing of raw materials for which the producers' associations are competent.

4. (39) The Conference invites the Governments of developing countries to promote regional and interregional financial support and cooperation among developing countries, on the basis of adequate guarantees and reasonable rates of return, for the establishment of commodity buffer stocks, market intervention or any other mechanism designed to maintain prices of commodities exported by developing countries at remunerative levels, to improve access to and to stabilize markets for them, and to guarantee the security of supply for importing developing countries. In this respect, consideration should be given to the establishment of an agency to finance and operate a multi-commodity buffer stock on agreed lines or to finance individual buffer stock and market intervention schemes organized by producing countries.

The Conference invites the governments of the developing countries to take note of the unfavourable effect of the recent developments in the international economic situation on the economies of the most seriously affected developing countries which are big importers of products indispensable to the subsistence of their populations. All developing countries should therefore elaborate, with the assistance of UNCTAD, a series of proposals which would be immediately effective and would aim at eliminating the above-mentioned unfavourable developments. This would, in addition, strengthen the justified endeavours of the developing countries to obtain remunerative and equitable prices for their raw materials.

5. (40) The Conference invites the Governments of developing countries to continue their joint efforts to ensure the establishment of a just and equitable relationship between the prices of their imports from developed countries and those of their exports to those countries, taking into account the development needs of the developing countries.

6. (41) The Conference invites the Governments of developing producer countries, taking account of world market conditions when technically possible, to consider the imposition of export duties or minimum export price schemes as a device for securing better returns for their exports and preferential terms for exports to developing countries where appropriate and technically feasible.

7. Moreover, the Conference invites these producer countries to grant the underprivileged countries favourable terms of payment with a view to solving the financial problems they encounter in their foreign trade.

8. The Conference invites developing countries to promote mutual cooperation in the transfer of financial resources with a view to stimulating their industrialization process through extensive processing on their own territories of their raw materials. This would reduce their vulnerability vis-à-vis other countries. In this respect the developing countries in a position to do so should grant low interest loans and credits and all other forms of assistance, financial or otherwise, which might contribute to the development of the economies of those countries. They should also increase the volume of their investments in the agricultural sector with a view to ensuring world food supplies and, in particular, the food supplies to other developing countries in order to lessen the dependence of such countries in respect of food imports from the developed countries and to enable them to enjoy comparative agricultural advantages and to plan and increase medium- and long-term production. The possibilities of setting up regional or inter-regional enterprises to process raw materials in the developing countries might also be considered. Such enterprises should be competitive in the international market in order to improve the present situation and to lay the foundations for a new international economic order in the relations between developed and developing countries.

9. The Conference invites the Governments of developing countries to increase their mutual trade by means of preferential trade agreements and the establishment of subregional, regional and inter-regional payments' unions.

10. (44) The Conference invites the Governments of developing countries to continue their efforts designed to perfect movements of regional, subregional or interregional integration with a view to accelerating the process of their national development, particularly in the field of primary commodities. In this connection the Conference invites the Governments of developing countries to stimulate regional and interregional financial support by providing national, subregional, regional and interregional financial institutions with medium- or long-term investment from available surpluses and at the same time to promote co-operation among developing countries for the establishment of payments arrangements and export credit schemes for the promotion of regional, subregional or interregional trade and economic integration among developing countries. Commodity trade between developing countries should be

stimulated by all possible measures, including the negotiation of long-term purchase and sale agreements between them in respect of commodities traded among them, and the orientation of the policies of their official procurement organizations in favour of importation from the developing countries.

11. (44 bis) The Conference invites the governments of developing countries also to continue their efforts by setting their sights on doubling the growth rate of their reciprocal trade as suggested by the Fourth Summit Conference of Non-Aligned Countries in September 1973. In this connection the Conference invites them to redouble their efforts to expand their reciprocal trade by joining the Protocol on trade between developing countries within the framework of GATT.

12. (45) The Conference invites the Governments of developing countries to encourage joint financing between them of common research and development efforts (whether in the production of natural products or in the manufacturing therefrom of end products) aimed at improving the competitive position of natural products exported by developing countries *versus* their synthetic substitutes, and to mobilize all available means to promote the transfer of science and technology among them, particularly in connection with the production and processing of their raw materials and other primary products.

13. In this connection the Conference invites the governments of developing countries to encourage the foundation of multinational institutions to facilitate active co-operation in research which developed countries have no interest in undertaking or communicating; and at the same time to study ways and means of strengthening their bargaining power in the market for patents and licences which is characterized by oligopolistic practices on a large scale. A group of experts might usefully examine the expediency and modalities for setting up a joint purchasing agency for buying techniques on better terms and also a multinational centre of technology to acquire technical know-how and put it at the disposal of national users at the lowest possible cost.

14. (45 bis) It also invites them to promote the establishment of national, regional, and interregional shipping companies which can compete with those of developed countries and with the fleets of transnational corporations, so as to promote the expansion of trade between developing countries, to bring foreign trade under the control of national institutions, and to improve the export earnings of developing countries.

(2) Invites the developing countries with surplus means of payment and importing foodstuffs to invest in the agricultural and stockraising programmes of the less developed countries on the basis of appropriate guarantees.

(3) Invites these same countries to exploit and put to use the non-exhaustible energy resources of the developing countries.

(4) Decides to create a permanent committee for technical aid which will be responsible for transferring technical know-how from the developing countries to the less-developed countries.

(5) Decides to convene an intergovernmental group of experts attached to the Bureau of non-aligned countries in order to implement a wider programme of action in favour of the less advanced developing countries in preparation for the United Nations Special Session in September.

The Conference,

Strongly requests the international community to take urgent measures to increase the import and export capacity of landlocked countries and to compensate for the disadvantages of the geographical situation of these countries, particularly in respect of transportation and transit costs in order to increase their trade possibilities.

Strongly requests the General Assembly to decide on the creation of a special fund in favour of the land-locked developing countries, in order to compensate for the damage caused to them by the increased transportation and transit costs.

Invites the governments of the developing countries to elaborate and take concrete and specific steps in order to assist the land-locked developing countries in their development efforts and in their international trading policy.

Requests developing countries with balance of payments surpluses to assist land-locked developing countries:

(a) to develop their national production capacity with regard to food produce and other resources, and

(b) to exploit and utilize non-depletable sources of energy which would not only contribute to the development of the countries concerned but would also be of direct assistance in the conservation of depletable sources of energy in the developing countries with balance of payments surpluses.

Recommends that all developing countries be included on the list of beneficiaries of the United Nations Special Relief Programme adopted at the Sixth Special Session of the General Assembly of the United Nations.

II. *International Action*

47. The Conference, reaffirming that the developing countries must display a political determination, in view of the increasing interdependence of international relations, which will enable the international community to apply the principles of the New York Declaration and Programme of Action approved by the Sixth Special Session of the United Nations General Assembly, referring in particular to the work of UNCTAD and other international bodies:

Recognizing that:
1. The developing countries have the right to establish a diversified, integrated and independent national economy by building a national industry based on their own resources and raw materials, exercising political sovereignty and in the spirit of self-confidence by mobilizing and organizing the forces of their working peoples and providing agriculture with modern technical equipment;

and considering that:
2. Mutual co-operation between the developing countries and, *inter alia*, the economic and technical co-operation granted by developed countries to the developing countries must be such as to assist the countries which enjoy such co-operation to reinforce national economic independence:

A. *Over-all integrated programme on commodities*

Invites all Governments to co-operate in the elaboration and implementation, before the fourth session of the United Nations Conference on Trade and Development, of an over-all integrated programme for commodities consisting *inter alia* of the following elements:

(a) The establishment of international stocking and market intervention arrangements to support prices at remunerative and just levels for a comprehensive range of commodities of export interest to developing countries. Stocking operations could be organized on a multi-commodity basis whereby a central agency would buy and sell stocks of a number of commodities in accordance with agreed criteria on operations, or on the basis of individual commodities, as appropriate depending on policies agreed to by producing countries or producing and consuming countries together.

(b) The creation of an agency or fund for the financing of stocking and market intervention arrangements which would attract investment capital from developed and developing countries in a position to invest from their own resources on the basis of guarantees and the collateral of stocks and reasonable rates of return. The international financing institutions might also provide funds either directly or through long-term loans on reasonable terms to participating countries. The agency or fund could organize stocking arrangements and market interventions in accordance with agreed criteria of operations provided in its constitution and/or provide finance for individual buffer stock schemes and market interventions of producing countries or producing and consuming countries.

(c) The substantial improvement of the facility for compensatory financing of export fluctuations so that the commodity export earnings of developing countries in real terms are stabilized, the period of repayments of loans extended, the ceiling on drawings eliminated and the terms on which loans are granted generally liberalized.

(d) A round of negotiations on international commodity arrangements including multilateral contracts and other techniques of market regulation to restructure the world market for raw materials and primary commodities, taking into account the need to maintain the commodity export prices received by developing countries in terms of the prices they have to pay for their imports, the interests of developing importing countries, and the need to provide exporting countries with sure outlets for their export supplies and importing countries with security of supplies.

B. *Access to markets*

Urges the Governments of all developed countries:

(a) To make structural adjustments in their economies in order to facilitate the expansion of their imports from developing countries.

(b) To take special measures to guarantee the increasing share of developing countries in their imports; to that effect:

    (i) They should reduce and eliminate tariff and non-tariff barriers as well as internal taxes and other duties on imports from developing countries of commodities in their raw, semi-processed and processed forms;

    (ii) Developed countries which are not in a position to eliminate internal taxes and other duties on imports from developing countries should refund the receipts derived therefrom to the developing countries concerned;

    (iii) They should take the necessary measures to encourage consumption of products originated in developing countries;

    (iv) They should refrain from taking unilateral measures, either general or specific, tending to restrict imports originating in developing countries;

    (v) In exceptional cases, and when products from developing countries compete with the national production of developed countries, the latter should, as a transitional step, assure a percentage in the consumption of such products to the imports from the developing countries.

(c) Wherever appropriate, to adopt specific commitments with regard to the sharing of their consumption needs between the national sources of supply and those of the developing countries, and make known bigger quantitative objectives for the import of competitive raw materials.

The Conference calls on Governments participating in the multilateral trade negotiations to give priority attention to the aforementioned measures guided by principles of non-reciprocal and preferential treatment for developing countries.

C. *Shipping*

Aware that excessive and too frequent increases in freight rates have had adverse effects on exports of raw materials from developing countries and their export earnings, urges all States to sign and ratify as soon as possible the Convention on a Code of Conduct for Liner Conferences.

D. *Transfer of technology*

Calls on Governments to establish a code of conduct on transfer of technology which should facilitate the transfer of technology to developing countries on easier terms and conditions contributing to accelerated economic and social development of these countries. The international patent system should be thoroughly revised so as to safeguard the special needs of developing countries.

E. *Energy Raw Materials*

1. Invites the international and intergovernmental organizations to elaborate a programme of action with regard to raw materials and particularly energy, to be responsible for the harmonious development of the developing countries, bearing in mind the progressive and predictable depletion in several decades' time of these raw materials and in particular fossil fuels, oil and gas.

2. *Processing of Raw Materials*

Invites the international organizations, in collaboration with the governments of the developing countries, to elaborate and implement an operational plan for training supervisory staff at the earliest opportunity, to enable the developing countries to control their own development, from the exploitation of their raw materials resources up to industrialization.

Relationship between export and import prices

Requests all Governments to co-operate with a view to bringing about just and equitable relationships between the market prices of raw materials, primary products, manufactured or semi-manufactured products exported by the developing countries and the prices of their imports from industrialized countries.

Marketing and distribution system

Stresses the need for urgent positive measures to ensure the developing countries' increasing participation in the marketing and distribution of the primary products they export, with a view to increasing the net receipts they derive from these exports. Invites all governments to obtain relevant information on the prices applied including the transfer prices of intermediate, primary and processed products, by transnational corporations which carry out the production, processing and marketing of primary products in developing countries and to make such information available to producing countries.

Synthetic and substitute products

Invites the developing countries to adjust their policies concerning the expansion of the production capacity of synthetic substances, primarily in the light of the high social cost of production of such substances and of the adverse effects it has on the economies and environment of both developing and developed countries.

Assistance to developing countries to expand the production of commodities and processing industries

Strongly urges international, financial, the developed and developing countries in a position to do so, to adopt coordinated measures, in accordance with the decisions of principle adopted by the Conference, with a view to effecting a substantial increase in contributions to a fund for developing countries in order to expand production of commodities including agricultural products and the processing of raw materials in the developing countries, taking particular account of the requirements of the least developed among the developing countries and the most seriously affected countries.

Interests of consumer developing countries

Strongly urges that provisions concerning the revaluation of the price of commodities exported to developing countries should include measures to safeguard the interests of consumer developing countries.

The burden of debt

Immediately invites the industrialized countries to agree to a moratorium for the reimbursement of debt contracted by developing countries until the objectives for which financial assistance was given are achieved and the basic products of the developing countries reach the markets of the industrialized countries in the form of raw materials, semi-manufactured and manufactured products. The Conference further proposes the cancellation or re-scheduling of debts contracted on unfavourable terms.

Invites all Governments to co-operate in reforming the international monetary system in order that developing countries might play a further and more effective part in the operating of the system and that an automatic system of transferring real net resources to developing countries should be set up and that a connection might be established between Special Drawing Rights and additional development financing.

The new international monetary system is to be established on a universal and equitable basis.

Multilateral trade negotiations

Invites the Governments taking part in multilateral trade negotiations to agree to a high order of priority for the lowering or elimination of barriers to the imports from the developing countries, in particular of basic commodities (including the processed ones), in conformity with the principles of non-reciprocity, non-discrimination and preference for the developing countries.

The Conference invites the Governments of the developing countries taking part in the multilateral trade negotiations to co-ordinate their positions and to co-operate, during the negotiations, in order to ensure additional net advantages for their foreign trade.

Generalized system of preferences

The Conference requests all developed countries to apply, improve and expand the generalized system of preferences for the export of manufactured or semi-manufactured products from developing countries to developed countries by transforming this system into a more regular and efficient one and by extending it to cover commodities (including processed and semi-processed commodities).

The Conference emphasizes that the system must not be used as an instrument of economic or political pressure, coercion or intervention in the policies of developing countries which produce raw materials. The Conference condemns these pressures as contrary to the system's nature and aims, and advocates the formation of a united front to oppose any measures designed to use the system as a means of economic or political pressure.

Processing raw materials

The Conference invites governments—especially those participating at the Second General Conference of UNIDO [United Nations Industrial Development Organization] which will be held in Lima in March 1975—to take steps to apply the programme of action adopted by the United Nations General Assembly at its Sixth Special Session in order to establish a new international economic order to enable developing countries to have a larger share of world industrial output. Such steps should make it easier for these countries to expand their existing industrial capacity and to create new capacities—more particularly for processing their raw materials and commodities, so as to make an effective contribution towards intensifying and diversifying their exports.

Annex B-4

Solemn Declaration
of the Algiers Conference of the
Sovereigns and Heads of State of
the OPEC Member Countries[1]

The strengthened solidarity evidenced by the Third World over the past two years—despite the dramatic accentuation of vast differences in the development prospects of its members as a result of the actions of the OPEC nations—is linked to the interaction between the newly rich OPEC nations and the other countries of Africa, Asia, and Latin America. Thus far, OPEC nations not only have successfully asserted their own interests vis-à-vis the developed world, but also have initiated development assistance programs far in excess of what had been anticipated in the period immediately following the first oil price increases and have successfully pressed for international discussion of issues of immediate concern to other developing nations as well as those of fundamental importance to themselves.

Thus the Solemn Declaration reprinted below is of particular interest in any assessment of the objectives of OPEC countries and those of the rest of the developing world and of the future ability of these disparate (and by no means homogeneous groups) to sustain cooperative action for mutual benefit.

The Sovereigns and Heads of State of the Member Countries of the Organization of the Petroleum Exporting Countries met in Algiers from 4-6 March, 1975, at the invitation of the President of the Revolutionary Council and of the Council of Ministers of the Democratic People's Republic of Algeria.

1.

They reviewed the present world economic crisis, exchanged views on the causes of the crisis which has persisted for several years, and considered the measures they would take to safeguard the legitimate rights and interests of their peoples, in the context of international solidarity and cooperation.

They stress that world peace and progress depend on the mutual respect for the sovereignty and equality of all member nations of the international community, in accordance with the U.N. Charter. They further emphasize that the basic statements of this Declaration fall within the context of the decisions taken at the VIth Special Session of the General Assembly of the United Nations on problems of raw materials and development.

---

[1]As reprinted in *The New York Times*, April 1, 1975.

The Sovereigns and Heads of State reaffirm the solidarity which unites their countries in safeguarding the legitimate rights and the interests of their peoples, reasserting the sovereign and inalienable right of their countries to the ownership, exploitation and pricing of their natural resources and rejecting any idea or attempt that challenges those fundamental rights and, thereby, the sovereignty of their countries.

They also reaffirm that OPEC Member Countries, through the collective, steadfast and cohesive defence of the legitimate rights of their peoples, have served the larger and ultimate interest and progress of the world community and, in doing so, have acted in the direction hoped for by all developing countries, producers of raw materials, in defence of the legitimate rights of their peoples.

They conclude that the interdependence of nations, manifested in the world economic situation, requires a new emphasis on international cooperation and declare themselves prepared to contribute with their efforts to the objectives of world economic development and stability, as stated in the Declaration and Programme of Action for the establishment of a new international economic order adopted by the General Assembly of the United Nations during its VIth Special Session.

2.

The Sovereigns and Heads of State note that the cause of the present world economic crisis stems largely from the profound inequalities in the economic and social progress among peoples; such inequalities, which characterize the under-development of the developing countries, have been mainly generated and activated by foreign exploitation and have become more acute over the years due to the absence of adequate international cooperation for development. This situation has fostered the drainage of natural resources of the developing countries impeding an effective transfer of capital resources and technology, and thus resulting in a basic disequilibrium in economic relations.

They note that the disequilibrium which besets the present international economic situation has been aggravated by widespread inflation, a general slowdown of economic growth and instability of the world monetary system in the absence of monetary discipline and restraint.

They reaffirm that the decisive causes of such anomalies lie in the longstanding and persistent ills which have been allowed to accumulate over the years, such as the general tendency of the developed countries to consume excessively and to waste scarce resources, as well as inappropriate and shortsighted economic policies in the industrialized world.

They, therefore, reject any allegation attributing to the price of petroleum the responsibility for the present instability of the world economy. Indeed, the oil which has contributed so significantly to the progress and prosperity of the industrialized nations for the past quarter of a century, not only is the cheapest source of energy available but the cost of imported oil constitutes an almost negligible part of the Gross National Product of the developed countries. The recent adjustment in the price of oil did not contribute but insignificantly to the high rates of inflation which have been generated within the economies of the developed countries basically by other causes. This inflation exported continuously to the developing countries has disrupted their development efforts.

3.

Moreover, the Sovereigns and Heads of State condemn the threats, propaganda campaigns and other measures which have gone so far as to attribute to OPEC

Member Countries the intention of undermining the economies of the developed countries; such campaigns and measures that may lead to confrontation have obstructed a clear understanding of the problems involved and have tended to create an atmosphere of tension that is not conducive to international consultation and cooperation. They also denounce any grouping of consumer nations with the aim of confrontation, and condemn any plan or strategy designed for aggression, economic or military, by such grouping or otherwise against any OPEC Member Country.

In view of such threats the Sovereigns and Heads of State reaffirm the solidarity that unites their countries in the defence of the legitimate rights of their peoples and hereby declare their readiness, within the framework of that solidarity, to take immediate and effective measures in order to counteract such threats with a united response whenever the need arises, notably in the case of aggression.

4.

While anxious to satisfy the legitimate aspirations of their peoples for development and progress, the Sovereigns and Heads of State are also keenly aware of the close link which exists between the achievement of their national development and the prosperity of the world economy. Increased interdependence between nations makes them even more mindful of the difficulties experienced by other peoples which may affect world stability. In view of this, they reaffirm their support for dialogue, cooperation and concerted action for the solution of the major problems facing the world economy.

In this spirit, the OPEC Member Countries, with increased financial resources in a relatively short period of time, have contributed through multilateral and bilateral channels, to the development efforts and balance of payments adjustments of other developing countries as well as industrialized nations. As a proportion of Gross National Product, during 1974, their financial support to other developing countries was several times greater than the average annual aid given by industrialized nations to developing countries during the last development decade. In addition, OPEC Member Countries have extended financial facilities to developed countries to help them meet their balance of payments deficits. Furthermore, the acceleration of their economic development and the trade promotion measures adopted by OPEC Member Countries have contributed to the expansion of international trade as well as balance of payment adjustments of developed countries.

5.

The Sovereigns and Heads of State agree in principle to holding an international conference bringing together the developed and developing countries.

They consider that the objective of such a conference should be to make a significant advance in action designed to alleviate the major difficulties existing in the world economy, and that consequently the conference should pay equal attention to the problems facing both the developed and developing countries.

Therefore, the agenda of the aforementioned conference can in no case be confined to an examination of the question of energy; it evidently includes the questions of raw materials of the developing countries, the reform of the international monetary system and international cooperation in favour of development in order to achieve world stability.

Furthermore, this conference may, for reasons of efficiency, be held in a limited framework provided that all the nations concerned by the problems dealt with are adequately and genuinely represented.

The Sovereigns and Heads of State stress that the exploitation of the depletable oil resources in their countries must be based, first and foremost, upon the best interests of their peoples and that oil, which is the major source of their income, constitutes a vital element in their development.

While recognizing the vital role of oil supplies to the world economy, they believe that the conservation of petroleum resources is a fundamental requirement for the well-being of future generations and, therefore, urge the adoption of policies aimed at optimizing the use of this essential, depletable and non-renewable resource.

7.

The Sovereigns and Heads of State point out that an artificially low price for petroleum in the past has prompted overexploitation of this limited and depletable resource and that continuation of such policy would have proved to be disastrous from the point of view of conservation and world economy.

They consider that the interest of the OPEC Member Countries as well as the rest of the world would require that the oil price, being the fundamental element in the national income of the Member Countries, should be determined taking into account the following:

(a) *the imperatives of the conservation of petroleum, including its depletion and increasing scarcity in the future;*

(b) *the value of oil in terms of its non-energy uses; and*

(c) *the conditions of availability, utilization and cost of alternative sources of energy.*

Moreover, the price of petroleum must be maintained by linking it to certain objective criteria, including the price of manufactured goods, the rate of inflation, the terms of transfer of goods and technology for the development of OPEC Member Countries.

8.

The Sovereigns and Heads of State declare that their countries are willing to continue to make positive contributions towards the solution of the major problems affecting the world economy, and to promote genuine cooperation which is the key to the establishment of a new international economic order.

In order to set in motion such international cooperation, they propose the adoption of a series of measures directed to other developing countries as well as the industrialized nations.

They, therefore, wish to stress that the series of measures proposed herein constitute an overall programme, the components of which must all be implemented if the desired objectives of equity and efficiency are to be attained.

9.

The Sovereigns and Heads of State reaffirm the natural solidarity which unites their countries with the other developing countries in their struggle to overcome under-development and express their deep appreciation for the strong support given to OPEC Member Countries by all the developing nations as announced in the Conference of Developing Countries on Raw Materials, held in Dakar between 3rd and 8th February, 1975.

They recognize that the countries most affected by the world economic crisis are the developing countries and therefore reaffirm their decision to implement measures that will strengthen their cooperation with those countries. They are prepared to contribute within their respective possibilities to the realization of the U.N. Special International Programme and to extend additional special credits, loans and grants for the development of developing countries.

In this context, they have agreed to coordinate their programmes for financial cooperation in order to better assist the most affected developing countries especially in overcoming their balance of payments difficulties. They have also decided to coordinate such financial measures with long-term loans that will contribute to the development of those economies.

In the same context, and in order to contribute to a better utilization of the agricultural potential of the developing countries, the Sovereigns and Heads of State have decided to promote the production of fertilizers, with the aim of supplying such production under favourable terms and conditions, to the countries most affected by the economic crisis.

They reaffirm their willingness to cooperate with the other developing countries which are exporters of raw materials and other basic commodities in their efforts to obtain an equitable and remunerative price level for their exports.

10.

To help smooth out difficulties affecting the economies of developed countries, the Sovereigns and Heads of State declare that the OPEC Member Countries will continue to make special efforts in respect of the needs of these countries.

As regards the supply of petroleum, they reaffirm their countries' readiness to ensure supplies that will meet the essential requirements of the economies of the developed countries, provided that the consuming countries do not use artificial barriers to distort the normal operation of the laws of demand and supply.

To this end, the OPEC Member Countries shall establish close cooperation and coordination among themselves in order to maintain balance between oil production and the needs of the world market.

With respect to the petroleum prices, they point out that in spite of the apparent magnitude of the readjustment, the high rate of inflation and currency depreciation have wiped out a major portion of the real value of price readjustment, and that the current price is markedly lower than that which would result from the development of alternative sources of energy.

Nevertheless, they are prepared to negotiate the conditions for the stabilization of oil prices which will enable the consuming countries to make necessary adjustments to their economies.

The Sovereigns and Heads of State, within the spirit of dialogue and cooperation, affirm that the OPEC Member Countries are prepared to negotiate with the most affected developed countries, bilaterally or through international organizations, the provision of financial facilities that allow the growth of the economies of those countries while ensuring both the value and security of the assets of OPEC Member Countries.

11.

Recalling that a genuine international cooperation must benefit both the developing and developed countries, the Sovereigns and Heads of State declare that parallel with, and as a counterpart to, the efforts, guarantees and commitments which the OPEC Member Countries are prepared to make, the developed countries must contribute to the progress and development of the developing countries through concrete action and in particular to achieve economic and monetary stability, giving due regard to the interests of the developing countries.

In this context, they emphasize the necessity for the full implementation of the Programme of Action adopted by the United Nations General Assembly at its VIth Special Session and accordingly they emphasize the following requirements:

(a) Developed countries must support measures taken by developing countries which are directed towards the stabilization of the prices of their exports of raw materials and other basic commodities at equitable and remunerative levels.

(b) Fulfillment by the developed countries of their international commitments for the second U.N. Development Decade as a minimum contribution to be increased particularly by the most able of the developed countries for the benefit of the most affected developing countries.

(c) Formulation and implementation of an effective food programme under which the developed countries, particularly the world major producers and exporters of foodstuffs and products, extend grants and assistance to the most affected developing countries with respect to their food and agricultural requirements.

(d) Acceleration of the development processes of the developing countries particularly through the adequate and timely transfer of modern technology and the removal of the obstacles that slow the utilization and integration of such technology in the economies of the developing countries. Considering that in many cases obstacles to development derive from insufficient and inappropriate transfers of technology, the Sovereigns and Heads of State attach the greatest importance to the transfer of technology which, in their opinion, constitutes a major test of adherence of the developed countries to the principle of international cooperation in favour of development. The transfer of technology should not be based on a division of labour in which the developing countries would produce goods of lesser technological content. An efficient transfer of technology must enable the developing countries to overcome the considerable technological lag in their economies through the manufacture in their territories of products of a high technological content, particularly in relation to the development and transformation of their natural resources. With regard to the depletable natural resources, as OPEC's petroleum resources are, it is essential that the transfer of technology must be commensurate in speed and volume with the rate of their depletion which is being accelerated for the benefit and growth of the economies of the developed countries.

(e) A major portion of the planned or new petrochemical complexes, oil refineries and fertilizer plants be built in the territories of OPEC Member Countries with the cooperation of industrialized nations for export purposes to the developed countries with guaranteed access for such products to the markets of these countries.

(f) Adequate protection against the depreciation of the value of the external reserves of OPEC Member Countries, as well as assurance of the security of their investments in the developed countries.

Moreover, they deem it necessary that the developed countries open their markets to hydrocarbons and other primary commodities as well as manufactured goods produced by the developing countries and consider that discriminatory practices against the developing countries and among them, the OPEC Member Countries, are contrary to the spirit of cooperation and partnership.

12.

The Sovereigns and Heads of State note the present disorder in the international monetary system and the absence of rules and instruments essential to safeguard the terms of trade and the value of financial assets of developing countries.

They emphasize particularly the urgent need to take the necessary steps to ensure the protection of the developing countries' legitimate interests.

They recognize that the pooling of the financial resources of both the OPEC Member Countries and the developed countries, as well as the technological ability of the latter, for the furtherance of the economy of the developing countries would substantially help in solving the international economic crisis.

They stress that fundamental and urgent measures should be taken to reform the international monetary system in such directions as to provide adequate and stable instruments for the expansion of trade, the development of productive resources and balanced growth of the world economy.

They note that the initiatives so far taken to reform the international monetary system have failed, since those initiatives have not been directed towards the removal of the inherent inequity in the structure of the system.

Decisions likely to affect the value of the reserve currencies, the Special Drawing Rights, and the price and role of gold in the international monetary system, should no longer be allowed to be made on a unilateral basis or negotiated by developed countries alone; the developed countries should subscribe to a genuine reform of the international monetary and financial institution, to ensure its equitable representation and to guarantee the interests of all developing countries.

The reform of the monetary and financial system should allow a substantial increase in the share of developing countries in decision-making, management and participation, in the spirit of partnership for international development and on the basis of equality.

With this in mind, the Sovereigns and Heads of State have decided to promote amongst their countries a mechanism for consultation and coordination for full cooperation in the framework of their solidarity and with a view to achieving the goal of a genuine reform of the international monetary and financial system.

13.

The Sovereigns and Heads of State attach great importance to the strengthening of OPEC and, in particular to to the coordination of the activities of their National Oil Companies within the framework of the Organization and to the role which it should play in the international economy. They consider that certain tasks of prime importance remain to be accomplished which call for concerted planning among their countries and for the coordination of their policies in the fields of production of oil, its conservation, pricing and marketing, financial matters of common interest and concerted planning and economic cooperation among Member Countries in favour of international development and stability.

14.

The Sovereigns and Heads of State are deeply concerned about the present international economic crisis, which constitutes a dangerous threat to stability and peace. At the same time, they recognize that the crisis has brought about an awareness of the existence of problems whose solution will contribute to the security and well-being of humanity as a whole.

Equally aware of the hopes and aspirations of the peoples the world over for the solution of the major problems affecting their lives, the Sovereigns and Heads of State solemnly agree to commit their countries to measures aimed at opening a new era of cooperation in international relations.

It behooves the developed countries which hold most of the instruments of progress, well-being and peace, just as they hold most of the instruments of destruction, to respond to the initiatives of the developing countries with initiatives of the same kind, by choosing to grasp the crisis situation as an historic opportunity in opening a new chapter in relations between peoples.

The anxiety generated by the uncertainty marking relations between those who hold power, coupled with the climate of uneasiness created by the confusion reigning in the world economy, would then give way to the confidence and peace resulting in an atmosphere of genuine international cooperation in which the developing countries would derive the greatest benefit and to which they would contribute their immense potentialities.

At a time when, thanks to man's genius, scientific and technological progress has endowed peoples with substantial means of surmounting natural adversity and of bringing about the most remarkable changes for the better, the future of mankind ultimately depends solely on men's capacity to mobilize their imagination and willpower in the service and interest of all.

The Sovereigns and Heads of State of the OPEC Member Countries proclaim their profound faith in the capability of all peoples to bring about a new economic order founded on justice and fraternity which will enable the world of tomorrow to enjoy progress equally shared by all in cooperation, stability and peace. They accordingly make a fervent appeal to the Governments of the other countries of the world and solemnly pledge the full support of their peoples in the pursuance of this aim.

About the Authors and
the Overseas Development Council

Mahbub ul Haq, who is presently Director of the Policy Planning and Program Review Department of the International Bank for Reconstruction and Development, was previously Chief Economist of the Pakistan Planning Commission. Mr. Haq is co-author, with Mrs. Khadija Haq, of *Deficit Financing in Pakistan* (1961) and author of *The Strategy of Economic Planning: A Case Study of Pakistan* (1963). He has written and spoken extensively on the subject of development planning. In January 1975, he was elected a member of the first Executive Committee of the Third World Forum (see Annex A-3, p. 178).

Ali A. Mazrui, a noted Kenyan scholar, is currently a professor of political science at the University of Michigan. He was previously on the faculty of Makerere University, Kampala, Uganda, and a visiting professor at various universities in several other countries. Most recently, he is the author of *World Culture and the Black Experience* (1974); *Who Are the Afro-Saxons?* (1975); *Soldiers and Kinsmen in Uganda* (1975); and *A World Federation of Cultures: An African Perspective* (1975).

Samuel L. Parmar was a member of the International Economics Faculty of the University of Allahabad, India, when he contributed his chapter to this volume. He is currently a consultant to the Office of Education of the World Council of Churches in Geneva. He has served as Chairman of the Working Committee on Church and Society of the World Council of Churches since 1968.

Félix Peña is presently in Buenos Aires as the Legal Sector Chief of the Institute for Latin American Integration and professor at the University of Salvador. He is co-author with Celso Lafer of *Argentina y Brasil en el sistema de relaciones internacionales* (Buenos Aires, 1973). Dr. Peña has also written several articles on Latin American integration, multinational enterprises, and inter-Latin American relations.

Krishna Roy is presently International Advisor at the Centro de Estudios de Población y Desarrollo (Center for the Study of Population and Development) in Lima, Peru. Dr. Roy has also been a lecturer in economics at Bwing Christian College in Allahabad, India, and has held a variety of research and planning positions in India. She did post-doctoral research in demography at Princeton University.

Soedjatmoko was the Ambassador of Indonesia to the United States from 1968 to 1972. In addition to his extensive diplomatic experience, Mr. Soedjatmoko has also served as Advisor to the Chairman of the National Planning Board in Djakarta. His many published works include *Economic Development as a Cultural Problem* (1958), *An Approach to Indonesian History: Towards an Open Future* (1960)—both issued in English by the Cornell Modern Indonesia Project—and *An Introduction to Indonesian History* (1965), of which he was the editor.

Soumana Traoré is the Director-General of the Societé Africaine pour Etudes et Development (African Institute for Research and Development) in Ouagadougou, Upper Volta.

Constantine V. Vaitsos is currently Director of the Division of Policies on Science and Technology for the Andean Common Market (Board of the Cartagena Agreement). He is also affiliated with the Institute of Development Studies, Sussex University, as a Senior Fellow on Trade and Technology. Dr. Vaitsos has written widely on investment practices and technology policies; his articles have been published in the United States, in Europe, and in Latin America. His most recent book is *Intercountry Income Distribution and Transnational Enterprises* (1974).

Bension Varon, currently Assistant Director for Policies and Projections of the U.N. Center for Natural Resources, Energy, and Transport in New York, was a Senior Economist in the Policy Planning and Program Review Department of the International Bank for Reconstruction and Development (with which he was affiliated in various capacities from 1965 to 1975) when he contributed his chapter to this volume. He has recently collaborated with Kenji Takeuchi on articles appearing in *Foreign Affairs* (April 1974) and in *The Annals of the American Academy of Political and Social Science* (July 1975).

Guy F. Erb, a Senior Fellow at the Overseas Development Council, was an advisor to the Central American Common Market prior to joining the ODC. Formerly, he was with the U.N. Conference on Trade and Development and the U.S. Foreign Service, where he served in the Office of the Special Representative for Trade Negotiations. Mr. Erb was Director of the North-South dialogue project, sponsored by ODC and the Charles F. Kettering Foundation, that led to the preparation of most of the essays compiled in this volume.

Valeriana Kallab is Executive Editor of the Overseas Development Council's publications program. From 1963 to 1972, she was a member of the publications staff of the Carnegie Endowment for International Peace in New York. At the Endowment, Miss Kallab edited, commissioned, and contributed articles—mainly on the evolution of U.N. activities in the economic development field—for the Endowment's quarterly, *International Conciliation*, and its special annual assessment, *Issues Before the General Assembly*.

The Overseas Development Council is an independent, nonprofit organization established in 1969 to increase American understanding of the economic and social problems confronting the developing countries, and of the importance of these countries to the United States in an increasingly interdependent world. The ODC seeks to promote consideration of development issues by the American public, policy makers, specialists, educators, and the media through its research, conferences, publications, and liaison with U.S. mass membership organizations interested in U.S. relations with the developing world. The ODC's program is funded by foundations, corporations, and private individuals; its policies are determined by its Board of Directors under the Chairmanship of Theodore M. Hesburgh, C.S.C. The Council's President is James P. Grant.

 ODC Board of Directors

Related Titles

Published by
Praeger Special Studies

*THE UNITED STATES AND WORLD DEVELOPMENT:
Agenda for Action, 1975
      James W. Howe and the staff of the
      Overseas Development Council

NEW DIRECTIONS IN DEVELOPMENT:
Latin America, Export Credit, Population Growth,
and U.S. Attitudes
(Overseas Development Council Studies II)
      Colin I. Bradford, Jr., Nathaniel
      McKitterick, B. Jenkins Middleton,
      William Rich, and Paul A. Laudicina

DEVELOPMENT IN RICH AND POOR COUNTRIES:
A General Theory With Statistical Analyses
      Thorkil Christensen

*DEVELOPMENT WITHOUT DEPENDENCE
      Pierre Uri

MULTINATIONAL CORPORATIONS IN WORLD DEVELOPMENT
      United Nations
      Department of Economic
      and Social Affairs

*PATTERNS OF POVERTY IN THE THIRD WORLD:
A Study of Social and Economic Stratification
      Charles Elliott, assisted by
      Francoise de Morsier

U.S. FOREIGN POLICY AND THE THIRD WORLD PEASANT:
Land Reform in Asia and Latin America
      Gary L. Olson

*Also available in paperback as a PSS Student Edition.